HEARING GOD'S VOICE

Alexa,
Happy Easter!
May God Bless you
and speak to you in new
ways so that you will hear
His voice and know His place
Fr. Mark Burger

FR. MARK BURGER

Cover design and book layout by Dan Evans
Cover graphic: St. John Church Prayer Trail, West Chester, OH

ISBN: 978-0-615-30666-7

Published in the United States of America by Fr. Mark Burger

This book is dedicated to

my Mom and Dad

And my siblings and their spouses:

Rick and Judy,

Mary Anne and Don,

Dan and Mary,

Dave and Lois

ACKNOWLEDGMENTS

"What did I ever do to deserve this?" How often have you found yourself saying or thinking those words? I know that I say or think those words quite often and when I stop to consider it, I believe that more often then not, it is at times of great blessings that I think or say those words the most. I know that I have been greatly blessed by God, far more then I ever deserve. Some of the greatest gifts that God has ever given me are the people who just seem to walk right into my life, each one at exactly the right time.

As this book is finally published, I am very much aware of how many people have played a part in bringing it about. I am truly grateful to God for the blessing that each one of these individuals have been to me. I want to offer my thanks to them for all that they have done. I want to give thanks to my friend Dan Andriacco for his assistance in editing the book. Thanks to another friend Dan Evans for his hard work in designing the cover and lay-out of the book. Others who have been a blessing to me are Carole Adlard, Nicol Courtemanche, Kaye Franks, Ken Franks, and Ruth Rechtsteiner for their painstaking work as proofreaders. I certainly cannot forget two great blessings who were the first to read and then type the manuscript for me, my mom, Mary Lou Burger and my sister, Mary Anne Veite.

A special thanks too for those whose belief in the book made it possible: Ned and Sue Bruns and Ken and Kaye Franks.

I want to thank Jim Strotman for donating his financial expertise to keep the business side of publishing the book on track. Also I cannot forget my friends and colleagues Karen Hake, for handling the order taking and distribution, Marianne Ball who handled the bookkeeping, and Kathy Mack who kept an eye on things as they progressed.

I also want to thank the people of my parish, St. John the Evangelist Parish in West Chester, Ohio. I have been called by the Lord to be a parish priest, and I thank the people of my parish for allowing me to serve them as their parish priest and pastor.

I thank the Lord for allowing me to share *Hearing God's Voice* with you. It is my prayer that these pages will offer you the opportunity to pause long enough to hear that still, quiet voice of the One who deeply loves you.

Fr. Mark Burger
July, 2009

INTRODUCTION: *THREE GRACES*

On that first day, as I knelt in the tiny chapel within the walls of a tiny monastery which was home to five Melkite monks, I was aware of three things: it was incredibly hot, it was overwhelmingly quiet, and I felt completely and utterly alone. As I prayed, my eyes were focused on the many icons, big and small, that decorated the iconostasis. The saints who looked back at me from their icons seemed to be glaring at me belligerently as if they were demanding to know what I was doing and what I wanted out here in this desert west of Jerusalem. I had no ready answer. Yet, I knew at the bottom of it all, it was God who had called me here. I had sensed that God wanted me here; my hope was that once I was here in the quiet of the desert, I would hear His voice.

I had been a parish priest for 16 years when I arrived at that tiny Holy Monastery of St. John of the Desert in 1996, but it was about five or six years prior to that when an inner call to a deeper prayer life had begun to surface. This was not just a call to pray more; it was something deeper. I began to experience an unrelenting pull to a concentrated time of prayer, away from everyone and everything. As I discerned what was happening in me, it became clear to me that God was calling me to live, for a short period of time, the life of a hermit.

So, when I finished my prayers on that very first hot day in that little chapel, one of the monks, Hieromonk Elisee, came and invited me to follow him to the small stone building that would be my hermitage for the next four months. The monk was young, kind and soft spoken. "Permit me to tell you something on behalf of my brother monks," he said: "We are happy to have a hermit living among us. It is our hope that you will find this little hut comfortable and that you will be able to find the solitude you seek. Perhaps you might even be given the grace to hear God's voice. We will pray that you are given this grace."

As it happened, I was given three graces in my short hermit life. In that time alone in the desert of Israel I came to experience silence in a new way. I learned in that time alone that we are never completely alone because we live in the presence of the Living God. And I learned that God is always speaking to us. Those three graces have changed my life and they continue to shape my life in new ways even now. I continue to crave silence, solitude (time alone with the Living God), and I try to pay close attention to God's softly spoken voice.

It was during my time in the desert that I began to understand the words Mahatma Gandhi said as he looked back over his life. He said that when he was young, he thought the most important thing in life was to be right, but after years of life had passed, he believed that the most important thing was to be awake to the moment. As I look back over my life, and especially as I return to those days in my hermitage, I have learned a lot. It was in learning to not run away from silence, and it was in embracing being alone in solitude that I came to realize that God talks to us all of the time, yet most of us miss it because we are not "awake to the moment."

Had I been awake to the moment on that very first day in the desert, I would have seen that God was even then already speaking to me. In my awareness of the oppressive heat that day, I now know after years of reflection that God was speaking to me of the oppressive nature of my life at that time, lived at so frenzied a pace. Had I been awake to the moment on that first day, I would have begun to understand that in that overwhelming quiet, God was inviting me into a silence that would allow me to hear His quiet voice. And again, had I been awake to the moment on that first day in that tiny, hot chapel, in those intense feelings of complete and utter aloneness, I would have known that it was God speaking to me of His desire for union with each one of us. In being awake to the moment today, I see now that those three graces – the heat, the quiet, and the utter aloneness – produced in me something that has not left me since then, an inner peace that no one else could ever give.

The following series of reflections were originally written for my parishioners. It is my hope that these daily reflections will give you an opportunity to learn to be awake to the moment and that you, too, might receive three graces - silence, solitude and the grace to hear God's voice. To echo the words of Hieromonk Elisee …

I will pray that you are given this grace.

Fr. Mark

January 1st
A New Year – A New Plan!

Last year someone sent me six New Year's resolutions that Erma Bombeck used to tape on the window over her kitchen sink. Here they are:

1. *I'm going to clean this dump just as soon as the kids grow up*
2. *I will go to no doctor whose office plants have died*
3. *I will follow my husband's advice and live within our budget; that will certainly put something new in our life!*
4. *I will apply for a hardship scholarship to Weight Watchers*
5. *I will never lend my car to anyone I have given birth to*
6. *And just like last year . . . I am going to remember that my children need love the most when they deserve it the least.*

We have just celebrated the beginning of a new year, and we are slowly working our way into a new millennium. Time is such a precious gift to us. It really is important to stop to consider what we plan to do with our time in this coming year. Each day brings with it a "clean slate", a chance to start over again and begin anew. How do you plan to use the time given you in this New Year?

January 2nd
A Doorway to Peace

Over the past few weeks, more than a few members of our parish have had some pretty grim news. Some have heard some hard words about the condition of their health; others have heard the sad news that their son or daughter is going through a divorce; still others have been told that they are losing their jobs. As one person said, "I woke up yesterday and everything was great. I went to bed last night and the world had collapsed around me! How will I ever get through this?"

How do people get through a terrible crisis? It seems to me that there are several ways to deal with a major problem.

You can get angry, curse a lot and carry on about how terrible the world is treating you and how unfair life is. You can and probably will do this at first. I think you will discover, however, that this response will only provide temporary relief. It might even increase your fear levels. It is more of a reaction than a response to the problem, and therefore will more than likely make you feel that nothing can help and you are totally alone.

Some people respond to problems by going off by themselves for a while to "take stock" of what is happening to them. Sometimes "stepping outside" the problem can give you some hints on what you might do next or whose help you might seek, or even who might need YOUR help in a given situation.

In my own life, there are two words that I often use when I am faced with some difficulty or personal problem or crisis. These two words are what I would call a "Doorway to Peace." These two words can give you a better perspective on your own life and on what is presently happening to you. What are these two words? The two words I use are "and yet ..."

Let me show you how to use them. Say, for example, you find out that you will lose your job next week. Simply state that fact for yourself and add the two words, "and yet ..." Fill in the space after "and yet ..."with as many positive things that you can about your given situation. You may be losing your job, AND YET you still have your talents, AND YET you still have many friends who can be of help in finding a new job, and so on.

By using these simple words you will be able to do something that each of us must do if we ever want to overcome any difficulty or hardship. When you use these words as I demonstrated, you begin your first steps in ACCEPTANCE. Acceptance is very important, because acceptance is the first step towards recovery. Anyone who has had to deal with any major crisis in their lives will tell you that they made no progress until they first accepted the situation as it was, and then began to work toward recovery.

If you have had some bad news in recent days and you don't seem to be able to find peace, pray first. Then state the problem and add two words. You will have opened a doorway to peace.

January 3rd
A Good Friend Is a True Blessing

I recently talked with a friend of mine who is a teacher. She told me about an assignment that she gave her class. They were to write a definition of a true friend. Some of their answers were rather interesting. One wrote, "A friend is someone who knows all about you but likes you anyway." Another definition submitted was, "A good friend is one who brings out the best in you." Another student said, "A true friend is there for you when everyone else would rather be somewhere else." Finally, one of the students who couldn't think of her own definition brought in a poster that she had in her room. In bright letters the poster proclaimed, "There are good ships and bad ships, but the best ships are friendships."

There are many important decisions that we need to make throughout our lives, but there is probably no decision quite as important as whom we choose to be our closest friends. In the Book of Proverbs it says that those who associate with the wise will end up being wise and those who associate with fools will end up being fools. In other words, we become like those with whom we associate, so choose wisely!

A good friend is a real blessing. If you are wise enough to have chosen good friends, or if you are blessed enough to have been chosen by others as their friend, why not take time to give thanks to God for such a blessing? Why not take some time to thank your friends for their friendship?

Remember, "The best 'ships' are friendships!"

January 4th
A Parable About Hurting Others

A man came upon a friend of his, named Joseph, who was muttering to himself and cursing his neighbor. "Why are you muttering to yourself, Joe?"

"Well, my neighbor has this very annoying habit of slapping me on the back each time he sees me. It drives me crazy. I've told him to stop, but he says he forgets. Well, I'll put a stop to it. I've put a stick of dynamite under my coat, so this time when he slaps me, he'll blow his arm off. That will teach him!"

This may seem like a silly way of handling a problem, but it is not unlike what happens whenever we strike out, intending to hurt another person. We always end up hurting ourselves. The next time you want to intentionally hurt someone in the family who annoys you, think of the man with the dynamite under his coat, and try to diffuse the situation in a less hurtful manner.

January 5th
A Positive Attitude Can Affect Others' Lives

Recently I came across a copy of a letter written many years ago by Martin Van Buren to President Andrew Jackson. Van Buren had heard that the President was about to do something rather revolutionary – he was about to take a ride on the railroad. The thought terrified Mr. Van Buren so much that he thought it his duty to write to the President to try to dissuade him. Here is part of what he wrote:

> *"As you may well know, Mr. President, 'railroad' carriages are pulled at an enormous speed of 15 miles per hour by 'engines' which, in addition to endangering life and limb of passengers, roar and snort their way through the countryside, setting fire to crops, scaring livestock and frightening women and children. The Almighty certainly never intended that people should travel at such breakneck speed!"*

How's that for a fearful attitude about life? Even though we might find Van Buren's letter amusing, I think that it serves to do more for us than simply make us smile. It can serve to make us stop and look at our own attitudes about life, and how we might be affecting those around us. Think for a moment – when someone spends a bit of time with you, do they go away strengthened and encouraged by your words and attitudes?

I once heard a mother of six children say, "In the past, when my children finished practicing the piano, I always asked them why they didn't spend more time at it so that they would get better. Then one day, I was visiting my neighbor. As I was talking to her, I could hear her daughter practicing the piano. When the young girl finished playing, she came into the kitchen where her mother and I were sitting. Her mother looked at her and said, 'I just love it when you play!' The girl's face lit up. From that day on, I made it a practice to encourage my children with positive remarks. No longer do I nag them about how long they practice; now I just encourage them by telling them how much I love to hear them play."

Can you imagine the difference it might make in the lives of your family, friends and co-workers if you chose to be more positive in your attitudes and in the way you share your attitudes with others?

January 6th
Active Ingredients

Have you ever taken the time to read the ingredients that are listed on the sides of some of the products you buy? Have you ever read the contents of some of the over-the-counter medicines you buy? I have, and some of those ingredients sound much worse than any ailment I might have! Anyway, have you ever noticed that some products list among their contents something called the "active ingredient"? I asked the pharmacist one time just what an "active ingredient" was. He said it was the main ingredient that makes the product do what it says it will do. That made sense to me. It also led me to ask a question of myself. Just what is MY active ingredient? What is it that makes me do what I do?

That's a good question for all of us to ask ourselves from time to time. Some people do what they do out of fear – so I guess their "active ingredient" might be fear. They are people who are so afraid that people won't like them that they try to do whatever they can to please everyone or to fit in with any crowd. And that's not the only "active ingredient" that a person could have. Some people are filled with guilt over past wrongs, some are filled with anger; still others are filled with jealousy, greed, or hatred. But even these are certainly not the only "active ingredients" at work in people's lives. There are many, many people who are filled with love, and everything they do is motivated by that love. The world is a beautiful place because so many people, whose "active ingredient" is love, have generously poured out their lives for others. And again, there are wonderful people whose "active ingredient" is compassion. These folks spend their lives healing others on a physical, emotional, or even a spiritual level. If you stop to think about it, there are probably as many kinds of "active ingredients" in people as there are people. The question we must ask ourselves then is: "What is MY active ingredient?"

January 7th
Alice Roosevelt Longworth

How easy it is for us to forget the power of words! Words can either heal or hurt, depending on how we choose them. It is said that Alice Roosevelt Longworth had a special pillow in her living room. Embroidered on the pillow were these words: "If you can't say anything good about someone ... sit right here by me!"

While this story might bring a smile to your face, it is good to remember that Ms. Longworth did have a reputation of being a gossip, and much damage was done to many people by that gossip. Her use of words was quite destructive. Whenever I think of how destructive words can be, I remember something I read by Pastor Chuck Swindoll, a prominent Protestant minister. He told of a woman in his congregation who had committed suicide. As her family struggled to discover what lead her to take her own life, they found an unfinished note that simply ended with the words, "They said ..." Swindoll says that the woman never completed the final thought, but that it was quite evident that whatever "they said" was so painful to her that she felt her only way out was to take her own life. This very sad story can help to remind us to weigh our words, and to remember that our words have very real power.

January 8th
It Came to Pass

One of my friends in Dayton who teaches a Bible Study class told me about one of her recent classes in which members of the group were asked to recite their favorite Bible quotation. One elderly woman in the group said that she had so many "favorites" that she couldn't choose just one. There was one quote, however, that she thought of on many occasions. It was just a part of a verse that her mother used to say to her whenever there was some difficulty or some suffering going on in the family. This verse fragment was "And it came to pass".

When the members of the Bible Study class asked for an explanation, the woman said that her mother used to say, "In all the rough times in my life, it's been a real relief to remember the words, 'and it came to pass' and realize that the Bible doesn't say, 'and it came to stay."

It's good for us to remember that almost all difficulties and worries eventually come to an end. The Lord invites us all to put our hand in His and to trust that He'll see us through the rough times. Why not spend some extra time in prayer deepening your relationship with the Lord?

January 9th
Am I "Connected"?

This past summer, I went to a museum which had displays of various forms of underwater wildlife. In one display, there were hundreds of various species of fish swimming and darting about, and in the center of the display was a man in a deep sea diving suit. As spectators walked by the display, the diver would wave and then, through an underwater microphone, tell the spectators about the antique diving suit he was wearing. "If I were not connected by this air hose to the life-giving air of the ship above," he remarked, "in just a few minutes I would be totally disoriented, and in a very short time, I'd be dead. I'm the only living creature in this display that must be connected to the air above or I'll die. All of these other life forms get what they need right in here."

I thought this statement was a good reflection on life in general. If we are not "connected to the life-giving air above" (God), it isn't long before we are disoriented and then in a rather short period of time, we are spiritually dead. It is vitally important for us to be people of prayer, people who spend time each day with our Source of Life and Love. The question this raises then for us is: Am I "connected"? We are the living creatures who must be connected to the Life above or we'll die.

January 10th
Appreciate the Gifts You Have

During World War II there was a shortage of sugar here in the States. Because there was a limited supply and because that limited supply was rationed, restaurants didn't offer much of it to their customers. One day a man in Washington, D.C. poured a bit of sugar into his coffee and then tasted it. He grimaced because it wasn't sweet enough. He leaned over the counter and called out to the cook, "Hey, I need more sugar in here!"

"Stir what you already got!" shot back the cook.

Have you ever felt like that man in the restaurant, finding life more bitter than you want it to be? I think that each of us can find things in our lives that are not as we would like them to be. In fact, some people find that their life is overwhelming. Yet, Jesus came to teach us what to do with the bitterness and the difficulties that life sometimes brings. To begin with, I think that Jesus wants each of us to do a kind of "inventory" of the gifts we have already received. What gifts do you already have as you face your present difficulties? Are you "stirring" these gifts into the mix of your life? In other words, are you taking advantage of all of the gifts, people and situations that are already in your life that could help you bear with your present difficult situation? If it feels like Jesus is not answering your prayers, perhaps, like that cook in the anecdote above, He is saying "Stir what you already got!" Maybe the "sugar" you're seeking to eliminate the bitterness you are experiencing is already in your life, within your grasp.

Take some time to do a "gift inventory" and then pause and give thanks for what you have already been given.

January 11th
Are We Giving God Scraps?

Imagine being invited to someone's home for dinner. Imagine being seated at a wonderfully decorated table at which a lighted candelabra, colorful flowers and sumptuous food create an elegant atmosphere. Pleasant conversation and soft music add to the ambiance. Course after course of delicious food is brought to the table as guests delight in the food that is put before them. As the meal continues, you notice one rather odd thing – as each course is served, you are asked to wait until the others have been served, and only then are you given the small portion of food that is left on the serving dishes; and not only that, the servings that are placed before you cannot actually be called "portions" because they are merely scraps of food that do not even fill half of your dinner plate. How would you feel?

I'm sure you would feel hurt, disappointed, angry and quite insulted. After all, isn't it proper to serve guests the best portions first? Wouldn't you serve them the best you had to offer and see to their needs first? I'm sure all of us would.

I raise these questions with you because of something that I have been hearing from lots of people lately in talking about spiritual direction. Often people will tell me that they know they should be praying more, they know they should spend more time with the Scriptures, and they know they ought to be using more of their talents for the benefit of the less fortunate but, by the end of the day, there's no time left.

What I tell people is what I've been saying to myself as I examine my own conscience – "If God is truly God in my life, if God is truly important, why am I giving Him half-hearted leftovers of my time, my talent, and my heart?"

Just ask yourself if during the past week you have given God, your special guest, the best portion of your time, your talent, your heart. Have you served God first, or have you waited until you have taken care of everything else first? I've been asking myself these questions every morning of this past week. It certainly has made me much more attentive to my prayer!

January 12th
Are You Really Rich or Truly Poor?

I was reading an interesting article about the extreme poverty that existed in America during the Great Depression. According to the article, the U.S. Government would send out agents to look for the poorest farmers from the remote mountainous areas of the nation in order to issue them some grant monies to help buy seed and feed for their livestock. The government sought out these farmers because they were believed to be the hardest hit by the Depression.

One agent reported that he had come upon an old woman from the hills of Kentucky living in a horrible little shack. It had no floor; the roof leaked, there was no glass in the windows, and there was very little heat in the winter. The old woman had just the very basic essentials and was barely able to survive.

The agent said to her, "If the U.S. Government were to give you $350, what would you do with it?"

Her answer was instant, "Why, I'd give it to some poor person!"

The agent was shocked and said, "Lady, how could you give the money to someone else when you are so poor yourself?"

"Who said I'm poor?" she snapped at him. "It ain't money that makes a person rich or poor, Mister! I may not have money, but I sure ain't poor."

It is true that there are many, many people who have lots of money who are, in reality, quite poor. And it is also quite true that there are many people who have little or no money, but are truly rich.

January 13th
Asking for God's Help

I was reading a novel the other day when I came upon a story, which became the focus for my prayer that night. The story is about a little boy back in the days of country stores. He used to go along with his mother when she did her shopping. When the woman was paying her bill, the storekeeper would set a large jar filled with candy in front of the little boy and invite him to take a handful of candy. The boy would never take any candy. The storekeeper would then reach into the jar and give the little boy a handful of candy. After a few months of this, the boy's mother asked "Why is it that when that man asks you to take a handful of candy, you never do?"

Her son smiled as he answered her, "Because his hands are bigger than mine!"

Sometimes when we pray for God's help, it's good for us to realize that we can often think too small. Our minds and our view of things can sometimes be like that little boy's hands – way too small. God knows how to give us what we need, and then he wants to give us what we need in far greater abundance than we could ever imagine. When you are asking God for something, how much do you trust God to give you what you need?

January 14th
Where Am I?

A priest was leading a pilgrimage and as the trip continued, the usually calm and serene priest grew more and more angry. After a few days, some of the pilgrims pulled the priest aside and asked him if they had done something to offend him.

"No, I'm not angry with you. I'm just becoming aware of something about myself as I watch all of you. I've learned that, no matter where we are, we're not there!"

"What do you mean?" they asked.

The priest thought for a moment and then explained: "When we arrived in London, members of our group immediately became anxious to know where we were going next. When they were told that our next stop would be Paris, they went and read all the pamphlets they could find on Paris. The whole time they were in London, they were mentally in Paris – they missed London. When we got to Paris, the group started to think of our next stop, Rome. Now they spent their time in Paris thinking about Rome! When I first noticed this, I was angry at the people I had observed doing this, but as I thought it through, I realized that I was really angry at myself because I was doing exactly the same thing. I realized that I was not only doing it on this trip, but I do it in my life every day. Instead of paying attention to the situations and the people who are in front of me right now, I keep looking ahead to the next event or the next person I will meet. In doing this, I'm missing so much of what is going on right in front of me. I need to change the way I live my life! When I get home, I'm going to put a sign on my desk with these words: Beware! If you're not careful, no matter where you are, you won't be there!"

That priest had learned a valuable lesson on that pilgrimage; he learned the importance of being aware of the world around you right now, in this place. This week, why not take a break from thinking ahead and worrying about tomorrow's events, meetings or problems and just concentrate on people or things around you, right now, in this place?

January 15th
Adlai's Gold Watch

A friend called several months ago, and in a rather uncharacteristically timid voice said, "I could use some advice or help or something."

"What's the problem?" I asked.

"Well, I can't put my finger on it, but I guess the best way to say it is that I feel like a Coke that has lost all its fizz. I don't know if I love my wife, I sometimes can't stand my kids, work seems pointless, and most days I keep saying things like, 'who cares?' or 'why bother?' What makes it all the more strange is that from the outside, no one can tell what I feel on the inside."

As he talked, a quote that I sometimes use in prayer kept running through my mind. The quote is attributed to Adlai Stevenson: "You can have an expensive gold watch with a perfect assembly of little pieces in it, but it is all worthless if the mainspring is broken." A couple of years ago while I was on retreat at Holy Spirit Monastery in Georgia, an old monk asked me to read that quote and to meditate on it using this question: "Is my life like Adlai's gold watch, neatly assembled, yet worthless because of a faulty mainspring?"

I guess I spent the better part of that week of retreat thinking about that question. When I went back to the old monk, he simply said, "Well, is there life in your love, and love in your life? The 'mainspring' of life is love, ya know!"

No matter what you do with your life, no matter how you package it, if there is not genuine love motivating you, you'll find yourself pretty empty in a very short time. The next time you pray, be sure to ask the Good Lord to keep you motivated by love. If God gives you that gift, you'll be so full of life, and so full of love that you won't ever feel empty. Your life won't be anything at all like that watch with the broken mainspring; it will be like those Timex watches that "just keep on ticking."

My friend and I have been meeting weekly for the past few months, talking about life. We've had some pretty good conversations. We've talked through a lot of problems, and we've even prayed together. We don't have all the answers, but we are trying to keep an eye on the "mainsprings" of our lives by asking God to fill us with love enough to keep our lives from ending like Adlai's gold watch.

January 16th
Be Not Afraid

A friend of mine called this past week to take me to lunch. As I was riding in his car, I noticed that he had a small statue of Jesus attached to his dashboard, and as he saw me looking at it, he blushed and said, "My wife gave me that. I sometimes pray in the car, and that little thing keeps me focused on whom I am talking to. Do you think I'm weird?" I assured him that I didn't think he was weird at all, and that I have a crucifix on my sun visor for the same reason. He smiled and then pointed to a colorful magnetic sign that was attached to his ashtray. "I read this out loud when I'm depressed or discouraged, it really does help a lot." What he pointed to was a quote from the Prophet Isaiah that is quite familiar to most of us because it is the basis for the song "Be Not Afraid". Here's the quote:

> *"Fear not, for I have redeemed you; I have called you by name, you are mine. When you pass through the rivers, they shall not overwhelm you. When you walk through fire, you shall not be burned, and the flame will not consume you. For I am the Lord, your God" (Isaiah 43:1-3)*

I hope to get one of those little signs to put in my car. In the ups and downs of life, I think that these words can be a real boost. Why not copy them down and put them in your car? Then when you're stuck in traffic, you may have some pleasant words to think about.

January 17th
Being Competitive

Someone was telling me the other day that he recently had a very interesting conversation with the abbot of a Trappist monastery. This friend, a family man who has five children, is a very successful salesman. Every year he goes on retreat, and this year he made his retreat at a monastery in the South. He was telling the abbot that one of the pitfalls of being a salesman is that it makes him too competitive. "You begin to see all of life as a great competition, and everyone you meet is your rival. Competition has become second nature to me. Is there any way that I can turn this 'second nature' into something for God?" he asked the abbot.

The abbot gave him a surprising answer. The abbot said, "Instead of competing with everyone you meet, just compete with one person – compete with yourself. At the end of the day, ask yourself, 'Was I kinder today than I was yesterday? Was I more compassionate today than yesterday? Am I closer to my family and to God today than I was yesterday?' And finally, ask yourself, 'What am I willing to do tomorrow to make sure that I'm better tomorrow than I was today?' It's okay to be competitive, the abbot said, as long as you're competitive about the right things!"

Are you kinder today than you were yesterday? Are you trying to be more understanding and compassionate today than you were yesterday? Are you making an effort to be closer to God and to your family than you were yesterday? Wouldn't we all be better off if we became a little more competitive with ourselves?

January 18th
Call Out to Jesus for Help

A mail boat was returning from the West Indies. Among the passengers was a man with a dog. A small child was playing with the dog, throwing a stick toward the front part of the deck for the dog to retrieve. One toss went too far and skittered off the deck into the ocean. At once, the dog jumped into the ocean after the stick. The dog's owner raced to the ship's captain and begged him to turn the ship around to rescue the dog.

"You want me to stop the mail for a stupid dog?" the captain screamed. "I can't do that!"

"Then you'll stop the mail for a man!" shouted the dog's owner, and with that, he jumped overboard. Of course, the captain had to stop the ship at this point so that both owner and dog were rescued.

So often people tell me that they feel worthless, that they feel like they are "drowning in a sea of troubles" and there seems to be no one who cares enough to save them. Well, we as Christians know that Jesus, much like that dog's owner, was willing to jump into our world to save us. He is also willing to jump into your sea of troubles to help you. If you are one of those who are feeling the need of a savior, why not call out to Jesus to help?

January 19th
Calming Angels

In 1777, a sculptor by the name of William Rush was standing on a battlefield near Princeton, New Jersey, when he witnessed the American army running away from an advancing British army. He noticed how frightened the Americans were, and how they just gave into their fear and took off running. Then all at once, the American soldiers stopped running and looked on in a kind of awe. General Washington had arrived on the field. Just his appearance on the field gave them courage. William Rush was amazed at the influence of Washington on the men. He said, "It was as if God had sent a calming angel. Once the soldiers saw General Washington, they knew that if he were present, all was not lost. The army turned back and fought the enemy, the retreat was over."

Isn't it amazing how one man can have such influence on others? Simply the sight of George Washington was enough to encourage those who, moments before, were terrified and giving up. If you took some time to think about it, would you discover some "George Washingtons" in your life? Can you recall people who have had, or perhaps even still have the power to calm your fears, the power to bring out the best in you, and the power to give you the courage to face some rather difficult circumstances? If there are such people in your life, pause and give thanks for them, for they are a true gift from God, a gift of "calming angels". While you are thinking along these lines, why not consider whether or not God is calling YOU to be a "calming angel" for others?

January 20th
Generating Warmth

An artist painted a picture of winter showing big trees covered and bent over with heavy snow, the sky dark, gray and dreary, a dark house casting long shadows on the snow as twilight appeared to be turning into darkness. It was a very impressive painting, but because it was so somber, so gloomy and so desolate looking, no one bought it. As the artist was closing his shop for the evening, he mentioned to a colleague of his that he thought he'd never be able to sell the painting. "Everyone comments on the painting. They are drawn to it. Everyone seems to stop and spend a few extra minutes looking at it, but no one buys it. How will I ever get someone to buy this painting?"

"I think I could do something to sell your painting," the artist's colleague assured him. "Just let me take it to my studio tonight and I will make a slight adjustment that will change everything."

The next morning, just as the artist was opening his shop for the day, his colleague came in with the painting. "Wait until you see your painting! I am absolutely certain that the first person who sees this painting will buy it. Take a look."

When the artist saw his wintry painting, he couldn't believe his eyes. It looked totally different. "I can't believe how two simple strokes of a paintbrush have changed everything! You are a true artist!"

The artist's colleague had made two small strokes of paint on the canvas, but, just as the original artist had said, those two strokes made all the difference. In one of the windows of that dark house, the colleague put a stroke of golden yellow paint, and on the snow outside that window he put just a tiny highlight of yellow. The effect was magical – it lighted the window so that the cold wintry scene was transformed into one of warmth and comfort. Within an hour, that painting was sold.

In this very same way, small gestures of kindness, compassion and understanding can, by the warmth they generate, transform a cold world into a place of tenderness and comfort. God has made you the artist and the paintbrush is in your hands.

January 21st
We Need to Act Like a Christian, Not Just Talk Like One

One of my favorite scenes from Victor Hugo's *Les Miserables* is the one in which the bishop arrives at his new home, a sixty-room mansion. After he has lived there a short while, he notices that there is a very small hospital directly across the street. The bishop goes over to the hospital and asks, "How many patients have you here?" He was told that there were twenty six patients. Then he asks, "And how many rooms are there here in this house?"

"There are six rooms in this house," he is told.

"Obviously there has been some mistake," the bishop said. "You shall have my house, and I will take yours. Move your patients."

The sick were moved into the sixty-room mansion, and the bishop moved into the six rooms in the little hospital. The people of the village are amazed and disturbed by these events. When they are asked by a bystander why they are so upset, the people reply, "Because he doesn't act like a bishop!"

That little scene was Hugo's way of poking fun of those churchmen of his time who may have called themselves Christians, but their actions spoke otherwise. Victor Hugo's "good bishop" does other kindly deeds, and by the end of the book, he is known for his goodness.

What do people say about you? Are you known for your goodness? Would people describe you as one who not only talks about being Christian, but truly lives like one?

January 22nd
God Planting Seeds

I read an article the other day about a special kind of evergreen tree known as the "lodge pole pine". It can be found in great numbers throughout the Yellowstone National Park. The amazing thing about this tree is that its pinecones hang on the tree for years and years without falling to the ground. Even when they do fall to the ground, these pinecones do not open up to disperse their seeds. The cone of the lodge pole pine will only open when it is exposed to extreme heat. When a forest fire rages through the park and all of the trees are destroyed, these pinecones, activated by the heat of the fire, release their seeds so that the first trees to grow in the devastated forests are the lodge pole pines.

Isn't it amazing how God takes care to ensure that even in the midst of a great disaster, the seeds of new life and hope are already being planted?

This is a good image for us to remember in our own life experiences. When devastating things happen to us, it is good for us to recall the lodge pole pine tree. Even in the midst of tragic events, God is already at work planting seeds of new life and hope.

January 23rd
Do We Know Where We Are Going?

Two young children took all the money they had and went to a county fair. As they looked around at all of the things "to do", they decided that they both loved the merry-go-round, so they put all of their money into buying merry-go-round tickets. They had been going around and around for a long time when their money ran out. As they got off the ride, their mother said, "Well, I see you finally got off that ride. Just tell me one thing. Where have the two of you been for all the money you spent?"

That's a good question for any one of us to ask ourselves as we consider our lives and how we are "spending" our time, our talents, our enthusiasm. Where have we been? Where did all of our efforts get us? If our lives are to mean anything more than "going around in circles," we have to take some time to consider a few questions. What's our purpose in life? Do we have a goal? What's our destination in life? Are we following a call of some kind? Does our life have meaning?

The Gospels are full of accounts of Jesus inviting us to follow Him. Perhaps today is a good day for us to stop, to check out where we have been and where we are going, to make certain we aren't going in endless circles.

January 24th
Molded

The world-famous artist Michelangelo is buried in the beautiful church of Santa Croce in Florence, Italy. As you approach his tomb, you notice a stone slab that is set into the floor. At one time it had an inscription carved into it, but over many years so many people have walked on it that the inscription is no longer legible. If you check with one of the ushers of the church, they will tell you that the stone slab marks the burial place of Domenico Ghirlandajo. Ever hear of him? Most people haven't. Although relatively unknown, he is probably one of the more significant people in the history of Art. He is significant not only for his own artwork, but also because of the talent he called forth from others. He was Michelangelo's art teacher!

That humble art teacher not only gave the world his own artistic works, but also gave the world a new great talent in his student. When tourists come to Florence to see the wonders of Michelangelo's work, they often include a visit to his tomb. For most of these tourists, however, the teacher's tomb goes unnoticed while the student's tomb is greatly honored. It's a bit of a tragedy that the markings on that stone slab have been allowed to fade away, for Ghirlandajo shaped one of the world's greatest talents.

Are there people like Domenico Ghirlandajo in your life? Is there a teacher or parent, grandparent or friend who has molded and shaped you into the good, talented person you are today? Do you give them the honor, respect and thanks that they deserve? Wouldn't it be a tragedy for that person to go unrecognized for their contribution?

January 25th
Don't Let Your Fear Stop You

Two caterpillars were crawling across the grass when a butterfly flew over them. They looked up and saw the butterfly dart from one flower to the next, sometimes flying very high, sometimes very near the ground. One caterpillar nudged its friend and said, "I can't even imagine it. You couldn't get me up in one of those things for a million bucks!"

Isn't it amazing how we let fear rule our lives and limit what we are willing to become? So often God sends opportunities in order that we become more than what we are today. However we pass up those opportunities because we let our fears set our limits. God has a grand plan for each one of us. The only thing that can get in the way of what God dreams for us is US.

God wants you to soar to new heights – let Him take you there.

January 26th
How's Your Driving?

A young mother was driving her kindergarten-aged son home from school one day when he remarked, "Mom, I really like it when you drive me home."

"Why?" asked his mother.

"Because it's so quiet – when Daddy drives me home, all the stupid idiots come out and he spends the whole time yelling real loud at them. And you know what else? Sometimes he says those words that you told me I'm never allowed to say!"

Bishop Sheen once said that one of the best ways to find out just how truly Christian you are is to examine what you are like when you are driving. So, using that criteria … How Christian are you?

January 27th
Stand on Your Own Two Feet

Theodore Roosevelt is credited with the story of two men who were talking politics. One man said to the other, "Tell me, just why are you a Democrat?"

"Because my father and my grandfather before him were Democrats, and I will follow in their footsteps."

The first man was very surprised by this answer, so he said, "Well, that's got to be the dumbest reason I've ever heard for being a member of any party! Don't you ever think for yourself? What would you be if your grandfather was a horse-thief and your father was a bank-robber?"

The second man thought for a moment feeling a bit insulted, but then he smiled and said, "Then I guess I'd be a Republican!"

Whether you are a Democrat, Republican or Independent, that story probably brought a devious smile to your face because you were thinking how you could change the party labels and use the story against a family member or friend who belongs to a party other than the one you prefer. Regardless of your party affiliation, what the story does point out is that no matter what our parents or other ancestors thought, eventually we have to make our own decision about our beliefs. This is not only true in the political realm, but also it is true when it comes to faith.

I had a conversation the other day with a man who was telling me that he has begun to question some of the things that the Church teaches. "I don't care for all of those 'odd religious practices' my parents did all the years I was growing up!" he said with a tinge of anger in his voice. "And I don't think I'll do any of them any more! I don't know what I think or believe, but I am NOT what they were!"

I suppose he expected me to be angry, because he was quite surprised when I didn't react in a negative way. I simply told him that it was time for him to stand on his own 'religious' feet and authentically search for God. I told him that this is exactly what Jesus wants from each of us. He wants us to choose to follow Him, not because our parents or friends have done so, but because we, in our own hearts, out of our own convictions, want to follow Him.

January 28th
Faith Is an Ongoing Learning Process

Albert Einstein often told the story of a time when he was sitting in a park quietly eating his lunch and looked up to see a 17 year old directly across from him also eating lunch. The young man looked at him and smiled and just to make conversation asked, "Hey mister, what do you do for a living?"

"I spend most of my time studying mathematics," Einstein replied.

"Really?" gasped the young man. "I finished math last semester! I can't believe there's that much more to learn!"

Einstein was amazed that some people think it's possible to know all there is to learn about a particular field of study. He was humble enough to know that there is always more to learn.

I think most of us would smile at that teenager's assumption that he had learned all there was to know about math since, like Einstein, we all know there's always more to learn. But there are many people who have a similar attitude about their faith. They assume that because they learned about Jesus and the Church and the Sacraments when they were children in school that they have learned all that there is to know. They often conclude that their religious education is complete when they leave school. The Lord offers us a share in the great riches of a spiritual life, but many do not partake because they assume that they already "know it all". This is far from the truth, however.

God wants to show us so very much, and there is always so much more to learn, that a lifetime is insufficient for us to comprehend even part of the knowledge He wishes to share with us. Therefore, it is important that we continue learning as much as we can about the Scriptures, the Sacraments, Church doctrine, and the spiritual life.

January 29th
Go Ask Them

If you were asked the question, "Are you a Christian?" how would you answer? I ask this question because I was reading a book by President Jimmy Carter in which he tells of a group of Christian lay missionaries who went through the countryside trying to make converts. One day they came near an Amish settlement, and hoping to make a new convert, they approached an Amish farmer and asked him "Brother, are you a Christian?"

The farmer scratched his head and asked them if they had a pen and some paper. When they had given him the pen and paper, the farmer began to write down a list of names. After a few minutes, he spoke to the missionaries. "Here's a list of the people who know me best. Go ask them if I am a Christian."

Jimmy Carter makes the point that the real evidence of one's faith is the fruit it bears. Does your life and faith bear enough fruit so that if your friends or neighbors were asked if you were a Christian, they'd be able to say yes?

January 30th
Forgetting Can Be a Virtue

I think it was St. Anthony of the Desert who said that one of the best things people can do for themselves is that each night as they undress for bed, they should also undress their heart and mind from the mistakes and failures of the day. He said that forgetting can be a virtue. The person who remembers hurts, personal slights, grudges or frustrations carries a burden that over time becomes a great affliction.

Thinking "I will forgive you, but I won't forget" is simply another way of saying "I won't forgive you". The person who wants to follow Jesus must learn the three "F's" of forgiveness: forgiven, forgotten, forever.

Suppose someone were to cut you with a knife. What would happen to that wound if you constantly ran around showing the wound to everyone? Even after it had been cleaned, medicated, and bandaged, you'd keep unwrapping the dressing to show others the injury. Wouldn't that wound most likely become infected? In the same way, if we keep examining over and over again in our minds the hurts, slights, or frustrations that occur on any given day, our minds and hearts can become infected with the bitterness that can destroy relationships.

I think St. Anthony was right. The fine art of forgetting can be a virtue!

January 31st
Cut Them Down

I've been reading a book about the last years of General Robert E. Lee. The book tells of one occasion, years after the Civil War, when General Lee was visiting old friends in Kentucky. His hostess led him to the remains of an old oak tree whose limbs were all broken down. There was just a slight sign of life in the charred old tree. "The damned Yankees and their artillery did that to my lovely tree," she said. "Every time I look at that tree, I'm filled with such rage that I don't know what to do with myself!"

General Lee looked at her and very kindly said, "I think you'd do yourself and the rest of your family a world of good if you'd chop down this old tree and forget it. The longer you let that anger and resentment grow in you, the more you are becoming like this tree, more dead than alive. Please cut the thing down. Let it go and forget it – maybe you might even begin to forgive and get on with living, rather than hanging on to dying."

I don't know what the old woman did about her tree. The advice she was given was certainly good advice that all of us could use. Do you have any "half dead trees" in your life that fill you with rage every time you look at them? Does your heart harbor resentments, old angers, old hurts and grudges? Do they continue to grow like that burned out old oak tree? Perhaps General Lee's advice would be of help to you – cut them down and forget them!

February 1st
Focus on Your Blessings

On a very cold, foggy day in February, someone calls to a young woman who is crossing the street to tell her that she's left her car's lights on. The woman stops in her tracks and goes back to turn them off. As she continues on her way, she is heard to mutter to herself, "I can see it's going to be one of those days when everything I do turns out bad!" She didn't stop to offer a word of thanks to the person who had spared her a dead battery. She didn't stop to think that this had already started out to be a good day because someone took the time to warn her about her lights.

It's pretty easy for us to forget how blessed we are as we muddle through these wintry days. If we'd simply stop at the end of each day to take a kind of personal "good things that have happened to me today" inventory, I bet each of us would be astonished at how much good happens in a single day. Gray winter days can tend to make whiners out of us. Perhaps the following poem can help to keep us focused on our blessings:

With feet to take me where I'd go,
With eyes to see the sunset's glow,
With ears to hear what I would know;

I'm blessed indeed. The world is mine.
Oh God, forgive me when I whine.

February 2nd
Broken Strings

Did you ever hear of the great violinist Paganini? I've been thinking about him these past few days. When I was in college, I had to take a music appreciation course in which the professor would take us to various concert halls to hear classical music – symphonies, chamber music, piano concerts, operas, and so on. When we returned, he would tell us stories about the people who had composed the music we had just heard. One day he told how Paganini had turned what everyone thought was going to be a terribly embarrassing concert into a magnificent performance.

It happened that Paganini was performing before a very distinguished audience when suddenly one of the four strings on his violin broke. The audience gasped, but Mr. Paganini just kept playing on the three remaining strings. Then, without warning, the second string snapped in two, followed immediately by the third string! The audience again was shocked and couldn't believe what was happening. Paganini stopped for a moment, raised his violin above his head and said "One string – and Paganini!" With that, he finished the concert playing the rest of the musical selection on just one string. When he finished, the audience was on its feet, wildly applauding his great skill and artistry.

I have been thinking about this incident in music history because many people have been telling me some of the major problems they are facing. There are many people among us who are trying to cope with great difficulties with such courage that they are, like Paganini, achieving great things.

I guess I bring this up as a reminder that from time to time, every one of us will experience a few "broken strings." We may have to face circumstances that look hopeless, and we may even feel completely helpless, but that doesn't mean we have to quit trying. God has given each of us a wonderful capacity to overcome seemingly overwhelming odds. It takes courage, and it takes faith, but it can be done. Are there any strings breaking in your life right now? Do you have the faith and courage to keep on playing?

February 3rd

Picture This!

A little boy came home from religion class talking about how much he liked the class. "What did you learn today?" his mother asked. "I learned how Moses led the Israelites out of Egypt" he replied smiling.

"Can you tell me how Moses was able to get the Israelites out of Egypt?" his mother asked.

"Well, I'll show you my drawing! You see here Moses hired some bridge experts and they built a very big bridge, bigger than any bridge ever built so that it crossed over the whole Red Sea!" he exclaimed.

"I don't think you have that story right" the boy's mother said, laughing.

"Well, if I told you the story that they told us in class, you'd never believe me!"

The story of Moses didn't sound reasonable to that little boy, so he came up with his own version that was easier for him to accept. While we may laugh at that little Bible student, perhaps we might stop to consider how we may be a lot like him. Most of us find it relatively easy to accept the stories in the Bible about how God was active in the lives of the Israelites or of the first disciples, but we waver when we are told that God wants to be involved in OUR lives. We assume that we aren't good enough, perfect enough, or holy enough for God to be involved in our lives. Yet, Jesus did come for each one of us – including YOU! God is interested in you and your situation. We hear those words preached to us, but we don't let them sink into our mind or into our heart. We, like that little Bible student, simply "draw our own picture" of how the story should go.

As the picture drawn for us in the Gospels reminds us, God is not the God of distant ages. As Jesus Himself said "God is not the God of the dead, but of the living!" God loves you and has chosen you for His own. He wants to be involved in your life. Tear up the "picture" you have drawn of your life. Give the pencil to Jesus and let Him draw a true picture of the Father's love for you.

February 4th
Going to Church on Sunday

"Dad, did you go to church every Sunday when you were a kid?" a young boy asked his father.

"Yes, son, I went every Sunday without fail," replied the father.

"Well, I bet it won't do me any good either. I'm not going anymore!" said the boy.

Does what happens in your heart on Sunday have any effect on who you are throughout the week? Does your coming to church on Sunday make a difference in who you are and the kind of person you are becoming? Can your children or friends tell that your coming to church on Sunday is not just to attend a service but also to meet Jesus, to hear His word, and to become a better person than you were yesterday? What's going on in your heart at church on Sunday?

February 5th
Three Golden Gates

One of the things that I like to do to keep me thinking the way the Gospel teaches me to think is to put little signs on my bathroom mirror as reminders of what is important. This week I put up a little sign that says, "REMEMBER THE THREE GOLDEN GATES!"

These words have become important to me because I've been meditating on how Jesus would want me to deal with the stories or rumors that I sometimes hear about others. As I was praying, I remembered a wise saying from one of the Desert Fathers of the early Church. (The Desert Fathers were men who went out to the desert to try to live the Gospel as perfectly as they could.) One of these holy men said, "If you are tempted to repeat a story told about someone, make sure you make that story pass through the golden gates before you let that story pass through your lips!"

What are the three golden gates? They are three questions that must be asked if you want to repeat the story you've heard and not break the "Golden Rule." If you want to be a true friend of Jesus, you must remember that all that you say about others must be able to pass through these three golden gates. Here are those three questions:

1. *Is it true?*
2. *Is it needful or helpful to anyone to repeat this story?*
3. *Is it kind?*

Throughout this coming week you will probably hear many rumors or stories about people. When you do "REMEMBER THE THREE GOLDEN GATES!"

February 6th
Great Things Happen When We Work Together

I read this week about a man named Herman Ostry, a farmer from Bruno, Nebraska, who faced a rather challenging problem. Mr. Ostry was at a loss as to what to do about the fact that local construction projects had altered the course of a nearby creek so much that his barn floor was 29 inches under water. He talked with his son and devised a plan to deal with the situation.

They determined that if they built a new foundation about 143 feet away from the barn's present site and were able to somehow move the barn to that foundation, all of their problems would be solved. So Herman's son, Mike, constructed a latticework of steel tubing and nailed, bolted and welded it to the inside and outside of the barn. Hundreds of handles were attached to the latticework. Mike calculated that the wooden part of the barn weighed about 17,000 pounds.

The Ostry's invited their neighbors and townsfolk to a barn-raising. They needed 344 people, one for each of the handles that had been attached to the steel tubing. After one practice lift, those 344 volunteers actually picked up the barn, each one supporting approximately 50 pounds, and slowly walked the barn up a slight hill 143 feet to the barn's new foundation. It took just 3 minutes.

Isn't that an amazing story? It's a great illustration, I think, of what

God wants from us. St. Paul teaches us that when the Body of Christ works together, great things happen. This is true whether it's just two or three members of the Body of Christ working on some project, or if it's an entire parish working at something. When we "share the load" we can move much more than a 17,000 pound barn!

February 7th
Spiritual Depth

The Japanese have made an art of growing dwarf trees. Trees that would otherwise have grown to be great oak trees or huge pine trees end up growing to be only 12 to 16 inches tall. How do the Japanese accomplish this? They cut the tap root of each tree so that the tree is forced to live and survive only on its surface roots. Without the ability to "go deep" for both water and nutrients via its tap root, the tree's growth is severely stunted.

In much the same way, our spiritual life and growth is very much determined by how "deep" we allow ourselves to go for water and nutrients. If we only allow our spiritual lives a few Sunday Masses a year, a quick prayer uttered here and there, or a few thoughts about the next life whenever we attend a funeral, we are apt to have a spiritual life very much resembling one of those Japanese dwarf trees. On the other hand, if we take our spiritual life seriously and constantly tend to it, nourish it with long periods of sustained prayer, practice the works of mercy and seek to learn God's will for our lives, our spiritual life will resemble great oak trees which soar toward the heavens and provide food and shelter for others. How deep are you willing to go in your spiritual life?

February 8th
Hang On To Your Enemies

I was reading about an event from the life of Abraham Lincoln that I have been using in my meditation. Mr. Lincoln gave his last public speech two days after Robert E. Lee surrendered to Grant. The speech took place in front of the White House where a large crowd had gathered to hear the President give a victory speech. Mr. Lincoln was not giving a wild, boastful speech but was talking about the need for reconstruction. People in the crowd were getting impatient with him and began shouting out questions and slogans at him. Realizing that his talk was a complete flop, Lincoln just kept quiet and stared at the crowd. Someone shouted, "What are you going to do with the rebel leaders?"

Before Lincoln could answer, the crowd started chanting, "Hang 'em! Hang 'em! Hang 'em!"

The President just stood there, not knowing how to reply. In the midst of all the noise, Tad, the President's eleven-year old son, tugged at his father's sleeve and said, "No Papa! Don't hang them. Hang on to them."

Quickly Abraham Lincoln raised his hands to quiet the crowd and then said, "There! My son Tad's got it right. Don't hang them, hang on to them!" Then he continued to speak of the need for healing and not vengeance.

Have you ever felt like you wanted to hang someone? Have you ever been that angry and hurt? Is there a division or rift in your family or among your friends? Are you carrying some kept hurts that make you want never to speak to someone again? Our first reaction may be to want to strike out at those who have hurt us, but where will that lead us? As Mahatma Gandhi once said, "A nation which chooses to operate by the 'eye for an eye and a tooth for a tooth' way of life will end up being a nation of blind, toothless people."

Jesus has called us to treat our enemies differently than the rest of the world treats its enemies. We are called to love them, not hurt them. Perhaps complete forgiveness and healing is not possible yet. But, maybe just deciding to "hang on to them" rather than "hang 'em" would be a good first step.

For the past week I have been meditating over young Tad Lincoln's words. Try it yourself. You'll be surprised what you discover about yourself.

February 9th
Winter Days

As we move through these cold days of Winter, it is amazing to hear the number of people who take the colder temperatures as personal insults from God or Mother Nature. It seems that wherever I go, people are talking and complaining about the weather. It reminds me of a story from the ancient Hasidic Masters that tells of a conversation between a shepherd tending his flock, and a friend who was visiting him.

Visiting friend: "What kind of weather are we going to have today?"

Shepherd: "The kind of weather I really like."

"How do you know it's going to be the kind of weather you like?"

"Since I found out that I can't always get what I really like, I have learned to really like whatever I get. So I am quite sure that I will like today's weather."

Isn't it amazing how much some people's happiness is affected by little things that they decide to take as personal insults? I see many people who have everything in the world that a person could ever truly want; yet they are unhappy. They are not unhappy because they don't have what they need, they are unhappy because they have decided to be unhappy. In fact, I know some people who have such a rotten outlook on life that they are not happy unless they have discovered a reason to be miserable!

Today it would be good for us to consider how loved we are, how much Jesus endured for us and just how blessed we truly are. We may not always get what we like, but we can learn to like what we do get. Happiness rests not in what we have or in how much we have, but rather in how much we appreciate what we do have.

February 10th
Savor the Time You Have

I was walking through church one day this past week when I noticed an older man, sitting in one of the pews, looking through a pocket calendar. When he saw me, he said "hello" and shook his head. "Can you believe a whole month of this new year is gone already?" he asked. "The older I get, the faster the time goes. It seems like I can't keep hold of a single moment."

He smiled at me and said, "You're probably too young to realize it now, but one day you'll look over your shoulder and realize that the years you have left number far less than the years you have lived already, and that's scary! Sometimes I wonder what I have to show for all the years. Remember to savor the time you have. It's gone mighty quick!"

It is amazing that we are already a week into February. There's a Chinese poem about time that sums it up:

Not Twice this day,
Inch of time foot of time
Each a gem.
This day will not come again.
Each minute is worth a priceless gem

Are you savoring the "gems" of time that God has given you? How are you using them?

February 11th
Let God Be God!

Isn't it amazing how often we are heavily burdened with life's problems? It seems to me sometimes that just as we finish one set of problems and are able to lay down a heavy burden, it's not too long before we find ourselves shouldering a whole new set of troubles.

I think this to be the one result that happens when we care for others. When those we love are hurting, we want to take on their hurts too. But don't you ever feel worn out from worrying about those you love and the problems that they face? I know that I do. I think the problem stems from trying to bear too much of the burden ourselves and not letting the Lord help us.

There is an old Jewish tale of a man walking along the road carrying a very heavy sack on his shoulders. A man came down the road driving a horse and wagon. The man driving the cart saw the man struggling with the heavy sack and offered him a ride. The man with the sack accepted the ride and climbed on the wagon. A few minutes later, the driver turned around to ask if his passenger was comfortable and was surprised to see the man was standing up in the back of the wagon with the heavy sack still on his shoulders. The driver remarked, "The wagon is going to carry the sack anyway, why not put down your load and let the horse and wagon do the work?"

When you bring your burdens to the Lord, are you like the man with the heavy sack – standing on the back of the wagon still struggling with the heavy load on his shoulders? Why not put that burden down and let the Lord "do the work"? We may find we're not so heavily burdened as we once thought ... if only we'd let God be God.

February 12th
Learning Through Suffering and Illness

One of the great writers of the twentieth century was Flannery O'Connor. She died at the age of 39 in 1964. From the time she was 25, she knew that she was suffering from a terminal disease, lupus, but she was determined not to allow it to be the focus of her life. She also suffered from a very serious disintegration of the bones, shingles, anemia, and a tumor. It was during these 14 years of suffering that she produced some of her greatest works. When asked how she was able to write in the midst of such suffering, she simply replied, "Many authors produce great works because of their extensive travels. I have never been anywhere but sick. In a sense, sickness is a place, more instructive than a long trip to Europe. I've learned so much from it. Sickness is a very appropriate thing, and I think that those who don't have it, miss one of God's great mercies."

It seems strange to speak of sickness as "one of God's great mercies" doesn't it? Yet Flannery O'Connor is not the only one who sees it that way. I read recently of a college student who went blind. After a long struggle with adjusting to his blindness, he confided to his minister that he was beginning to see life differently. He began to see his blindness as a "talent" given to him by God. Not "talent" in the sense of a special ability, but "talent" as used by Jesus in the parable of the "talents." The young college student said that he wanted to use his blindness in such a way that when Jesus called him home, he could say that he had done something great with what God had given him in blindness. He didn't see his blindness as a burden, but rather as an opportunity.

In your own life right now, do you find yourself dealing with sickness or suffering? Do you feel like Flannery O'Connor who was "never anywhere but sick?" Perhaps, like that young blind student, you can "invest" your illness in such a way that it will bear great fruit for God's kingdom.

February 13th
Kindness Is a Seed That Always Bears Much Fruit

The owner of a drive-through coffee business in Portland, Oregon, reported how surprised she was one morning when one of her customers not only paid for her own mocha, but she also paid for the person in the car behind her. It put a smile on the owner's face to tell the next customer that his drink had already been paid for. That second customer was so happy to have had someone pay for his coffee that he gladly paid for the customer behind him. The owner of the coffee shop couldn't believe it, but the kindness of that first customer turned into a string of kindnesses – one customer paying for the coffee of the next customer – continuing on for 2 hours and 27 customers.

"It restored my faith in humanity to see a simple act of kindness get passed on for two hours!" she said.

One of the Desert Fathers once said, "Kindness is a seed that always bears much fruit." Why not take some time this week to plant a few seeds of kindness?

February 14th
Love Your Enemies

One of the people I enjoy reading about is General Robert E. Lee. A man of outstanding character, he was known for his faith as well. General Lee believed that his faith should not just be a "Sunday faith" but rather it should be integrated into the way he lived his life every day. There is one anecdote about General Lee which illustrates that he was indeed more than a "Sunday Christian".

General Lee was asked by a reporter what he thought of one of his fellow officers in the Confederate Army. The officer in question was widely known to be making terribly derogatory remarks about General Lee. In fact, the officer had attacked just about everything General Lee said or did. "Well, General Lee," the reporter asked, "What do you think of that officer?"

"I believe him to be a fine officer who possesses great military skill," replied the general.

"But sir," the reporter asked, "Don't you know what that man is saying about you, both privately as well as in the press?"

"I know what he says," Lee answered, "But you asked me what my opinion was of him, not his opinion of me."

Jesus tells us to love our enemies and to do good to those who persecute us. General Lee was a man of Christian principles. He had the ability, the opportunity and the national forum to destroy his fellow officer, yet he did not. To do so would have been against his Christian faith.

Have you ever been hurt by what someone has said about you? Haven't you felt like getting even by reacting in a destructive way? Probably all of us have had that experience and yet all of us know that we are called to act differently. Robert E. Lee's desire to be more than a "Sunday Christian" led him to act differently than most people would act. Perhaps our own desire to be more than "Sunday Catholics" will lead us to do what he did.

February 15th
Being a Friend to the Poor

I've been reading the life of one of the most influential saints of the Church, St. Basil the Great. He was the bishop of Caesarea, who lived from 330 to 379 AD, and is famous in the Eastern Catholic Church, (like St. Benedict in the West) as the "Father of Monasticism." Most monks today follow the ways of both Benedict and Basil in their attempt to live a holy life.

You might ask, "Since I am not a monk, what would Basil have to teach me?" Well, I think he has much to teach us, because in addition to being a monk and a bishop, he was well known as the "best friend of the poor." Basil said, "As a Christian, you must realize that the coat hanging unused in your closet belongs to the one who needs it; the shoes rotting in your closet belong to those without shoes; the money you put in the bank because you don't need it now belongs to those without money. You do wrong to everyone you could help, but fail to help."

This basic Christian teaching of Basil is centuries old, yet it is as applicable today as it was so many years ago. In these difficult days, it might be good for us to keep those holy words of St. Basil the Great in mind. We might take some time to consider what we might have in our own closets that is not being used that could be of great value if given to those who have little or nothing.

God has given all of us many gifts. With each of these gifts comes a great responsibility to share with others some of the bounty we have received. St. Basil knew this and lived it. That's why the Church refers to him as Basil the Great, the friend of the poor.

February 16th
Simple Truths

Some students were asked to write what they thought were the most important things to believe about God. One student wrote, "I don't much care that God knows everything. I know He does. What I really think is important is the fact that God knows me." Another student wrote, "I think it is not as important to know that God is everywhere as it is to know that wherever I am, God will be with me." A third student added, "I agree with what both of you have said, but I would add how important it is for me to always seek to know God, wherever I am, and to seek to find Him wherever I find myself."

These are very simple, but very profound truths.

February 17th

Jumping to Conclusions

I came across an interesting story that can serve to remind us that jumping to conclusions can be dangerous.

On a wintry night, a motorcycle driver decided to wear his jacket backwards so that the biting winds and freezing rain could not penetrate the openings between the buttons. Wearing the jacket backwards was a little uncomfortable, but it did serve his purpose and he was much warmer. As he sped along the road, the motorcycle skidded on an icy spot and crashed into a tree. When the ambulance arrived, the EMT pushed through the crowd to get to the man to tend to his injuries. He asked a man who was standing over the victim what happened. "Well," the man replied, "the guy was in pretty good shape after the accident, but by the time we got his head turned around to face to the front, his neck was broken!"

One of the most important lessons any of us can learn about life is that jumping to conclusions, taking action, offering advice, or making decisions before we know the whole story, can be very destructive. Sometimes, as in the story above, jumping to conclusions can cause a great deal of pain, pain that could have been avoided. Taking the time to get to know the whole story is an act of true charity.

February 18th
Know Your Limitations

A young mother put her two children to bed. She then changed into one of her husband's oversized sweatshirts, put on a pair of his old jeans and then began to wash her hair. As she was shampooing, she could hear her kids getting louder and wilder. As soon as she was finished, she wrapped a bath towel around her head and ran into her kids' room and screamed, "Damn it, you kids quiet down right this minute, and I mean it!"

The two little boys were instantly quiet and they stared at her with their mouths hanging open. She turned around, switched off the light and slammed the door. After she was gone, the two-year old asked his older brother, "Who was that?"

Sometimes the circumstances of our daily life can be so aggravating and frustrating that we turn into people that even those closest to us don't recognize. This isn't because we are bad or evil people, but it is because we often fail to remember that we do not have unlimited energy or strength. We are human beings who can only do so much for others. If we forget this, we end up doing others and ourselves a great deal of harm. I think many people live "outside" their limitations because they deeply love their families and friends, and they want to do as much as they can for them. What usually happens is when we live outside our limitations, we often end up angry and frustrated. We try to do so much that we can do none of it well, and some of our loved ones end up bearing the brunt of our anger. An ugly scene follows, and everyone feels hurt and confused.

Perhaps we ought to begin our day with a simple prayer: "Lord, teach me to know my limitations and to live accordingly."

February 19th
A Universal Medicine

At dinner one night, a little girl was excited to tell her parents that there was a new student in her class. "Where is she from?" her father asked.

"She is from Thailand," the little girl replied.

"Does she speak English?" her mother asked.

"Nope," the child answered.

"That must be pretty hard to understand each other," said the mother.

"It doesn't really matter too much. She laughs in English," the little girl said.

Perhaps one of the best gifts that God ever gave us is the ability to laugh. Someone once said that laughter has no foreign accent. It's the one human activity that can cross cultures and bring us all together as one family. There's nothing like a good laugh to clear up a quarrel or to brighten an otherwise gloomy day. Laughter can "lighten up" tense situations and relieve a great deal of stress.

What a wonderful gift we have been given in humor and laughter. I know a doctor who says he often writes out a prescription for his most seriously ill patients that simply reads "laugh 3 times each day." He goes on to explain that laughing people seem to heal quicker. Maybe that old saying is true. Maybe laughter really IS the best medicine.

February 20th
What Do They Know Anyway?

One of the most important things to learn is when NOT to listen to what other people tell you. The great American poet, Carl Sandburg, flunked English class and was told that he should learn to use his hands because he certainly couldn't write well. What if Carl Sandburg had listened and didn't write? Thomas Edison was told by his teacher in grade school that he was stupid and that he didn't know how to think. Einstein could not speak until he was four years old, and did not read at all until he was eight years old. He too was told he was stupid. Beethoven's music teacher wrote an evaluation of his student and concluded by saying, "Mr. Beethoven – as a composer, he's hopeless." What if Beethoven had listened to his teacher and had given up music? F.W. Woolworth couldn't get a job; in fact he was told that he wasn't smart enough even to wait on customers. Walt Disney was fired by his newspaper editor because, as the editor put it, "Mr. Disney doesn't have any good ideas or original thoughts." And finally, the great opera star Caruso was told by his voice teacher, "You can't sing, you have no voice at all. You are wasting my time!"

All of these great people have given the world some truly wonderful gifts. What would have happened if they had listened to what other people had said to them? It is important to learn when NOT to listen to what other people tell you.

February 21st

New Heights

Earlier this week, I was reading part of a Jesuit missionary's journal. He described the many difficulties he had endured in India. He wrote about the harshness of his assignment and the terrible loneliness that was creeping into his soul. He went out one afternoon near the mountains where he observed a nest of eagles. As he sat and watched the eagles, the priest began to pray and to ask God to give him the courage and the strength to persevere with his mission. He asked God to show him how he should deal with all that he had been enduring.

As he sat praying and watching the eagles, the priest noticed that a heavy storm was brewing at the edge of the valley. He wondered what the eagles would do as the storm rushed through the narrow valley. Would they fly to try to outrun the storm? Would they fly into the storm? Or would they be dashed against the rocks?

To his amazement, the eagles set their wings in such a way that the harder the wind blew, the higher it took the eagles until they were soaring far above the storm. The eagles didn't fight the storm, but they used it to reach greater heights. It came to him that the eagles' soaring above the storm was God's answer to his prayer. The priest was facing his own storms, but they didn't have to be the end of his mission. He, like the eagles, could use the storm to reach new heights.

In your own life, are you facing storms that appear to be on the verge of overwhelming you? Like that Jesuit priest, we can all take a lesson from the eagles and let our present difficulties launch us to new heights. As you come before the Lord in prayer, ask God to give you the courage and trust to step out in faith so that you can soar with the eagles.

February 22nd
The Work of Mercy

A 45-year old woman named Catherine living in 19th century Ireland inherited 24,000 pounds sterling from a Quaker couple with whom she had lived for 20 years after the death of her parents. In addition to inheriting that silver, Catherine also inherited her friends' traditional Quaker ways of doing things, especially their strong emphasis of being like Jesus for others. She had always been impressed by their habit of giving to causes that made Jesus more visible and real to the world. They were very charitable people, and so too, because of their example, was Catherine.

Catherine decided that she shouldn't just fritter her inheritance away on useless things. She was going to do good things with it. 24,000 pounds sterling would go a long way in 19th century Ireland. In fact, it was worth about one million U.S. dollars! The "good" that Catherine wanted to do with her money was to attack the terrible poverty she saw all around her. She wanted to care for the sick, to educate poor people, and to improve conditions that were quite hazardous for women. Other Catholic women (Catherine was a Catholic) asked if they could help with her work. They began not only to work together, but to pray together as well. They nursed the sick in hospitals and in their own homes. They taught school. They provided safe quarters for working girls. They even opened an employment agency for young girls who wanted to work as servants for wealthy people. The women worked hard and their work prospered. They did it because of their love for God and for people. The houses that Catherine and her friends opened became known as "houses of mercy." Little did Catherine McAuley know that she had founded Sisters of Mercy with her 24,000 pounds sterling. Catherine McAuley was a Catholic girl with a Quaker background who simply loved God, saw there was work to be done, and knew that she had the talent and the means to do it.

At one point in the Gospel, Jesus is troubled because he sees the people who are like sheep without a shepherd. He tells his apostles that the "harvest is rich, but laborers are few." Then Jesus calls his apostles and sends them forth. What was true in Jesus' day is true in our own. There are many people who are like sheep without shepherds. Catherine McAuley saw it in her own day and responded. This week, as you take time to pray, ask the Lord to show you where He needs your hands, your heart, and your service.

February 23rd
Your Treasure

Take a few moments to consider this question: What is your greatest accomplishment in life? How would you answer it?

I read an interview with former President George Bush, Sr. in which he was asked this same question. The interviewer tried to prompt his answer by asking him, "Is it when you were a fighter pilot during World War II and were shot down and survived?"

President Bush simply said, "No, it's not that."

The interviewer went on asking, "Was it when you were U.S. Ambassador to China, or when you were head of the CIA or Vice President, or was it being President?"

Bush again just simply said, "No." Then, after a long pause, the former President said, "I think my greatest accomplishment is that my children still come home to be with Barbara and me."

Having read George Bush's response to that question, what is your answer now? Would you see your family or the relationship you have with others as your greatest accomplishment? Would you see your faith and living the Christian life as one of your greatest accomplishments? Jesus said, "Wherever your treasure lies, there will your heart be." (Luke 12:34). If you want to know what your greatest accomplishment is, check out what you treasure. Is what you treasure worth giving your heart to?

February 24th
Holding On

One of the tourist attractions in Dayton, Ohio is the home of Paul Lawrence Dunbar, the famous poet. When Dunbar died, his mother was so grief-stricken that she decided to leave his room exactly as it was on the day that he died. She would not let anyone touch a thing, not even the papers that Dunbar had strewn across the top of his desk. The room became her shrine to her son, and that turned out to be unfortunate.

After Dunbar's mother died, her friends discovered that Paul's last poems were lost forever. Because his mother had made his room into a shrine and not moved anything, the sun had bleached the ink on the papers strewn across his desk until most of the words written there were completely bleached out. The last few poems of his life were lost forever.

One of the things that anyone who wants to grow in the spiritual life learns is that when we try to "hold on" too tightly to people or things, we are apt to end up losing them. As difficult as this truth may be to grasp, we should not be surprised, since Jesus taught that "Whoever wishes to save his life will lose it, but whoever loses his life will save it."

Maybe this might be a good time for us to examine our own attitudes toward life. We can approach life filled with fear, "white knuckling" our way through it, or we can see all of life as a gift, holding all of it loosely and remembering to give thanks for all the people and things that are given to our care.

February 25th
Listen!

After having been urged for two years by his adult children, an older man finally admitted that he was hearing impaired, and purchased a hearing aid. He was amazed at how much his hearing improved, and went around telling those he met that he could "hear every word they were saying." He was beside himself with joy and wondered why he had put off getting his hearing aid for so long. The man's children were overjoyed as well because it had been years since they had seen their father so happy and so involved in life. In addition, they were happy that they didn't have to repeat themselves so much.

About a month after their father got his new hearing aid, one of his daughters noticed that he wasn't wearing it. Thinking that he had merely forgotten to put it on, she reminded him to do so.

"I hate that stupid thing!" he said.

"But I thought you loved it," she answered.

"Well, I used to till one day I went for a drive in my car. Why, that thing sounds horrible! I wouldn't be caught dead in a car that sounds so bad! And to think that I always thought that car was so quiet. The hearing aid ruined my car! I won't wear that silly thing ever again. If I continue to wear it, who knows what terrible things I might discover? I'd rather be deaf and happy!"

If you made a concerted effort to listen better, what new "discoveries" do you think you might make? Would you find that the car that you thought was in great condition is really on its last legs? If you listened better to your family and friends, would you discover anything new about them? If you took the time to listen to the things that you say to other people, would you discover that you're not the "kind" person you thought you were? It would probably be a real eye-opener if we all "tested" our hearing from time to time. Who knows what discoveries we might make?

February 26th
Playing Second Fiddle

There is a fable about two thirsty animals, a lion and a tiger, which arrived at a watering hole at the same time. They immediately began to argue about which of them was most important and deserved the right to drink first. The argument became very violent – they would rather die than give up the right to drink first. As the fight continued, both animals happened to look up to see a flock of vultures circling patiently, waiting to see which one would lose the fight and become their lunch. When the lion and tiger realized what was happening, they both drank and quietly withdrew back into the jungle. Being first was not worth becoming someone else's lunch!

This fable reminds me of a comment made by the famous conductor, Leonard Bernstein, when he was asked what instrument in the orchestra was the most difficult to play. His answer was immediate – "Second fiddle. I can get plenty of first violinists, but finding someone who can play second fiddle with enthusiasm is the problem. Yet if there is no one to play second fiddle, there is no harmony."

Even though our society often urges us to "be number one," Jesus teaches us that being number one is not the goal of life. The goal of our lives should be to serve others. Are you ready and able to put aside being first so that you can truly serve others and bring about real harmony?

February 27th
Good Deeds Done for Us

Are you aware of how much other people do for you, and do you show them any appreciation for all that they do? I asked myself that question this past week when someone told me about an incident which occurred in a post office in Washington, D.C. A man was writing at a post office desk when he was approached by an older gentleman with a postcard in his hand. The old man said "Mister, could you please address this postcard for me?"

The man gladly did so, and then agreed to write out the message the old man wanted on the card. "Is there anything else you want me to add to this message?" the younger man asked.

The old man thought about it for a few minutes and then said, "Why yes, at the end could you put, 'P.S. Please excuse the sloppy handwriting?"

How would you have reacted to what the old man had said? I don't know how the young man in the story actually did react, but I'm sure he was at least a bit shocked by the old man's final statement. After I thought about how I would have reacted, I began thinking about an even more interesting and important question. "Have I ever been like the old man, showing a lack of gratitude for a simple act of kindness someone has done on my behalf?"

Probably each one of us is on the receiving end of many acts of kindness every day. Perhaps this week would be a good time for us to become more aware, not only of the many good deeds done on our behalf, but also to become more aware of our response to them.

February 28th
No Rain

A Native American man was invited to attend a Sunday morning church service. The preacher delivered his sermon with much shouting and lots of pulpit-pounding. The Native American showed no emotion or reaction to the sermon. On the way out of church people gathered around him and asked him what he thought of the sermon. His response was "High wind, big thunder ... no rain!"

From time to time, it's good for us to consider how well we are living out the Gospel. Is our following of Jesus just a matter of lots of "high wind and big thunder", or does the faith we profess produce the "rain" that Jesus calls us to produce? Is there a recognizable difference in the way we as Christians care for others, respect others, listen to others and respond to the world around us?

February 29th
Rules for Living

A few years ago, the son of some friends of mine went off to college and ended up living in a student residence. The director of the residence was an older woman who had raised nine of her own children, so that taking care of a house of 22 college boys was something she could handle quite well. When new students arrived, she would meet with them individually. At the end of their conversation, she would ask each new student to take a copy of the following "Golden Rules for Living" and to post it on the door of his room. She reminded them that this was their new home, and they should live accordingly. Here are those rules:

If you open it, close it. If you turn it on, turn it off.
If you unlock it, lock it up. If you break it, admit it.
If you can't fix it, call in someone who can.
If you borrow it, return it. If you value it, take care of it.
If you make a mess, clean it up. If you move it, put it back.
If it belongs to someone else and you want to use it, get permission.
If you don't know how to operate it, leave it alone.
If it's none of your business, don't ask questions.
If it ain't broke, don't fix it.
If it will brighten someone's day, say it.
If it will hurt someone or their reputation, don't say it.

March 1st
Honesty

A United Methodist minister was hired as the new pastor of a Midwestern congregation. About two weeks after the minister moved into the parsonage, a local man stopped by to introduce himself. The young man informed the minister that because he was young and just starting out in life, he wouldn't be able to contribute much to the parish. After thinking for a few minutes, the young man informed the pastor that even though he couldn't give much money, he could "fix" the parsonage electric meter so that the minister's bill would be next to nothing. In addition, he offered to "pirate" cable into the parsonage so that the minister and his family would have cable TV free of charge!

When the minister informed the young man that what he wanted to do was dishonest and immoral since it amounted to stealing, the young man was shocked. "Why, those big companies expect us to cheat. They raise prices to cover it. We're just getting what's coming to us!" the young man exclaimed.

I don't know what the minister finally did to convince the young man. I do know that the man never got the chance to "fix" the electric meter or acquire free cable TV for the minister. I imagine that the young man got quite a sermon on honesty.

I think it was Woodrow Wilson who wrote that his father taught him that the most important virtue to have was honesty. Whenever Woodrow went to school to take a test in mathematics or science, his father would give him the same speech. "Today you will not be taking one test, you will be taking two – one in mathematics and the other in honesty. I hope that you will fail the mathematics test rather than the honesty test. There are many good people in the world who cannot pass a math test, but there are no good people in the world who cannot pass an honesty test!" The speech made a big impression on the future president. He made it his number one goal to be honest.

We are all well aware of the fact that we live in a culture of dishonesty. Our society has so rationalized dishonesty that many truly believe that dishonesty is only wrong if you get caught. You can steal electricity by "fixing the meter" or hijack cable TV, or steal from your employer, as long as you don't get caught. How are we supposed to respond to such a world view?

When St. Francis of Assisi discovered that much of his home-town citizens were dishonest and corrupt, his response was not to point a finger at anyone. He decided that his response had to be a Gospel response. His response was to look into his own heart and begin immediately to root out any dishonesty, sin or corruption that he found there. He felt that he wasn't holy enough to point out other people's scandalous behavior. Francis felt that God wanted him to simply root out his own sin, and by that example, challenge others to do the same.

As we continue to hear news reports of dishonesty or corruption in government, in business or in society, perhaps we, like St. Francis, can take the opportunity not to point a finger at anyone, but simply to look within and examine our own conduct and root out any dishonesty or sin we may find there.

March 2nd
Limiting Words

"If you have to talk at all," the doctor said, "make sure the total of your words each day is not more than 50 words. If you disregard what I tell you to do, you may never be able to speak again."

Can you imagine what it would be like to have your doctor give you this advice? Can you imagine how frustrating it would be to be unable to speak as often as you want? I had a conversation this past week with a man who is suffering from throat cancer and was told by his doctor to "speak as little as possible". The man told me that at the beginning of his treatment he was allowed only 50 words a day. I asked him what it was like to be so limited in speech, and if he had learned anything profound from the experience.

"I've learned three things (so far) from this bout with cancer. First, most of us talk too much anyway and what we say is not very helpful in making the world a better place. Second, talking is not the only way to communicate. Your eyes can say a lot if you let them and if other people take the time to 'read' what you are trying to say; and third, if you're not talking, you have a better chance to do more listening. I was surprised how much I didn't know about my wife and kids. I had been talking so much and listening so little that I had missed a lot of important information!"

The man went on to tell me that while cancer has been a terrible experience in his life, he has learned to love the silence it imposed on him. "I've really come to enjoy listening to people. I used to think I loved to talk with people, now I love to listen to people. I know now that listening, not talking, is the most important part of communication."

The conversation I had with this man has certainly made me think twice about what I would learn if I suddenly found myself unable to speak. If you had to limit the number of words you said each day and was forced to do more listening than talking, how do you think it would affect you, and what do you think you'd discover?

March 3rd
Look at the Big Picture

There is a tribe in the country of Borneo know as the Diaks. A few years ago, they were suffering from a severe malaria epidemic and many of them died. In response to the crisis, the World Health Organization decided that they would have to take some action to combat the epidemic before the entire tribe was wiped out. The W.H.O.'s response was to spray DDT over the jungle area to kill the mosquitoes that carry malaria. It was a great success. Almost all of the mosquitoes were killed. Health and happiness returned to the Diaks, but not for long.

Soon new disasters befell the Diaks. First, one by one the thatched roofs of their homes began to collapse. Home after home was destroyed. Shortly after that, rats began to overwhelm their villages. The W.H.O. investigated and discovered that the DDT killed not only the malaria-carrying mosquitoes, but also all of the parasitic wasps that eat the thatch-eating caterpillars.

Since there were no wasps around to eat the caterpillars, those caterpillars multiplied and literally ate the roofs off of the Diaks' homes. At the same time, the bugs that had been killed by the DDT were eaten by the lizards that are native to Borneo. The lizards were in turn eaten by local cats. The DDT-laden lizards turned out to be so deadly to the cats that all of the cats died. With no cats, the rat population grew so fast that rats overwhelmed the island.

In response to this situation, the W.H.O. decided that drastic measures had to be taken. Hundreds of cats were collected from around the world and were parachuted into the "de-catted" island. The organization is waiting to see if this solves the problems that the "solution" to the malaria epidemic caused.

Isn't it amazing how often what we think is sure to solve a difficult problem turns out only to worsen the problem? So often we try to "fix" people or situations without thinking our solutions through or without looking at the "big picture".

For example, parents who want to protect their children from pain intervene in their child's daily activities to "fight their battles for them", or when their child misbehaves in school, they often intervene and blame the teacher rather than deal with their child's bad behavior. The result is that the child realizes he doesn't have to change, and the situation grows worse.

The same thing can happen with family members who are living with an alcoholic. Even though they know there is a problem, rather than deal with the real issue, they choose to ignore the drinking and may even help the alcoholic get out of the trouble that their drinking causes. Instead of improving the situation, they make it worse. The alcoholic gets sicker, and the marriage and the family begin to collapse.

The next time you decide to "fix" a situation or help a person with a problem, think of the Diaks of Borneo. Take time to ask yourself just how the action you are planning to take is going to affect the "big picture". Take care. If you don't, you may end up in a worse situation than you were at the beginning. You may even end up having to parachute in hundreds of cats!

March 4th
Look Up

A man by the name of Halford Luccock wrote the following poem:

"If your nose is close to the grindstone rough
And you hold it there long enough,
In time you'll say there's no such thing
As brooks that babble and birds that sing.
These three will all your world compose,
Just you, the stone, and your old nose!"

How aware are you of the world around you? How aware are you of the people around you and their particular needs? It is quite easy for us to get so caught up in our own little world and in our own little opinions and ideas that we can miss the vast world that surrounds us. Some people get so caught up in their work that they become strangers to their own families. Some people get so caught up in their own fears and worries that they forget that life is full of simple joys and pleasures, and some people get so caught up in their own little world that they forget the great gift that God has given us in the world of nature.

Take some time this week to become aware of the great gift of life that is beginning to bud all around us. Take your nose away from the grindstone of the mundane and the ordinary and look around you. God is very much at work right in our midst – don't miss it!

March 5th
Love Is Stronger Than Death

Very often when I am working on homilies or retreat talks, in order to collect my thoughts, I end up walking through Spring Grove Cemetery. It's an inspiring place with many beautiful monuments surrounded by lush flowerbeds, picturesque lakes, and colorful flowering trees. In addition to enjoying the natural beauty of the cemetery, I also enjoy reading the various tombstones. It may sound a bit morbid, but reading tombstones is a way of reading local history, because each monument "tells a story".

A few weeks ago, I saw a rather large tombstone, beautifully inscribed, commemorating a Mr. & Mrs. Osterkamp. I was most impressed by the lines of poetry chiseled below their names.

Under Stella's name are the following verses:

"Beloved Wife & Pal. True to me, kind to me, never deceiving;
Cheering me, helping me, ever believing.
Sad for me, glad for me, never apart.
Dear to me, near to me, Pal of my heart."

Under Ben's name are these verses:

"Clean hearted, warm hearted, all the way through;
Fair to me, square to me, life's dearest part.
Best to me, blest to me, Pal of my heart."

Aren't these wonderful sentiments? I don't know who the Osterkamps were. The tombstone indicates they died in the 1930s, but the message they left on that tombstone shows how true the words of Scripture are, that "love is stronger than death." While the words this couple had on their tombstone gives the world a glimpse of their love for each other, I am sure that the love they shared probably cannot really be captured in words carved in stone, but only by sentiments far beyond mere words, which were written in their hearts by the One who gave them to each other. Look into your own heart and see what words are inscribed there by, and about, the ones you love. Pause … and give thanks to the One who gave them to you.

March 6th

Sloth

Is there anything that you have been meaning to do for others for quite some time, but have not been able to find the time to do it? I don't know about you, but I have stacks of notes to myself about things I've been planning to do, but a lack of time has kept me from getting to them. A friend of mine sent me a little note this week to remind me that it had been a whole year since I last wrote to her. She said that she didn't want to pester me, but had written a year ago to ask my opinion on a certain matter, and she thought it was high time that I replied to her letter. She ended her note with a smiley face and a brief poem by the American poet, Theodore Roethke:

The Sloth
In moving slow, he has no peer
You ask him anything in his ear,
He thinks about it for a year!

Well, needless to say, I answered her letter right away! After I wrote to my friend, I made a resolution to make time for those things I have been meaning to do, but have not allowed myself the time in which to do them. I wonder if this might not be a good practice for you too. Try to set aside some time each week to do those things you've been meaning to do –

especially those little kindnesses that would make someone's life a little brighter!

March 7th
Crown or Chain

While in Israel I saw an interesting poster. The poster was of a king, magnificently dressed, frowning as he made a chain from his beautiful gold crown. At his feet sat a slave, smiling as he formed his iron chains into a beautiful crown. Underneath the scene was the following: "Life is what one makes it, no matter of what it is made."

Isn't it amazing how true that statement is? Perhaps this poster could serve as an examination of conscience for each of us. Very often, material things can bring people great happiness and freedom to help others. But just as often, material wealth or success can make people feel trapped by greed or worry over losing the wealth or material goods that they have acquired. It all depends on whether you own your wealth or your wealth owns you. This is not only true of material goods, but of everything that life offers us.

As we seek spiritual renewal and growth and examine our lives, perhaps we need to ask ourselves whether or not we are making a crown or forging a chain with the things that life brings our way.

March 8th
Many Roads Lead to God

Some farmers were discussing their views on religion as they drank coffee and waited in line at a local mill where they were to have their wheat crops prepared for market. One farmer began to tell the others that they were wrong in the way they practiced their faith and wrong in the way that they prayed. Then he proceeded to tell them the proper method of prayer and that they should listen to his preacher, the only "good" preacher worth hearing. Tempers began to get a bit hot as he continued to tell all those around him that they were not true Christians unless they did as he did. Some rather unfriendly words were exchanged, after which there was a long pause in the conversation.

Finally one man who had not taken part in the debate scratched his chin and said, "I suppose there must be a least a half a dozen roads that lead to this mill, and I can come up with a variety of ways to get here. I can also tell you that not once in all the years I've been coming here has the miller ever asked me how I got here. The only thing he wants to know is whether or not the wheat I bring him is any good. It seems to me that God must be a lot like that miller ... He only wants to know whether or not the wheat you bring Him is any good."

It's pretty easy to get caught up in the "externals" of faith and forget that the most important thing is what is in our heart. The Lord will probably not ask us by what road we came to Him. He will ask though, about the condition of our hearts. Are they filled with love, compassion, forgiveness, understanding, faith and trust?

March 9th

Motivated by Love

One of the famous stories of Mother Teresa concerns a newspaper man who was accompanying her on her daily rounds. As Mother Teresa was visiting with some of her sisters who were picking up a starving woman whose filthy body and pus-filled sores created an intense stench, the reporter turned away from the scene and got very sick. On the way back to the motherhouse, the reporter told Mother Teresa, "Mother, I wouldn't do what you sisters do for a million dollars!"

Mother Teresa smiled at him and very gently said, "Neither would we. We only do this for love. Money means nothing to us. It does not motivate us, only love does."

What motivates you? What moves you to live the way you do, to treat others the way you do, to act as you do? If we want to take our faith seriously, we must, from time to time, examine our motives. Authentic disciples of Jesus are, like Mother Teresa, motivated by love.

March 10th
Moving Fences

In 1923, in southern Poland, a Protestant nurse (a Quaker, in fact) died. In the area there was only one cemetery, a Catholic cemetery. Because she was not a Catholic, church officials declared that she could not be buried there. Finally, after much discussion, the church officials decided that she could be buried just outside the fence of the cemetery.

Because the nurse had been such a wonderful example of Christian charity and because most of them had benefited from her love and her healing ministry, some of the local peasants came in the middle of the night and moved the fence. In the morning, when the caretaker arrived for work, he saw that the grave of the young nurse was no longer outside the fence.

This is what being a Christian is all about – moving the fences of our hearts to include more and more people. Are there people in your family, your neighborhood, your parish, your city, your country or the world that need to be included within the fences of your heart?

There's an old song which says, "Don't Fence Me In;" perhaps our song needs to be "Fence Others In."

March 11th
Cracks

Did you know that the largest bell ever cast is in Moscow, and weighs 219 tons? One of the Czars had the bell made, but he never heard it ring because of a very small amount of water. It happened that as the bell was being cast in a mold, a huge fire broke out in the bell works factory. As workers tried to put out the fire, they inadvertently allowed a small trickle of water to get into the bell mold, which caused a crack to form in the metal. When the bell was freed from its mold, it was ruined, for a cracked bell cannot be rung. It may be the biggest bell in the world, but it is of little use since it cannot do that for which it was made – ring.

That bell could be a symbol for many of us at times. We were made to produce a "joyful sound" for God, yet a little bit of negativity or pettiness can create a crack in your attempts to be more like Jesus. Just think for a moment, does the way you speak to your spouse or children, other family members or co-workers "ring true" to the Gospel Jesus preached? It's good for us to examine our lives to see if our way of living the Gospel conforms to the One in whose image we have been molded.

March 12th
Love Heals

I spent some time the other day with a man who is very ill. He was telling me that he thought the treatments he was receiving made him feel sicker than the disease he was fighting. I asked him what he thought the best medicine was for his illness. He looked at me for a while and then smiled and said, "I think it's the kind of medicine that we take for granted." "What medicine is that?" I asked. Then he went on to tell me about someone he had been thinking about as he was sitting in the waiting room at the hospital.

"Toward the end of his last term in office as the Speaker of the U. S. House of Representatives, Sam Rayburn announced that he had been diagnosed with cancer and was returning to Bonham, Texas. When Mr. Rayburn was asked why he wanted to go back to a small town like Bonham when the best medical care and newest treatments could be found right there in Washington D. C., Rayburn simply told the reporters that he was going back to his little hometown rather than stay in Washington because Bonham is the kind of place where people know when you're sick and they give a damn when you die."

The man looked at me again and then said, "The best medicine, Father, is the love of the people in your own family and the love of your friends." He said, "I'm convinced that love does more to heal than any chemotherapy or radiation. If I am fortunate enough to get better, I'm sure it will be because of the love that is all around me."

We can never underestimate the power of love to heal. It heals both the recipient and the giver. Take time this week to reach out to those around you in simple gestures that show your love and concern. Your love after all, is the best medicine there is.

March 13th
Unfinished Treasures

John Steinbeck wrote a famous story called "The Pearl," in which a man finds a very precious, beautiful pearl. The problem is that when the man looks at the pearl, he sees a tiny flaw in it. He realizes that if the pearl didn't have that tiny flaw, it would be the biggest and most valuable pearl in the world. So he picks up the pearl and peels off the first layer of the pearl's skin, but the flaw still remains. He continues to take off layer after layer of the pearl until finally, there is no more pearl! The flaw is gone, but so too is that beautiful pearl.

There is a great lesson in that story for each of us. Have you ever done to one of your family members or to one of your friends what the man in that story did to his pearl? Have you ever ruined a perfectly beautiful relationship by "picking at" flaws or shortcomings? We can do this to others or we can even do this to ourselves, and every time we do it, we end up destroying something that God gave us as a great gift. Each of us is an unfinished treasure. God gives us to each other and asks us not to pick at each other, but to love and cherish each other.

March 14th
Nourished

As a man was placing a bouquet of roses on the grave of a friend, he noticed a Chinese man placing a bowl of rice on a nearby grave and laughingly asked him, "And when do you expect your dead friend to come up from that grave and eat the rice you brought for him?"

The Chinese gentleman was a bit surprised by the rather rude remark, but he simply smiled and said very quietly, "I guess about the same time as your friend comes up from his grave to smell those roses!"

When the man realized that he had insulted the Chinese man, he apologized and then asked, "What is the significance for you of putting a bowl of rice on a loved one's grave?"

"It's both a tribute and a reminder," the Chinese mourner said. "It's a tribute to the deceased because it is a symbol of our belief that this person has nourished us by his life and love. It is a reminder to us to be aware of those who are still alive who are nourishing us each day, and it reminds us that we too have an obligation to nourish others."

The next time you visit the grave of a loved one, take some flowers, but why not also take some rice as well; after all, we all need to be reminded of both how we have been nourished and how we are called to nourish others.

March 15th
Oil of Kindness

I recently read about a man who was considered a bit odd, somewhat strange and most certainly eccentric. People often laughed at him because he had this habit – he always carried a little can of oil with him wherever he went. If he opened a door and it squeaked, he put a little oil on its hinges. When he came to a gate that was difficult to open, he oiled it. Whenever he found anything squeaking or rusty, or not in good working order, he set to working on it with his little oil can. He was never seen without his oil can. When the can was empty, he quickly filled it with more oil, for as he put it, "the world is full of squeaky, creaky, rusty things that need a good dose of oil." When asked why he went to all the trouble of carrying his oil with him, he said, "I just want the people who come after me to have an easier time of it. Their life should be a bit better because I was here first."

Are there people in your life who "squeak, creak, or are a bit rusty?" Perhaps God is asking us to be like that "eccentric" man and his can of oil. Maybe we are to bring what the Bible calls the "oil of kindness" or the "oil of gladness" to others. If we carry our own "can of oil" with us wherever we go, maybe those who follow us will find the world a better place because we were here first.

March 16th
Open Up Before You Blow Up!

Have you ever been really frustrated with someone who continues to do things that annoy you? Has a member of your family or a good friend continued to do things that you wish they wouldn't do? I'm fairly certain that this has happened to you because it seems to be a part of the human condition. How have you dealt with it? Have you ever decided that you would swallow your frustration, to just "let it go", but found out that it surfaced again in the middle of an argument about a totally different subject? I know this has happened to me.

I was talking to an old friend the other day about just this kind of thing. She told me that her grandmother kept a sign over her kitchen sink (where she did all of her profound thinking) as a reminder of what she needed to do when she felt frustrated. The message on that sign was:

"If you're frustrated, and your feelings are beginning to boil, they've got to come out. You can bury a stone or a stick or an old tin can, but you cannot bury a worm. That worm will eventually come to the surface."

Hiding or pretending that nothing is wrong will not make things better. Burying things will only make things more intense. The world would be a much more peaceful place, each of us would experience a greater sense of peace of mind and heart, and our lives would be much happier if we would only learn to open up before we blow up!

March 17th
Open Your Heart to God's Grace

It is estimated that 500,000 tons of water rush over Niagara Falls every minute. That's a lot of water! Did you know that on March 29, 1948, the falls suddenly stopped? It was the middle of the night when it happened, but people within the sound of the falls were suddenly awakened by the overwhelming silence. The flow stopped for thirty hours. Some thought the world was coming to an end. Others thought a drought was coming. Some others thought it was a sign of God's anger.

What caused it? It seems heavy winds had set the ice fields of Lake Erie in motion and tons of ice jammed the Niagara River entrance near Buffalo and stopped the flow of the river until the ice shifted again.

Just like the great power of Niagara Falls could be blocked by cold winds, so the power of God's grace at work in our lives can be blocked by our own ice-cold hearts. We can turn our backs on God and block His grace for a while, but He keeps coming at us until we warm up to His influence.

I saw a poster the other day that sums it up pretty neatly: "Your worst days are never so bad that you are beyond the reach of God's grace. Your best days are never so good that you are beyond the need of God's grace."

We've all got to keep our hearts open to the flow of God's great love which is much more powerful than 500,000 tons of water.

March 18th
Our Choices Influence Others

A few years ago when I was on sabbatical, I spent some time in Egypt in the Valley of the Kings, where many of the pharaohs are entombed. One of the guides who was leading our group through the tombs explained the meaning of the symbols that were used to decorate the walls of the tombs, and he also taught us the significance of the various beautifully carved statues. I was fascinated by the fact that on every representation of the pharaoh, there were two symbols that were wrapped around the pharaoh's head. The first was a representation of a vulture; the second was an image of a cobra. Our guide explained those symbols in this way:

"The vulture is a bird that eats dead things and rotten meat. The cobra is a powerful snake that attacks and kills anything that threatens it. The pharaoh, as leader of our people, must guard his thoughts. If rotten, dead thoughts come to his mind, the vulture is there to consume them. Our people are protected then from rotten thinking. On the other hand, if poisonous, hateful thoughts come into his mind, threatening our people, the cobra, the fastest of the snakes, is there to pounce on these thoughts and to kill them at once. Thus, our people are protected once again."

I believe those ancient Egyptians were onto something. They were well aware of the power of our thinking, and they wanted to be sure that their leaders were in the practice of guarding their thoughts. The pharaohs of Egypt had great influence over thousands of people. If their thinking was bad, many people could be hurt by it, so they posted a guard at the mind of their leaders.

Now, even though most of us will never have the kind of influence that a pharaoh might have had, each one of us does make a difference. So it would be a good thing for each of us to take some time now and then to examine our thinking. Evil thoughts and bad thinking can paralyze us and lead us to make destructive choices. It is vitally important for us, therefore, to pay close attention to the way we think about things. Perhaps we might ask the Lord to send an angel to guard our minds and hearts from rotten, hateful thoughts so that our families and our people will be protected from them, just like those thousands of Egyptians so long ago.

March 19th
Our Real, Live God!

Recently I read a story from Japan about a man named Seko. The story of Mr. Seko is a legend in Japan that is often told to young people. According to the story, when Mr. Seko was a very young child, his parents would tell him wonderful stories about dragons. From the time he was a child, he wished and wished that he would one day see a real dragon. He collected stories and images of dragons. Dragons actually became his hobby. He grew so fond of dragons that eventually they became his life. He became an artist, and as you might have guessed by now, his subject matter was always a dragon. His art made Mr. Seko famous all over Japan. People came from distant places to look at his paintings, and many would not leave until he had agreed to sell them some of his art.

Mr. Seko's love for dragons was so well known that he was no longer called Mr. Seko. Everyone simply called him "The Dragon Man."

According to the legend, one day a real live dragon heard about the

"Dragon Man" and thought to himself, "If the Dragon Man loves paintings of dragons so much, he will love me, a real dragon, even more." So the dragon went to Mr. Seko's studio and stuck his head right through the open window!

The story ends with the artist fleeing in sheer terror. His love for painted dragons had in no way prepared him for the real thing. The moral of the ancient story is that just as painted images of dragons had not prepared the artist for the power and magnificence of the real dragon, so too our love for our images of God in no way prepares us for an encounter with the Real God. If you read through Scripture or read about some of the great saints who have encountered God in various mystical experiences, you find that no one has words to describe the great and awesome Lord God. This week, as you pause to pray, take some time to consider the power and glory of the God we have not yet seen face to face. Our artistic images and even nature itself pale in comparison to our Real, Live God!

March 20th
How Are You?

I recently finished reading a biography of John Quincy Adams in which the author relates the following story. One day when Adams was about 80 years old, a friend met him on the street in Boston. "How is John Quincy Adams?" the friend asked.

"John Quincy Adams himself is very well, thank you. But the house he lives in is sadly dilapidated. In fact, it is tottering on its foundations. The walls are badly shattered, and the roof is worn. The building itself trembles with every wind, and I think that John Adams will have to move out of it before too long. But Mr. Adams, himself, is very well." And with a smile on his face, John Adams happily continued on his way.

John Quincy Adams was wise enough to realize that one's physical health is not the only measure of how well a person is doing. In a culture like ours, which is so preoccupied with physical health and beauty, it is good for us to remember that there is much more to us than the condition of our bodies. What about our level of enthusiasm for living, for learning, and for loving?

So, the next time someone asks you, "How are you?" remember John Quincy Adams and recall how much more there is to you than the mere state of our body.

March 21st
Picking Up The Pieces

One of the most magnificent cathedrals in Europe is the beautiful French cathedral at Reims. It has a great history and has some of the most breathtaking windows in the world. The great rose window is the cathedral's claim to fame, and most people who visit the church are told an amazing story about that window. During World War II, a bomb hit the cathedral and completely shattered the rose window.

The people of the town were devastated, but not defeated. Following the disaster, the villagers left their homes and gathered up all of the bits and pieces down to the tiniest shard of glass. When the war ended, they commissioned some highly skilled artisans to rebuild that shattered rose window using the pieces they had gathered together from the old window. The new window was even more beautiful than the first one. It was all made possible because the villagers ran out and together "picked up the pieces."

I tell you this story because many times devastating things happen to people right around us. When these things occur, a great opportunity opens before us. We, like the villagers of Reims, can help others "pick up the pieces" of their lives. By thoughtfulness, kind words, and charitable deeds, we can scoop up the pieces of the broken hearts of the bereaved, bring healing to the sick or terminally ill, and be a support to those going through the pain of divorce or separation. Sometimes we may feel helpless before the tragedies that may happen to our friends or neighbors, but we are not really helpless. We can help by picking up one piece at a time, by one simple act of love and tenderness at a time. And in the end, when healing finally comes, we can step back and see that the healing has come, not in one great act of healing, but in many small, shard-like acts of charity.

March 22nd
Godlike

A cruise ship was in the middle of its voyage when it ran into a terrible storm. One of the passengers was getting a bit nervous and went to the captain and asked, "Captain, are we in any real danger?" "No, madam," replied the captain, "not yet. Just keep your eye on the sailors. If they are still cursing and swearing, everything's okay. If you hear them start to pray, put on your life jacket!"

If you are like me, you probably found yourself smiling when you read that story. You are probably smiling because you could see yourself in those sailors. The implication of this story is that sailors only pray when they are in trouble. God certainly wants us to approach Him when we are in trouble, but He doesn't want us to stop there. God wants our prayer to be richer and deeper than fear.

Year after year, Mother Teresa was able to work with the poor 16 to 18 hours a day, all of it filled with disease, poverty and death because she had been a person of prayer. In fact, she said it is not possible to work very long with the sick and dying without being a person of daily prayer. Prayer has to be more than a "helping hand" when you are in trouble. Prayer is meant to form us in God's image.

St. Anthony of the Desert said that the more you pray, the more your prayer changes from "God, give me this … to God, mold me, and change me." The more time we spend with God, the more we come to know Him and the more we come to resemble Him.

March 23rd
Prepare for a Better Day

The other day, I was talking with an elderly man who had taken great pride in his abilities as a fisherman. In the course of our discussion, we spoke about how my ministry as a priest is very much like his life as a fisherman. "Let me remind you," he said with a big grin, "that Jesus actually said, 'I will make you fishers of men' so the two of us have lots in common!"

After many comparisons, we came to the subject of spending a lot of time working hard at something with little or no tangible results. He said, "I learned a long time ago something about that. In my life, there have been days, weeks, and sometimes whole months when nothing seemed to turn out right. After one really bad period in my life, I told my old granddad about how depressed I was. My granddad told me to learn to 'fish or cut bait.'"

"What did your granddad mean by that?" I asked.

"Well, I think he meant that when I experience bad periods and things aren't going very well, I should go home and prepare for better days. I should go home and get a fresh look at things and come back on a new day with a new approach and a new attitude. Sometimes when you've been at it for a long time, you can get tired and lose heart. Going home to 'cut bait' means going back to find your heart again. It doesn't mean to quit or give up. It means not to waste your time worrying about failure."

"Fish or cut bait" sounds like a great philosophy for life. How about your life? Do you experience periods in which everything feels wrong and nothing seems to be what you hoped it would be? Have you felt like giving up on life, on your family, your marriage, your work, or yourself? Perhaps this is an opportunity to "fish or cut bait" – to go home and take a breather, to find your heart again, to prepare for a better day and to find a new approach.

After all, Jesus has called each of us to be "fishers of men" and like all good fishermen, we have to know how to "fish or cut bait."

March 24th
A Dead Cat

A crisis developed in a family recently. The family cat, Boots, suddenly died. Everyone was very upset, but the youngest child was clearly having the most difficult time. In order to console her daughter, the little girl's mother sat her down and said very gently, "Erin, God has taken Boots to heaven."

With very wide eyes, Erin looked at her mother and asked, "What would God want with a dead cat?"

When I first heard this story, I laughed. But after thinking about it for awhile, I realized that there is a message in this little story. Don't we all just assume that if God is going to take someone or some "cat" to heaven that He would give it new life and, therefore, He would not be taking a dead cat to heaven, but rather a live cat? Obviously, this little girl didn't make that assumption. I think she has something to teach us.

Don't we do what she did when we come to God with our problems or worries? Don't we assume that God sees our problems in the same limited way that we do? Aren't we like little Erin, seeing only a dead cat in front of us? What God sees is something entirely different–God sees new possibilities.

The next time we are confronted with a crisis, perhaps the first thing to do would be to take a few minutes in prayer to ask God to help us see beyond the immediate problem to the new possibilities that might come about if we tried to see things as God sees them. If Jesus could raise the dead to new life, I'm certain that He could give new life to a pet cat and even more so, He could help us, His beloved, to cope with whatever crisis we face. Trust Him!

March 25th
Where You Are

Have you ever heard of King Henry III of Bavaria? He lived in the eleventh century and was King of Bavaria for a short time when he realized that he didn't like being a king. He felt that court life was tedious, and the pressures of being a ruler were overwhelming. He didn't like being surrounded by some rather unsavory and unethical people, and he hated the feeling of "living in a glass house". As time went on, he became more and more unhappy and began to spend much of his time praying for a solution to his misery. Finally he decided to go to a monastery and become a monk so that he could close himself in the monastery and spend the rest of his days in prayerful meditation. King Henry went off to speak with Father Richard, the abbot of a local monastery.

"Do I understand, Your Majesty, that you wish to become a monk here?" asked Abbot Richard.

"Yes, indeed I do!" said the king.

"But, why do you want to be one of us?" asked the abbot.

"I find it too difficult to be a true Christian at the palace among all those people at court. I think it will be much easier for me here in this monastery," the king replied.

"Do you understand, Your Majesty, that to be a monk, you will have to be completely obedient to me?"

"Yes, I understand that; from this day on, I will be absolutely obedient in all that you tell me to do."

"In that case, Sire, I will tell you what you must do. Go back to your throne and serve God faithfully. If you cannot be a Christian there, you certainly could not be one here within the monastery. You must be willing to serve Jesus where he has put you if you want to be his real friend and disciple. Jesus has put you there on purpose." King Henry did go back to his throne and it is said that he was a good king because he knew what it meant to be obedient to Jesus.

Why did I tell you this story? It is because each of us from time to time thinks that it would be much easier to be a Christian if we were in some other situation or some other place. Haven't you ever thought you could be a better Christian if you just had the patience of some neighbor or friend? Haven't you ever thought it would be a lot easier to be a good Christian if you had just married someone else, gone to school some other place, or found a different job? Haven't you ever thought that you'd be a better Christian if you didn't have any teenagers driving you crazy or if you didn't have to work with that strange woman next to you at the office? I think we all have times when we think we could be a better person if only our circumstances were different.

I think that King Henry can serve as a reminder to us that God has a purpose for putting us in the place where we are. It is precisely in the particular place and among a particular group of people that God wants us to serve faithfully. God is not found somewhere else, but right where we are.

March 26th
Seeds of Discouragement

There is a legend about a man who found Satan's barn. In this barn, Satan stored all of the seeds that he would sow in the hearts of men and women.

There were seeds of hatred, seeds of jealousy, seeds of pride and seeds of envy. The most numerous of all the seeds were in big bags marked with the letter "D". "What are those seeds, and why are there so many?" the man asked Satan.

"Why, those are seeds of discouragement," Satan replied, "and there are so many because they will grow in almost any heart."

"Is there any heart where these seeds won't grow?" the man asked.

Reluctantly the Evil One said, "There is only one place these seeds will not grow, and that is in the heart of a grateful person."

If the cold and darkness of winter is making you feel a bit discouraged, perhaps it's time to take an inventory of all of the things that you have for which to be thankful.

March 27th
Asking for Directions

I read a magazine article about recent psychology studies that show that men and women find their way differently when driving places. The study indicated that women find their way by relying on familiar landmarks. They memorize where landmarks are and do all of their navigating by them. Men, on the other hand, navigate by "vectoring", meaning that they find their way by taking a basic direction that they believe to be the right one hoping that eventually they will "stumble across" the place they intend to go. When women cannot find their "landmarks" they will quickly find someone to give them direction. Men, however, are very reluctant to ask anyone for directions. Many men, in fact, will never ask for directions.

For most married couples these "psychological studies" have not provided any startling new discoveries. Women have known for years that men will not ask for directions! Many a vacation has been "dampened" by someone's refusal to ask for directions.

Navigating life, especially our spiritual life, is never easy. It requires both a sense of direction and "landmarks" to help us negotiate it well. Seeking direction from Scripture, from wise and holy people along the way is the best way for us to keep from being lost. This week, take some time to consider where your life is headed. Is it time for you to seek some helpful direction?

March 28th
Sixty Miles

During the Revolutionary War, a minister by the name of Peter Miller was preaching one Sunday morning when one of his neighbors came into the back of the church and started heckling him. The more Reverend Miller spoke, the louder the heckler got. Finally, some ushers had to remove the heckler from the church. Each Sunday after that, the neighbor would come and sit in the back of church, making noise and generally trying to disrupt the service. Each time he became too loud, he would be ushered out of church. This went on for several months until one Sunday morning, the heckling neighbor failed to show up. The minister was quite surprised, but also a little bit happy. The following week, the heckler failed to show again. The minister finally concluded that he would now finally have a quiet church on Sundays. Then, after the Sunday service, one of the members of the congregation informed Reverend Miller that the heckler hadn't been in church because he had been accused of treason, was tried and found guilty, and condemned to be hanged.

Reverend Peter Miller immediately set out on foot to appeal to General Washington for a pardon for the man. It was a 60 mile trip. When he arrived, he met with General Washington and begged for the condemned man's life. When Washington replied that he could not grant his appeal for his friend, Miller exclaimed, "My friend? Why, he's not my friend. He's my worst enemy! He has done me nothing but harm."

"Do you mean to tell me that you have walked 60 miles to save the life of an enemy? That puts this whole affair in a new light. Your request is granted. The man is hereby pardoned," Washington declared.

With the pardon in hand, Miller set off to the place of execution, hoping to get there in time. He arrived just as the prisoner was being led to the scaffold. Noticing that it was Reverend Miller coming, the condemned man shouted, "So you've come to get your revenge by watching me hang, eh?"

Reverend Miller walked up to him and said, "No, I've come to do what every Christian is called to do, 'to set the captive free'."

With that, he showed the officer in charge Washington's pardon, and the prisoner was released.

Reverend Miller said that he had come to do what every Christian is called to do, to set the captive free. In the Gospel, Jesus announces that he has come to set the captives free. Are there any "captives" in your life that you are being called to "walk 60 miles" to set free?

March 29th
Seeing Our Way Clear

As a man was talking with his farmer friend, he noticed a cow straining to look over a stone wall. "Why do you suppose that your cow is trying to look over that stone wall?" asked the man.

"Well, it seems fairly simple to me," explained the farmer; "my cow is looking over that stone wall because she has no way of seeing through it."

Are there any "stone walls" in your life right now? Are there problems in your marriage, problems with one of your children, a serious illness, death or grief, or any other difficulty that you just can't "see" your way through? Perhaps today is a good day to try to see over those "stone walls". How? I always begin my "straining to see over the wall" with lots of prayer. Spending time in prayer puts us in contact with real power. Probably the best thing that prayer can do is to help us to think more clearly and to know that we are not alone. Prayer can convince us that we are not the only ones who are going through terrible times and that many people have gone through similar problems before us. Thus, another great source of strength is our friends. There's nothing that can help us to see over the "stone walls" quite as well as crying on the broad shoulders of a good friend. By sharing our burdens with God and with trusted loved ones, we can "see" our way clear of those terrible "stone walls" that block our paths from time to time.

March 30th
Words Are Like Matches

One of the great gifts that God gives us is words – and through them, the ability to communicate with one another. Since we use words all day long in our conversations and in our thinking, we have to realize that words are not to be used carelessly.

I like to compare words to a book of matches. You can strike a match to light the candles on a beautifully set dinner table, and in the soft glow of the candlelight, enjoy a wonderful meal with family and friends. You can strike a match to light a campfire, gather friends and family around, tell ghost stories, roast marshmallows, and create warm memories that will last a lifetime. By the same token, however, you can strike a match to set a forest fire or commit the crime of arson by which people are horribly burned or murdered.

Simple little matches have tremendous potential in them for both good and evil. In the same way, simple little words have tremendous potential for good or evil. In both cases, it all depends on how you choose to use them.

From the time we were little children, we were warned not to play with matches. Perhaps we should also be warned from childhood not to be careless with our words.

March 31st
Little Things Mean a Lot

I read the novel, *The Agony and the Ecstasy*, which tells the story of the famous artist, Michelangelo. The novel is filled with many anecdotes about the artist's life and times. One such story describes him watching stonecutters working huge slabs of marble in the mountains. He watches the stonecutters strike the stone many times, but it is not until the 201st blow of the hammer that the crack in the marble appears. What was different about that 201st blow? When the stonecutter was asked that question, he simply replied, "It was not the last blow that split the stone, it was those 200 or so before that last blow that did it."

So often as we strive to be good Christians, good spouses, good parents, good workers, or just plain good people, we can get discouraged by the mundane, routine little things that we are called upon to do, that seem not to be making much of a difference. But these little acts do, in fact, make a big difference. If our lives are to bear "good fruit", it will be because of the sum of all those little mundane things that we have been willing to do day in and day out. Every act of kindness and compassion, no matter how insignificant it may seem, will in the long term, bear much spiritual fruit.

April 1st
Solve Problems One Step at a Time

Did you know that experts say that there is a best time to ride a bicycle up a hill? Those who ride bicycles say that the best time to ride a bicycle up a hill is at night. When I first read that, I immediately thought that it made sense, since it is usually cooler at night, and riding up a hill would probably be easier than riding in the heat of the day. But that is not the reason. The experts say that hills which seem to be almost impossible to ascend during the day are more easily negotiated at night because at night the cyclist can see only a few feet in front of him and the hill seems either level or not very steep. He is lead to feel that he can go the few feet that his light shows are ahead of him. During the daylight, the cyclist will see the whole hill and become overwhelmed by the thought of such a huge incline, and usually is defeated before he even begins the climb.

When we are faced with difficulties or problems, aren't we like those daylight bicyclists? Don't we often feel like we are going to be overwhelmed by our problems? Perhaps the nighttime cyclists have something to teach us. Just as they realize that success in conquering a hill is achieved by concentrating on a few feet at a time, so too we might best achieve success in dealing with our own personal crisis by dealing with the few feet that the light we have right now allows us to see.

We may not be able to solve or overcome the whole problem, but we can deal with part of it. That may be the best way for us to climb that hill.

April 2nd
On Hold

I was at the hospital the other day to anoint someone, and as I was riding the elevator to the intensive care unit, a woman saw my Roman collar and asked me to pray for her son who was quite ill. After I reassured her that I would pray for her son, she started to ask me questions about God, about heaven and hell, and finally, about prayer. She asked me if I thought that God really answers prayers. I told her that I do believe that God answers prayers. "Well, I think that God always gives me the same answer – 'NO!'" she said. We laughed. Then she asked me, "Do you get any 'yeses' when you pray, or do you get all 'no's' as I do?" I thought about it for a minute.

"I certainly get many 'yes' answers from God and I get some 'no' answers too, but I think I get another kind of answer from God as well. Sometimes I get the feeling that God is saying, 'wait.' Sometimes God doesn't say 'yes' or 'no', He simply says 'wait, because the time isn't ripe yet.'"

In our prayer life, it can get pretty discouraging when it seems as if God is always saying "no" to us. Perhaps if you look at how some events in your life have eventually turned out, you might discover that God had not really said "no" to you as you first thought, but rather God said "wait." If you are discouraged right now, perhaps once again, God is simply saying, "Wait!"

April 3rd
Spend Time With People Who Are Close to God

"I want a deeper and stronger relationship with God. What's the best way for me to do that?" a young man asked his parish priest.

"There are many things to take note of when you are trying to grow in your relationship with God," the priest replied. "But one of the most important things to be aware of is the company you keep."

"What do you mean by that?" the young man asked.

"When I was young," the priest explained, "my father made me write out an ancient saying on the front of my school books. In addition, he put a little card with the same verse on my desk. I still remember that saying: 'Play with fire and you'll get burned. Play in the dirt and you'll get dirty. Expose yourself to infectious diseases, and you'll get infected. Spend most of your time with good people and you'll become a good person. Spend most of your time with bad people and you'll become ... ?'" The priest concluded, "By spending your time with people who are close to God, you can't help but grow closer to God yourself. I can't think of an easier way to grow closer to God."

Are those with whom you spend most of your time leading you in a direction that takes you closer to God or further away? Do those who spend their time with you find themselves moving closer to or away from a deeper love of God?

April 4th
Spiritual Maturity

Do you consider yourself a mature person? What are the signs that mark the life of a mature person? Is it simply a matter of age or physical development? We all know that age is not a true marker for maturity, and having a physically developed body certainly doesn't make someone mature. But what is it that makes one a mature person? An important question we have to ask ourselves as we grow older is not just whether or not we are physically or emotionally mature, but rather, "are we spiritually mature?"

When I was in the seminary, I heard about the oldest living clergyman, a Methodist bishop by the name of Welch. He was 103 years old. On his 103rd birthday, he was asked if he thought a lot about death and dying. "I think about it from time to time," he said, "But I don't worry too much about it. In fact, I don't worry about it at all because after all, when was the last time you heard of a Methodist bishop dying at 103 years of age?"

I remember that old bishop not just because of his sense of humor, but also because of some other comments he made. He had been asked to comment on spiritual maturity and the "signs" that a person was becoming more spiritually mature. "The spiritually mature person," he said, "is the person who knows that he/she is imperfect, that there will always be a struggle to be good, that sorrow, suffering and loss are all part of life, and that regardless of how often we may fail, we are still deeply loved by God. There's one more thing – a spiritually mature person prays a bit differently too. In my early days I found that most of my prayers began with the words, 'God give me …' and now that I am older, I find that my prayers begin with, 'God make me …' I no longer worry about what God can do for me, but rather what God can do with and through me."

Because of a long, long life of prayer and devotion, Bishop Welch grew into a spiritually mature person. One hundred and three years of prayer had produced abundant fruit. Even though we may not be 103 years old, we too are called to grow more deeply in holiness. Perhaps one step in the direction of spiritual maturity that we can all take is to be more willing to be used by God and formed by God into the person that He wants us to be. Why not take the next step in your spiritual maturity journey by spending more time this week in prayer learning to know His plan for you?

April 5th
Surrounded by Gifts

A desert wanderer came upon a spring of cool, crystal-clear pure water. The water was so delightful that he decided that he wanted to take some to his king. He loved his king more than anyone because they had been in the war together and endured many hardships and because he knew that the king was a genuinely good man. "I owe him the best," the man said to himself, "and since this is the best water I've ever tasted, I want to share it with him." After he quenched his own thirst, the man filled his leather canteen and began the lengthy journey through the hot desert to the king's palace.

When he reached his destination, the water had become stale because of the old leather container in which it had been stored. The king graciously accepted the gift and was overjoyed at seeing his old friend. He tasted the water with a grand expression of gratitude and delight, and the wanderer went away from the palace with a joyful heart. He knew he had given the king a great gift.

After he had gone, the other members of the king's court came forward to get a taste of the water. As each one of them tasted the water, they spat it out in disgust because the water was indeed putrid. "Your majesty, how could you look so pleased and be so grateful when you tasted this horrible water?"

"Ah," the king replied. "It was not the water I tasted, but the spirit in which it was given."

Jesus has called us to be both the wanderer and the king in this parable above. He wants us to be generous and so full of love that whenever we discover any true gift, we immediately seek to share it with someone. Jesus also wants each of us to be like the king, who can see beyond the surface of things to discover the real gift that is being given by those around us. In the kingdom of God, we are surrounded by gifts – gifts we are meant to give to one another and gifts we are meant to receive graciously from one another.

April 6th
You Choose

Eleanor Roosevelt was a remarkable person. From her earliest days, she was told over and over again how ugly she was, and she was often the butt of cruel jokes. Even when she became the First Lady, she continued to be ridiculed because of her lack of physical beauty. Despite all the terrible things that people said and did to her, Eleanor refused to return insult for insult, meanness for meanness. She was always a compassionate woman filled with kindness for all those she met. How did she do it?

Mrs. Roosevelt wrote to a friend that she never let those around her dictate how she would live her life. She said that she knew that she lacked physical beauty, but she decided that she would never be an ugly person or act in an ugly way. Then she went on to tell an old story she had heard as a little girl.

"It happened there was a young princess who was very unhappy because she was not pretty A kind old aunt told the young princess that it was much better to concern herself with not acting ugly rather than not being ugly. So, that old aunt taught the princess to do three things: to smile at everyone she met, to look for all the beauty she could find in each person she met and in every place she found herself, and to never leave a person without having said something kind to them.

The princess took her aunt's lessons to heart and lived them. In time, the people of the kingdom loved her more than anyone else, and many of the people remarked that they were blessed to have such a beautiful princess."

Do you let the people around you or the circumstances in which you find yourself dictate how you choose to live? Eleanor Roosevelt's little story is a great reminder that we all can choose how we will respond to the world around us. When the world treats you in an ugly way, how will you respond?

April 7th
Take Time Away

Someone recently sent me this little anecdote:

> *"I needed your advice on a very important matter yesterday, but when I phoned, they said you weren't in," said a woman to her pastor. "I'm sorry, but yesterday was my day off," replied the priest.*
> *"Well, I don't believe you should get a day off!" sniffed the parishioner. "You know the devil never takes a day off!"*
> *Smiling, the pastor replied, "You know, you are absolutely right, the devil never takes a day off, but if I didn't take a day off, I would be just like him!"*

Did you know that one of the major causes of the breakup of marriages and families is that people don't know how to "take a break"? There are some people who never take a break from their hectic lives because they feel guilty about wasting time. Others feel that the work they are doing is just too important, or that if they don't work as much as possible, they will end up a failure.

One of the things Scripture says that Jesus did often was to "go to an out-of-the-way place for prayer." He often spent the night alone on a mountain in prayer. At other times, Jesus took his disciples to deserted places to "rest a little".

When was the last time you "took a break"? When was the last time you and your spouse were away for a weekend alone? Taking time away together is one of the best ways to deepen a marriage, strengthen a family, or renew your own spirit. Why not take some time to be more like Jesus rather than end up acting more like the Devil?

April 8th
Taking Time for Jesus

A priest was giving a sermon on the proper use of time, when he advised his parishioners to be "good stewards of time." A little girl in the congregation leaned over and asked her mother, "Why do we have to be sewers of time?" The mother said she would explain it all when they got home.

Upon arrival at home, the young mom explained that the word was "steward" and not "sewer". Then she asked the little girl to get 10 pennies out of her piggy bank and to put them on the kitchen table. "If you are going to be a good steward of time for Jesus," the young mother explained, "here is what you must do. Put nine of your pennies on one side of the table, and one penny on the other. Those nine pennies are now yours, and that other penny belongs to Jesus. That's being a good steward of your time for Jesus. It's called 'tithing'. What do you think of that?" she asked.

"Poor Jesus!" cried the little girl.

If you laid out the hours of your day like that little girl laid out her pennies, how much of your time would you be giving to Jesus? Is the time you give to Him proportional to the many gifts that He has bestowed upon you?

April 9th
Teach By Being Good

Anthony De Mello tells the story of a holy man who was addressing his disciples about teaching morality. Here is the story.

The holy man said, "When I was a teenager, my father warned me about certain places in the city. He said, 'Don't ever go into a nightclub, son.'

'Why not, Father?' said I.

'You'll see things in there that you shouldn't!' This of course roused my curiosity, and the first chance I had, I went into a very evil nightclub."

The holy man's disciples asked him, "And when you went into that nightclub, did you see anything you shouldn't have?"

"Yes, indeed I did," said the holy man. "I saw my father!"

Anthony De Mello doesn't say what effect this episode had on the holy man, but I'll bet the young teenager was shocked. I'm sure that irreparable damage was done to their relationship. That teenager never saw his father in the same way again. Seeing his father in such an evil place put his father in an entirely new light.

The most effective way to teach about morality is not found in talking about goodness, but in being good. One truly precious gift we can give our young people is to be a good example to them.

April 10th
Teaching Responsibility

Recently I was standing in the kitchen of some friends of mine as dinner was being prepared and I was "reading the refrigerator" when I found the following story behind a large magnet. (You can tell a lot about a person by what they have on their refrigerator!). Here is the short story that was posted:

"There's a story about four men named Everybody, Somebody, Anybody, and Nobody. There was an important job to be done, and Everybody was asked to do it. Everybody was sure that Somebody would do it. Anybody could have done it, but Nobody did it! Somebody got angry, because it was Everybody's job. Everybody thought that Anybody could do it, and Nobody realized that Everybody wouldn't do it. It ended up that Everybody blamed Somebody, when actually Nobody did what Anybody could have done!"

I asked my friends why this story was posted on their refrigerator, and they told me that they were having problems with their kids not helping out. The mother of the family went on to say that she feared for their family if everyone was "out for themselves" and didn't take time to consider the needs of the others in the family. "These kids just don't think enough, they take, and take, and take and they seldom give. I put that story up there and every time one of my kids comes near the refrigerator, I make them read it aloud. They roll their eyes at me, but they do seem to help out more," she said.

April 11th
Thank God for Friends and Neighbors

Did you know that in the last century in Ireland and Wales, one of the ways that many families were able to support themselves was to be bee-keepers? Selling honey became a very profitable industry in which there was fierce competition. It wasn't long before the business became regulated, and many laws were enacted to protect the public to assure that the honey that was sold was pure. One law that I think has much to teach us was the 3rd year law. The law required that every third year each bee-keeper had to distribute some of his honey among his neighbors free of charge.

Why? It served as a reminder to all of the bee keepers that the nectar with which their bees produced their honey had originally come from the flowers all over the neighborhood, not just from their property.

We owe a lot to our friends and neighbors. Wouldn't it be great to have a law that served to remind us how blessed we are by our friends and neighbors? It's so easy for us to fall into the false notion that any of us are truly happy or have been successful totally on our own merits or talents. Our friends and neighbors bring so much wealth and depth to our everyday life that it would be a sin of ingratitude to fail to acknowledge at least in some minor way what God has given us through them. Why not take time this week to thank God for your neighbors and friends, and then take some time to let your friends and neighbors know how much you appreciate them?

April 12th
Gifts

I heard a talk one time when I was on retreat that made a lasting impression on me. The preacher, a Trappist monk, explained to us that we cannot force anyone, even God, to give us what we really want or need. Furthermore he explained that by meditation, we realize that what we most need for true peace and serenity has already been given to us. The monk then gave us a list for study and meditation. At the end of our meditation, we were asked to pray before the Blessed Sacrament and give thanks to God daily for the many gifts given to us, but that we take for granted. Gifts from God, that if they were taken from us would make us truly miserable. Give thanks to God for all of those things which you cannot force someone to give you, yet God has already given you.

Here is the list:

- *You can force yourself to put food in your mouth, but you cannot force yourself to have an appetite.*
- *You can force yourself to lie in bed, but you cannot force yourself to sleep well.*
- *You can force yourself to pay someone a compliment, but you cannot force yourself to feel admiration.*
- *You can force others to tell you a secret, but you cannot force others to trust you.*

- *You can force others to be civil to you, but you cannot force anyone to love you.*

The best things in life cannot be forced or willed into being. They are simply gifts for which we must always give thanks.

April 13th
Sixty-five Thousand Miles

I have a question for you. How many miles do you think you have walked in your life so far? I recently learned, by flipping through the channels yesterday and landing on an old "Mister Rogers" program, that the average person walks about sixty-five thousand miles in their lifetime! If Mister Rogers is right, I also learned that that's like walking two and a half times around the world! Now that is a lot of walking.

As I thought about all of that walking, I began to ask myself where my feet have taken me so far in life. I was amazed at all of the places my feet have taken me. Just in traveling around the world, I think I've been in 31 countries and almost as many states. In ministry roles I have been in countless hospital rooms, homes, nursing homes, hospices, missionary schools, dispensaries, parishes, retreat centers, jails, homeless shelters, rehab centers and even out to a tiny hermitage in the desert. I know that I've been to a lot more places, but, I got that far when I began to get a headache, so I stopped thinking about it!

I wonder, if you were to take a few moments to consider all of the places your feet have carried you in your walk through life, what would your travelogue look like? In your love for your family, where have your feet taken you? Try to recall just how many places you have walked to in support of those you love. Consider how far you've walked in your journey to pursue an education, to secure a job, or find a home. All of that is a whole lot of walking!

As my headache faded and I began once again to consider those sixty-five thousand miles that Mister Rogers had talked about, I had an inner voice ask me another question, "How far have you walked in your search for God?" That question got me thinking not only about the past but about the future. It led me to a time of deep prayer as it began to dawn on me just how many miles God has walked in pursuit of me.

So, let me ask you to consider those very same questions - How far have you walked in your search for God? And How far has God walked in searching for you?

April 14th
The Call to Serve Others

I've been reading the autobiography of Dr. Albert Schweitzer. Winner of the 1952 Nobel Peace Prize, he was a theologian, concert musician, philosopher, scientist, biblical scholar, physician and missionary. Because of his wisdom, many people sought him out for advice. A young teenager wrote to ask Dr. Schweitzer for advice concerning a future career, "What career can my friends and I follow which will be a sure road to our own happiness?"

The wise doctor replied, "I don't know what your destiny will be, but one thing I do know: the only ones among you who will really be happy are those who have sought out and found a way to serve others."

In our world today, many people are looking for happiness, and many hope to find it in money or material possessions. Dr. Schweitzer had material possessions and was a very famous concert musician before he felt "called" to serve the poor in equatorial Africa as a physician and missionary. He was middle-aged and had not yet even been to medical school when he realized what he had to do. Yet age and success in his academic and musical careers did not deter him. He chose to put aside his own welfare and offer his life in service to the poor of Africa. Toward the end of his life, Schweitzer said, "I have known great joy and deep happiness because I accepted the call to serve others."

If we are authentic followers of Jesus, we, like Albert Schweitzer, need to be attentive to and answer the call to serve others.

April 15th
Nurturing Relationships

I was browsing through a garden store the other day when I discovered a beautiful display of seeds. There must have been 500 different kinds of seeds, neatly packaged in brightly colored envelopes with magnificent pictures of the flowers or vegetables that the seeds within could produce. Just looking at the pictures made me want to buy them all. If I bought those seeds and planted them, my "world" would be turned into a garden of delight! I couldn't resist.

I was just about to buy several dozen packets, when I remembered what would always happen to me at this time of the year when I was a kid. I'd be in a hardware store, I'd see fantastic flowers, and would just have to buy some seeds because I could imagine wonderful floral displays in our yard. It would be great. I'd buy two or three packets of seeds, go right home and plant them, being sure to give them a great amount of water to "get them started". Then I'd wait for the greatest flowers in botanical history to appear in my garden. I waited a long time. They never did show up. Instead of the huge, beautiful vivid and aromatic blossoms I'd imagined, I ended up with green stalks that looked like they had been through a nuclear holocaust! I could never understand why my flowers didn't look like the ones on the packets.

It never occurred to me that I had to do more than just plant some seeds and pour water over them. I didn't know about creating the best possible conditions for the seeds, or about fertilizing, weeding, and all the nurturing that the flowers really needed. I just thought that buying the seeds and putting them in the ground would give me the flowers I liked in those pictures. It was not to be. Those kinds of flowers take lots of hard work.

This can serve as a good parable on our spiritual development. We can look around our world and see truly holy, caring people who are living out the Gospel, and we are impressed. We can look around and see a couple who are truly loving and committed to each other, their marriage seems to be "made in heaven", and we want a marriage like that, too. We all say "That's the kind of person I want to be," or "That's the kind of marriage I want," or "That's how I want to raise my kids." It all looks so easy and effortless, but we know better than that. Relationships take a lot of work. If we want to produce "good fruit", we have to be willing to do more than stand on the sidelines and "be impressed". We've got to tend to all the conditions that could affect our relationship with God, with our family members, with friends, and with ourselves.

In the next few weeks, you might be out shopping and find a display of seeds. I'm sure you'll be so impressed by all the colors and photographs that you'll want to buy some right away. Be careful – there's more to those seeds than meets the eye - and there's more to love and holiness as well.

April 16th
The Gift of the Eucharist

A man whose wife was sick decided that he would do the cooking. He did quite well until one day he decided he would try to bake bread. Thinking that bread is eaten so quickly and that he had limited time, he decided to make a large batch, so he quadrupled the recipe. Misreading the directions, he added two pounds of yeast to the dough. Faithfully following all the other directions, he put the dough near the heat and waited for the dough to rise.

Some time later, his wife called down from the upstairs bedroom, "Have you put the dough in the oven yet, dear?"

Frantically he replied, "Put it in the oven? I can't even keep it in the kitchen!"

Jesus told us that the Kingdom of God is like yeast in bread – it's very tiny, but when it is put in the right environment, it expands far beyond itself. Has the "yeast of the Gospel" found a "warm spot" in your heart and begun to expand? Are you spending time in the warmth of prayer so that the leaven of Jesus' words will reshape your life? On the Feast of Corpus Christi, when we celebrate the gift of the Eucharist, may each of us take time to be nourished by Jesus, the Bread of Life, and grow in His likeness.

April 17th
The Jesus Boat

While on sabbatical, I had an opportunity to see a very interesting artifact. It's called "The Jesus Boat" and it is a fishing boat that has been carbon-dated to the time of Jesus and the apostles. Archeologists who have studied the boat say that it is a typical light fishing boat and could certainly be the type of boat that Peter, James and John would have used in their fishing business.

It was in 1986 that two brothers who lived in a kibbutz near the Sea of Galilee made the discovery. These two Israeli fishermen were out checking their equipment when they noticed something "different" sticking out of the mud along the shoreline. Because there had been a very severe three-year drought, there was an unusually low water level in the sea. The low water level exposed the boat which had been on the bottom of the Sea of Galilee for almost 2000 years.

It really was fascinating to be able to see such an old boat and to be able to picture more accurately what life was like for Jesus and His apostles. The part of this story that I find even more interesting is the fact that the boat itself would never have been discovered by those two Israeli brothers had it not been for the three-year drought. The lowering water levels of the sea was, I'm sure, seen by everyone as a real disaster from which nothing good could possibly emerge. But without the drought, there would have been no discovery.

There is a lesson for us in this story. Often those events in our lives which appear to be complete disasters turn out to be the doorway through which we make new discoveries about God, about ourselves, and about life. If you are experiencing some terrible times right now, if you feel overwhelmed and feel that nothing good could ever come out of your situation, perhaps you are enduring a "three-year severe drought" which will "lower the water levels" enough for you to make some startling new discoveries.

The rains eventually returned to Israel and the water level of the Sea of Galilee is back to its normal level. Because the level was allowed to be lowered for a period of time, the world was given a wonderful gift. If your "water levels" are lowered for a brief time, perhaps you too will be given a wonderful gift.

April 18th
The "Mountain" Within Ourselves

Have you ever had to face a situation in your life that seemed to be too big for you to handle? Sometimes I think that we get overwhelmed by the duties and the difficulties that life sets before us, and we begin to feel that things are hopeless. These are natural feelings, but they can't be our final stance toward life.

Sir Edmond Hillary, the world famous mountain climber, was asked which mountain provided the most challenge to him. Hillary thought about it a moment, and then said, "It's not the mountain itself that we conquer, but ourselves. The most challenging thing we have to face is the 'mountain' within ourselves. It's our attitude about facing difficulties that makes the difference."

We often look at our problems and think they are too big for us. When I have difficulties or problems to face, I read the story of David and Goliath. I like this story because it can teach us how to "see" our problems. When the Philistines sent Goliath against the Israelites, the Israelites thought he was too big to conquer. They thought they would soon be slaves, and they were about to give up hope. The young shepherd boy named David saw things quite differently however. When David put his trust in God, he looked at Goliath, and picking up five smooth stones to put in his slingshot, thought that the giant was simply too big to miss!

In the same way, when we face problems that seem like mountains, when we face a future that seems too big and too frightening, we have to put our trust in God, and start "seeing" things from a new vantage point. We have to realize that our greatest mountains are within us, and they can be overcome.

April 19th
The Power of Prayer

A famous missionary priest went traveling through the countryside and came to a small village where, in one of the large houses, a young girl lay seriously ill. Her parents begged the priest to pray for their daughter in the hopes that he could cure her. The priest knelt by the young girl's bedside and prayed over her.

An uncle of the girl was standing nearby. He was not at all pleased to have a priest praying for his niece. He thought the girl needed more medicine, not some preacher's words. So he said to the priest, "You're nothing but a charlatan! How can a few words mumbled by you do anything to cure my niece? Words are useless!"

To the uncle's surprise, the priest turned on him and with eyes blazing with fury, the priest began to yell at him "You understand nothing," he exclaimed "you ignorant fool!"

The uncle was utterly shocked and offended by the priest's words. His face went red, and he began to shake with rage. He was just about to strike the priest when the priest began to smile.

"If just a few words can make a man like you hot and angry," the priest said, "why do you doubt the power of a few words uttered by a priest to his God to make this young girl well?" The uncle was speechless. The young girl was healed within the hour.

There is a tendency to underestimate the power of our words. This is also true when we speak of the power of the words we say to God in prayer. We must never forget that there is a great power in a few words uttered with faith to God. If you find yourself in a difficult situation, or if you are feeling a bit overwhelmed with life, why not turn to the Lord in prayer?

April 20th
Improving on the Silence

A man who was visiting a small town in Vermont on business decided to stay at a bed and breakfast inn. In the evening, he thought he would join a group of men sitting on the front porch. As he sat there among the "locals", he attempted to strike up a conversation with them six different times. Each time he either got a nod of the head or a one word answer. Frustrated, the businessman finally cursed at the men and said, "Is there a law in this town against talking, or what?"

One of the natives spoke right up and said "Mister, there's no law around here against talking, but we all have an understanding that no one speaks unless he is sure he can improve on the silence."

We live in a world filled with a lot of chatter. From time to time, it's good for us to consider whether or not the things we say improve the silence. Do the things you say improve the silence by building up the world around you and fostering harmony in your family or among your friends? On the other hand, do the things you say plant seeds of mistrust and dissention? The words we speak have great power to do good or ill. How are you using that power?

April 21st
The Story of the Word, "Hello"

Did you know that after Alexander Graham Bell invented the telephone and it began to be used by the general public that a controversy arose over what a person was to say when they answered the telephone? Bell told his customers that he thought they should use the nautical term "ahoy" when they answered the phone. Most people just couldn't use that term. It seemed much too silly to pick up the phone and say "Ahoy!"

One of Bell's friends, Thomas Edison, who was helping him perfect the telephone, created a new word for the English language to solve the controversy. The word was "Hello". In a short time, it was used by most people. In fact, the first telephone operators were called "Hello Girls".

I think the story of the word "hello" can serve as a reminder to us that we need to continually find new ways to better communicate with one another. It has been said that about 90% of the hurt in the world is caused by poor communication. Perhaps, like Alexander Bell and Thomas Edison, we too should be searching for new and better ways to help people communicate with each other. In your relationship with your friends, your family members or your spouse, what can you do to improve the quality of your communication? What practical steps can you take today to make that happen?

April 22nd
There Can Be Good in Every "Mess"

In 1995, a garbage man named Craig from Peabody, Massachusetts, was throwing bags of trash onto his garbage truck when one of the bags burst open, spewing refuse all over the street. He was disgusted at having to pick up the pieces of trash and was grumbling as he went about his task. He noticed a fast food soft drink cup with a contest sticker on its side. Since he had won a chicken sandwich the week before, he decided to check this sticker out, hoping he might win some fries or a coke. Instead, as he peeled the sticker, he discovered that he hadn't won a sandwich, fries, or a coke, but rather $200,000!

When asked what he thought about the discovery, Craig replied "It just goes to show you that right in the middle of a big mess, God can give you big gifts if you just take the time to look for them."

April 23rd
There Is More Than One Way to Preach The Gospel

One night last week, a rather interesting man came to the rectory door. He asked if there was a priest available who could bless something for him. I told him I would be happy to bless whatever he wanted. He smiled broadly and opened the top three buttons of his shirt to reveal a rather large bandage covering his chest. As I stood there he carefully removed the bandage to reveal a tattoo that covered most of his chest. It looked very sore, so I asked him if he was concerned about infection.

"I'm not worried about that at all. I just want you to bless it. It is religious you know. I've saved for quite a long time to pay for this thing." The tattoo was a picture of Jesus with a crown of thorns. Under the picture of Jesus were the words, "HE LOVES YOU".

"Does it hurt?" I asked

"No, not too much. I want people to know I'm Christian, and since I can't really talk in front of crowds, I thought this would do my preaching for me. We are all supposed to preach the Gospel you know! I figured this was a good way for me to do it. Besides, if I ever get bummed out or feeling low, all I have to do is look down at my chest and I'll feel 100% better. Not only that, if I ever get to feeling like I don't want to be Christian anymore, I'll just look at my chest and know it would be pretty tough to change my whole chest, so I'll just have to hang in there."

"It sounds like you've got this all figured out," I said as I admired the detailed work of the tattoo.

"Yeah, I've been thinking about it for a long time. I had it put on my chest because my mom was always telling me that if I had anything to say, I should go and 'get it off my chest'. I guess I just took her literally! Can you bless this thing or not?" he asked as he laughed at my surprised look.

I blessed the man's tattoo just as he wanted. He went away very pleased with himself. I blessed his chest, and I wondered how many other people would be blessed by the image on his chest. There's more than one way to preach the Gospel!

April 24th
Thermometers and Thermostats

This week I thought I would offer a few thoughts on, of all things, the weather. Hasn't it been wonderful with the rising temperatures and sunny days? Isn't it interesting that when there is a change in seasons, we all seem to pay attention to the temperature? It's not uncommon to hear people discussing the weather in general and the current temperature in particular. I've noticed that I've looked at the thermometer a lot more often these past days; I suppose just to confirm that it really is as warm as it feels. It's funny to me that we all seem to talk about the weather as if we can do something about it. All we can really do is report what is happening. We can't change things all that much. Yet, we go on talking about it as if we can.

The changing temperatures remind me of two things. The first is that I'm not in control of everything in my life. Some things (probably most things!) are not under my control, and I have to adapt to changing circumstances and let go of those things I have no power to change. Secondly, there are some situations on which I can have a great influence if I choose to do so. I believe that God wants us to pay attention, and to come to know the difference.

I think this is best explained with an example. There are two devices for measuring temperature - a thermometer and a thermostat. The thermometer simply measures what the temperature is. That's all it has the power to do, and it is quite useful in that limited way. A thermostat, on the other hand, not only measures the temperature, but when attached to a furnace or air conditioner, can also change the temperature.

In some situations in our lives, we can only be thermometers. We can only indicate what the temperatures are. In other situations, we can bring about real, needed changes. How do we discover whether we are being called to be a thermometer or a thermostat? There's no easy answer, but I think we begin with the simple prayer:

"God grant me the serenity to accept the things I cannot change,
The courage to change the things I can,
And the wisdom to know the difference."

As the weather continues to change, it's good for us to take time out prayerfully to consider what the Lord is asking us to be.

April 25th
Thinking of Heaven

A young doctor went to check on one of his patients who was just coming out of anesthesia following surgery. As the doctor was checking the patient's blood pressure, far-off church chimes began making beautiful music. The patient opened her eyes and when she heard the chimes, she said "I must be in heaven." Then she saw her doctor and murmured, "I can't be in heaven, there's my doctor and he certainly wouldn't be here!" I don't know what the doctor thought, but I don't think I'd want to see her bill after that comment!

Do you ever think about heaven? I'm certain that all of us spend some time thinking about the next world, but probably few people realize how important it is for us to think about it. I was reading C.S. Lewis the other day when I found a statement that has been part of my meditation this past week. He said,

"If you read history, you will find that Christians who did most for the present world were precisely those who thought most about the next. It is since Christians have largely ceased to think of the other world that they have become ineffective in this one."

Just how we view this world and the next one will determine how we choose to live our lives and how happy we will be as well. Let me explain this with a story.

A very prominent wealthy man was dying. As he lay in his bed in a huge, lovely home surrounded by a few family members, some business associates, all of the top doctors and the most expensive medical equipment that money could buy, he looked around and whispered, "I'm leaving home! I'm leaving home! What will become of me?" Across town there was another man dying. This man was not surrounded by wealth or the best doctors. He had with him his family, a few possessions, a priest and a visiting nurse. He looked around and said with a gleam in his eye, "I'm going home! I'm going home!"

It is vitally important that we take time to think about heaven. What we think about it will make all the difference in how we choose to live. How we see the next world will very much determine how we live in this one. How we live in this one will very much determine what we see in the next one.

April 26th
Time for One Another

A father kept bringing work home night after night. This really disturbed his 7 year-old daughter because he no longer played with her or helped her with her homework. When she asked her father why he had to bring so much work home from the office, he explained to her that he was so busy at work that he just couldn't get it all finished during the day.

"Well then," she said, "why don't they put you in a slower group?" When the father heard his little girl's question, it dawned on him that he was busy doing lots of things but not doing the right things. It occurred to him that his child was going to be a little girl for only a short period of time. If he kept himself as busy as he had been, he would miss her childhood and she would miss out on his love and guidance. He made a decision that he would look for a new job, a job that would be at a much slower pace and give him more precious time with his daughter.

In a world that keeps us all rushing from one thing to the next so that we never have time for one another, we all need to be put in a "slower group". Time and attention – we all need to receive it and we all need to give it.

April 27th
Trees or Fence Posts

I think it was St. Francis DeSales who said that when he looked out over the congregation before him in church, he realized that there were two basic kinds of Christians – trees and fence posts. If you plant a tree and water it regularly, it drinks in the water, takes in nutrients from the soil, produces leaves, then blossoms, and eventually bears fruit. If you plant a fence post and water it regularly, it may soak up the water, but that is all it can do, for it has no life in it. If fact, if you keep watering the post, it will simply rot.

If you took inventory of your life, which would you be, a tree or a fence post? In your marriage or relationships with others, are you a tree that is producing growth, leaves, and fruit, or are you simply soaking up water and slowly rotting from within? With regard to your job or school, which are you, a tree or post? If you took an honest look at how you live your faith, which are you, a tree or a fence post?

April 28th
True Christians

A group of women went once a week to visit an elderly woman named Maggie who was confined to her bed due to a serious illness. Sometimes they would take her some beautiful flowers to cheer her up or take her some magazines to read. Maggie enjoyed their visits, but always frowned when, as they were leaving, they'd say, "We'll pray for you this week, Maggie."

After a few visits, the women asked Maggie why she always frowned when they said that. "Well, my dears, it has to do with what goes through my mind when you all say those pious words."

"What goes through your mind?" they asked.

"Are you sure you won't get mad at me?" asked Maggie. They reassured her they wouldn't get angry, and she said, "Well then, this is what goes through my mind when you tell me you will pray for me – I can do my own damn praying, what I really need is somebody to mop these dirty floors of mine!" They all laughed and said, "Maggie, how about we pray for you while we mop your floors?"

"If you will do that, I'll take your prayers as coming from true Christians!" Maggie laughed.

If we are going to be "true Christians" there has to be more to our "praying" than just words, and our service to one another has to be more than just "good deeds."

April 29th
True Compassion

Have you ever heard of Sir William Osler? He was one of England's most famous doctors who worked, among other places, in a British military hospital during World War I. He was a skilled surgeon filled with a professional concern for his patients. He was famous for his skill in surgery and he was also noted for his happy disposition. In fact, everyone knew he was on the ward or in the hospital because wherever he went and whatever he was doing, Dr. Osler always whistled as he moved from patient to patient.

One day while he was examining a patient, a telegram arrived informing him that his young son had been killed in battle on the fields of France. Friends recalled that from the moment he heard the news, he was not the same. As soon as he could, the doctor returned to his work, but the joy had left him – the whistle was gone, and there was a slight stoop to his shoulders from that time on. Friends also noticed that something new was a part of Dr. Osler's routine. Now, instead of standing at the bedside of his patients, he sat down and looked directly into his patients' eyes. When his patients spoke, he listened, as the doctor himself put it, "just the way I would have wanted a doctor to listen to my son's complaints. I've seen suffering from a whole new point of view now, and I don't think I'll doctor the same way ever again. I can't see someone suffer now and not be moved by it. I've been hurt in such a way that I can never again be indifferent to pain." His friends say that William Osler was the finest doctor who ever lived – but never quite as fine as after his son was killed in battle.

Isn't it true that only after we have suffered a loss or setback that we truly understand the pain of others? True compassion has its roots in having experienced pain and suffering ourselves. The Gospel teaches us that the best way for us to cope with our pain and suffering is for us to reach out to others who are in pain. Sharing in another's burdens lightens two loads – theirs as well as your own.

April 30th
Trust Him

"If you had faith the size of a mustard seed, you could say to this sycamore, 'be uprooted and transplanted into the sea' and it would obey you." With these words, Jesus reminds us of the importance of little things. Our modern culture often tries to convince us that in order to make a difference in this world, you have to be the biggest, the strongest, the toughest, the wealthiest and the most influential person around. Yet, if you take some time to think about it, you'll soon come to understand that we must never underestimate the power that each one of us has for good. A simple candle in your house when there is a power outage can prove to be more useful than all the stars in the heavens. Or again, when you want a drink of water, the kitchen faucet is of more use to you than Niagara Falls could ever be. Our small powers and gifts, when placed in God's hands, can accomplish whatever is needed.

If you are at a point in your life when everything seems to be overwhelming you and it seems that everything is bigger, stronger, and more powerful than you, perhaps Jesus is calling you to a deeper faith, a deeper trust. If your strength or power is only the size of a mustard seed, now is the time to put that tiny amount of strength in God's hands, along with a mustard seed of faith, and great things will be accomplished. Trust Him!

May 1st
We All Bring Light to the World

A school teacher grew so exasperated with one of her students that she sent him home with a note for his mother. The teacher wrote to the mother, suggesting that she take the boy out of school because he was much too slow to learn. In addition, the teacher thought that since the boy was partially deaf, there was not much more that could be done to further educate the child.

The mother decided that she would have to teach her son herself. She began by making sure that he understood that learning came from being curious. She taught him well – her son was Thomas Edison, who said that most of his inventions grew out of his own curiosity.

At the time of his death in 1931, Thomas Edison held patents for 1,100 inventions, and there were many, many more on his drawing board. The President of the United States ordered that, as a sign of mourning and gratitude, the nation should turn off all electric lights for one minute as Edison's funeral began. The temporary darkness served to remind the nation just how much "light" that "slow," partially deaf student had given to the world.

It doesn't matter how slow, deaf, or uneducated we may think we are; all of us, because we are God's children, are capable of bringing lots of light into the world.

May 2nd

We Are Called to Be Missionaries

A young man wanted to find God, so he went to a beautiful church in his neighborhood. He thought that under the beautifully painted dome, in the light of the colorful stained glass windows, and in the presence of graceful statues of the saints, he would experience God's presence. As he sat surrounded by all the beauty, he thought to himself, "I'll just sit here and see if God allows me to feel His presence." Then he put his head down on the back of the pew in front of him.

It wasn't long before he felt a tapping on his shoulder. Looking up, he saw a young woman. "Are you okay?" she asked. "If you need someone to listen, I would be more than happy to spend some time with you, or if you're hungry, I'd be glad to give you a few bucks to get something to eat."

Realizing the risk that the young woman had taken and the loving kindness behind it, the young man thanked her and assured her that he was just fine. As he left the church he realized that he had been in God's presence in more than one way.

The Church constantly reminds us that all of us are called to be missionaries. Some people will go off to foreign lands to preach the Gospel. Most of us, however, will be missionaries right here in our own "back yard" or maybe in our own beautiful church, just as the young woman had been.

In what ways are you spreading the Good News of Jesus Christ?

May 3rd
We Are Victims of Busy Lives

A young lawyer tells this story about her father. When she passed the Bar exam, the young attorney was offered a job in a city 350 miles away from home. Because of the distance between them, she and her father had not seen each other for several months, and her father was getting a bit lonely. He telephoned his daughter and asked her, "When are you going to come and see me? I miss your pretty face and the sound of your voice, and I miss you!"

She responded by explaining how busy she was; being the lowest-ranking person on the staff, she had much to do, a busy court schedule, and a host of meetings that she could not miss. It was just impossible for her to visit with him if she wanted to advance in the law firm.

In the following weeks and months, the father called again and again asking her to visit. She encouraged him to get involved in a senior's group or to do other things because it was not a good time for her to get away. Finally the father got on a bus and made his way to his daughter's home.

"You must tell me something I've been wondering about for some time now," he said to her. "When I die, do you intend to come to my funeral?"

"Daddy!" she replied, "I can't believe you'd even ask such a question! Of course I'd come to your funeral."

"Good," he said smiling, "Let's make a deal. Forget about coming to my funeral. Just come sometime to see me. I need you now more than I will at my funeral."

The famous passage from the Bible about the "Good Samaritan" who stops to care for the man along the roadside comes to mind here. Perhaps not all of those in need of our compassionate assistance are the victims of robbers. Some might just be victims of our overly hectic, overly scheduled lives.

May 4th

Putting Our Hands Together

Isn't it wonderful how God puts people together? I just don't mean physically, but spiritually as well. I've been thinking about two elderly women I saw on one of those news magazine shows. This is their story.

In the Spring of 1983, Margaret Patrick arrived at the Southeast Senior Center for Independent Living, to begin a program of physical therapy. Millie McHugh, a staff manager at the Center for quite some time, introduced Margaret to the other residents as they sat in the dining room eating their lunch. Millie noticed Margaret looking at the piano in the corner of the room and she saw what she thought was a tear in the old woman's eyes. "Is there something wrong?" Millie asked her.

"No," Margaret said softly, "It's just that seeing the piano brought back a flood of good memories. Before my stroke, music was everything to me."

Millie glanced at Margaret's right hand as the elderly black woman told her of her music career. She could tell that her right hand was paralyzed. Suddenly Millie said, "Wait right here. I'll be back in a minute." She returned moments later, followed closely by a small white-haired woman in dark thick glasses. The woman struggled with her walker as she approached.

"Margaret Patrick," said Millie, "meet Ruth Eisenberg." Then she smiled. "She too played the piano, but like you she has not been able to play since her stroke. Notice, she has a good right hand and you have good use of your left hand, and I have a feeling that if you two worked together, something beautiful might result."

The two elderly women made their way over to the piano. "Do you know Chopin's Waltz in D flat? Can you play your half of it?" Ruth asked. When Margaret nodded that she knew it, the two sat together on the piano bench and began to play. Two healthy hands-one with black fingers, the other with short, plump white fingers-moved across the ebony and ivory keys.

Since that first day they played the piano together, Margaret and Ruth have played hundreds of times for countless audiences. Many people have been touched by their charm and their grace. They have been in many cities and even on television performing in hope of raising people's spirits, especially those who have had strokes or other debilitating illnesses. They call themselves, 'Ebony and Ivory' and people love them.

In their years together, they have found out that they share more than just physical challenges of paralysis. They both are widows, great-grandmothers, both have lost sons, and both have great faith. Both have suffered a stroke and both thought they had little to offer the world, until they met each other.

It's a wonderful story of how God puts people together and uses them to touch others. God has called all of us to do something beautiful for God. We have all been called here to make beautiful music together. God calls us with our strengths and weaknesses to care for each other, to reach out to each other, to encourage one another, and to be for others the face of Jesus. The Lord is inviting all of us, just like Ruth and Margaret, to put our hands and hearts together for others. Can you play your half of it?

May 5th

What Consumes Us?

Three men were having lunch, discussing and "solving" all of the world's problems. They had determined that almost all of the world's problems were caused by consumerism. The first man said, "The problem with the world today is that most people consume too much."

"Oh, I don't think that people consume too much, I think the problem is with what they choose to consume," said the second man.

The third man thought for a few moments and then said, "I think you are both right, partially; but I think there is a more important point to be made. It's not how much we consume or even what we consume; it's what consumes us that is important."

That third man was certainly wise in his observations. While it is important that from time to time we take stock of both how much we are consuming and just what we are consuming, it is more important to know what consumes and drives us. Is it a spirit of generosity and gratitude or a spirit of greed and selfishness that motivates us? Is it a spirit of trust and fidelity that marks our relationships, or are we consumed by a spirit of suspicion and second-guessing?

When it comes to consumerism, I think that these are the kinds of questions that Jesus would ask us to consider, because what consumes us makes all the difference in how we live our lives.

May 6th
Wholeheartedly

I recently saw an interview with the Reverend Billy Graham in which he was asked how he came to know what God wanted him to do. Billy Graham smiled and said that after he experienced a conversion to Jesus he had all kinds of ideas about what he was going to do for God. "None of my plans went anywhere," Mr. Graham said. "Then a friend told me not to tell God what I was going to do for God, but rather let God tell me what God wanted done."

"So, what did you do?" the interviewer asked.

"Well, every day I just said a short prayer – 'God, let me do something – anything for You!'"

"What happened?" the interviewer asked.

Smiling, Billy Graham simply said, "The rest of my wonderful life happened."

Billy Graham has indeed had a wonderful life. What made that life possible? It was the generosity of his heart, and his willingness to be used by God in any possible way. God wants to give each one of us a wonderful life too. That wonderful life is offered to each of us.

When I was on sabbatical living as a hermit, I spent a lot of time sitting before the Blessed Sacrament praying with these words from the Old Testament: "The eyes of the Lord roam over the whole earth, to encourage those who are devoted to Him wholeheartedly."

What a wonderful life awaits those who turn their hearts over to Him and say, "Use me, Lord, in some way ... in any way You want."

May 7th
Following Your Compass

An experiment was recently conducted at a national university sociology department to determine just how susceptible individuals are to the influence of a group.

Here's how the experiment worked. Seven pieces of string precisely two feet long were placed side by side on a black background. Placed next to those seven pieces of string was an eighth piece that was obviously six inches shorter than the other seven pieces. Six people were then brought into the room. Prior to being brought in, five of the six individuals were secretly told that all eight pieces of string were the same length, that the shorter string was in reality the same length but that the black background caused an optical illusion, making the eighth string look shorter. Thus, when all six people were brought into the lab to observe the string, each of the five who had been coached did, in fact, say that the strings were all the same length. Having heard the other five people say "yes," the sixth person was asked if all eight pieces of string were the same length. In three fourths of such experiments, the sixth person answered "yes." When one was asked why he answered in that way, he replied, "Well, I thought these other guys must know something I don't. I'll agree with them since all of them can't be wrong." When the experiment was repeated and the sixth person in each group was brought in alone without the other five to "prejudice" him, ten out of ten people said without hesitation that the eighth piece of string was shorter.

So what does all this prove? It says that very often we allow other people to be our "compass" or guide. I'm sure you've been in meetings where everyone agrees with what the first few speakers have to say. Everyone seems to "fall in line" behind the most popular voices. People can be led or misled by a simple majority opinion or by a particularly attractive statement. Sometimes we "go along" to "get along." We don't put a lot of thought and consideration into it. We may just look to what everyone else is saying or doing and we just follow along.

Who or what is the "compass" of your thought and belief? Do you form your opinions on what your heart tells you, what Jesus would tell you, or merely on what others tell you to believe?

May 8th
Starting, Finishing

Recently I was visiting some friends when one of their college-aged sons came home from work. "How're things going?" the young man's adoptive father asked.

"Terrible," the son answered.

"What's so terrible?" the father asked.

"I hate my life! Nothing good ever happens. In fact, nothing at all ever happens. I just go to work. I come home. I go to a bar with friends. I come home. It's always the same thing day after day, week after week. I hate life!" the boy muttered as he went to the refrigerator, got a beer, then sat down on the couch. Looking at me, he asked, "How do I get out of this boring life?"

I looked at him and said, "You know, Mike, when you were talking, I began thinking about Buddha."

"Buddha? I thought you were a Catholic priest, what's with Buddha?" he asked.

I told him about the last time I was down at the Abbey of Gethsemani near Bardstown, Kentucky. While on retreat there, I met a Buddhist monk with whom I had many conversations during the eight days we were together. I had told the monk in one of our conversations that part of my prayer on retreat was to discern what God wanted me to do. He smiled and said that he was asking God the same thing. Then he told me that one of his spiritual masters had given him one of the sayings of Buddha to help him "hear" what God was saying. I asked him what the saying was. The monk wrote it out for me and this is what he wrote:

> *"It was the Buddha who said, "There are two things that keep great projects from coming to life: 1. Not starting, and 2. Not finishing."*

After I read the saying, I looked at the monk who was smiling at me.

Then he said, "My master taught me that if I wanted to know what God wants me to do on any day, ask myself two questions "What in my life needs starting? What in my life needs finishing?"

The monk just stood there looking at me and smiling. I thanked him for the wise saying he had given me. Then he said that he was returning home and wished me well.

"So, what does all of that have to do with me?" the young college student asked. I just smiled and said, "What needs starting in your life? And what needs finishing? Answer those questions, and maybe you'll feel differently about life."

About a week ago, I got a card from that young man on which was written just a brief note: "I've discovered I need to start thinking of other's needs rather than only my own and I need to finish growing up. I like old Buddha!"

Take a few minutes this week to ask yourself: "What in my life needs starting? What in my life needs finishing?" And then, why not begin doing both?

May 9th

What We Honor Defines Us

Recently I read some of the writings of the novelist Salman Rushdie. He described in one article what it was like in his home when he was growing up in India. He said that in all of the devout households in India, there is a custom of kissing the "holy books" or the books of scriptures. The custom is to kiss the books before you read them and after you have finished reading them; if by some accident you should drop such a book, you are obliged to kiss the book as a kind of apology. Rushdie said that while most households practiced the custom of kissing the holy books, his family kissed not only holy books but also kissed all books. He commented, "We kissed not only holy books, but dictionaries, atlases, novels, Superman comics, magazines, and if I had ever dropped the telephone directory, I would have been obliged to kiss that book too!"

Rushdie's conclusion is that it is no surprise to him that he ended up being a writer of books. "Having grown up with such a reverence for books, how could I not dedicate my life in some way to them?" he said.

Those thoughts reminded me of a saying from one of the ancient Christian Desert Fathers: "What we honor defines us." That brings up a good point for us to contemplate, "If what we honor defines us, and I examine my own life for what I honor by the amount of time, energy, resources, and how much of my heart I put into it, who am I?" What do you honor in your life? How has what you honor shaped who you have become? If you are not happy with the person you have become, what must you begin to honor in order to become the person you want to be?

May 10th
Fearful Things

I read about a man who awoke with a start one night because he felt a mysterious, dark presence in the room with him. He just sensed that he was not alone, and he grew more and more terrified. As he stared into the dark, he could make out a vague shape. His heart pounded. He didn't move, but the dark shape did. He dreaded the blow of a knife, hammer, or an ax. Three long hours passed, the dark form was still there. Finally, dawn came, and the first rays of the sun revealed the nature of the dark intruder. It was a Mickey Mouse balloon! His son had been given the helium-filled balloon for his birthday, and it had been hanging on the ceiling. Through the night, as the helium began to leak out of the balloon, it descended until it was just beside the bed. It had been moving about with the breeze coming through the window. When the man realized what had been terrorizing him all night long, he laughed out loud. He thought about it for a minute, and then said to himself, "If only I had had the courage to switch on the light, I could have avoided a rather fearful, fitful night."

Have you ever found yourself in a situation in which you are terrified about what might happen? St. Francis of Assisi said that one of the best antidotes to fear is the light. Fear has more power over us when we are "in the dark." When we are faced with fearful things, the best way to deal with them is to bring these frightening things out into "the light" by sharing them with a good friend, and by taking it to God in deep prayer. I've found in my own life that when I do that, most of the things that have been so frightening turn out to be just like that Mickey Mouse balloon.

May 11th
Nearby

A woman was leaning over an accident victim as a crowd gathered around. Suddenly she was roughly pushed aside by a huge man with a very deep voice who said, "Step back lady, I'll handle this. I've had a course in first aid you know!" The woman watched as the man began to look at the victim's wounds. As she watched him, the man began to look a bit confused. She calmly said, "When you come to the part where you have to send for the doctor – I'm already here!"

Have you ever noticed how we often try to solve all our problems alone when true help and expertise is already right around us?

Every so often, it is good for us to take a look at the people who are right around us. It is an amazing thing to discover that God has planted great talents and resources around us in the many people who have gifts that we need. It's also a little humbling to realize that God has placed us where we are because there are people who need the gifts that we have. If you ever find that you are in need of some kind of help, look around. The people who can be of help to you are probably already there and ready to help. Then again, look around and take note of those people very near you who need the kind of help and compassion that you can offer. They would be surprised to know that you are already there, ready to help them.

May 12th
Bullies

A writer by the name of Jack Hanley tells of an experience that he had as a young teenager at school. He said there was a terrible bully in his class who would threaten him and demand his lunch money every day. After a few days of going hungry, Jack decided that he would fight back by taking some karate lessons. "I took the lessons," Jack remembers, "until one day the karate instructor informed me that I had to start paying $5.00 a lesson. Since $5.00 seemed like a fortune to me, I decided I'd go back to paying the bully – it was cheaper."

While Jack Hanley's story is funny, it does illustrate a not-so-funny reality. How often do we find it easier to "pay a bully" rather than defeat him? When I first read Jack Hanley's story, I laughed until I thought of all the alcoholics and drug addicts I have worked with who find it much easier to continue using or drinking than it is to get into and stay in recovery. Very often, they'd rather "pay the bully" than deal with the real issue. How often do parents allow their children to do things that are not good for them, simply to avoid a "scene?" They, like Jack Hanley, "pay the bully" rather than defeat him. How many of us in social situations are tempted to "go along with the crowd" so that we don't feel or look out of step?

Jesus came to set us free. He tells us, "The truth will set you free." He does not want any of us to live under the tyranny of any bully. If any evil is bullying you, do not pay it any dues. Join hands with Jesus and work to defeat it.

May 13th
Morning Offering

Saint Paul seems to have given a lot of advice. In one of his more famous letters, his First Letter to the Corinthians, he gives loads of advice, but there is one little snippet of advice that is neatly tucked away in the 10th chapter: "Whatever you do, do it all for the glory of God."

Whenever I come across that quote I am reminded of an old nun who taught 3rd grade at the grade school I attended. She would teach us that the most important thing each of us had to do each morning, before we did anything else was to say a very important prayer, The Morning Offering. I remember complaining to her one day that I couldn't remember all of the words to that prayer, and since that was such an important prayer, God was probably not happy with me. Her response to me was simple. "God loves you. If you can't remember the prayer, simply say this, "God, everything I do today is for you!"

I've said that prayer just about every day since then and I am glad that I learned it at an early age because it taught me to pay attention to what I do, and how I do it. I've learned that the simple things we do can have a great effect on the world around us if we do them with God in mind.

There are very few people who have not heard or read the famous quote of Mother Teresa of Calcutta, "We can do no great things; only small things with great love." I think she came to this conclusion by her own experience of offering everything she did for God. The world has been blessed by what she did. She paid close attention to "doing." We too need to pay attention to our "doing."

A few weeks ago I read an article by a professional writer on the craft of writing. She said that when she teaches young people about the art of writing, she always begins by telling them to pay attention to their lives and what they are doing. "What you do and how you do it is important," she told them. Then she gave her students a little sign to tape up over their desks. It says: "Planning to write is not writing. Thinking about writing is not writing. Talking about writing is not writing. Researching to write; outlining to write; none of this is writing. Writing is writing. If writing is what you want to do, then write."

What is it that you do? If you were to take a few moments right now to consider your days, what are you doing with them? Why are you doing what you do? For whom are you doing the things you do? How is what you are doing shaping who you are?

May 14th
Into Your Day

At a retreat not long ago, I spoke with a woman about her prayer life. I asked her when she thought that her prayer had been at its best. Her answer was a bit surprising to me. She said, "You know, what ruined my prayer life was the invention of permanent press clothes! I used to spend a lot of time ironing my family's clothes, and it was during that time that I did my best praying. When I ironed one of my husband's shirts, I'd start to think about him and what he had said to me that morning, whether I agreed with him or (more often than not) disagreed with him. Then I'd think about his needs or his worries, and I'd naturally start talking to God about him Next, I would start to iron one of my daughters' blouses and I'd do the same thing I had done when ironing my husband's shirt. I'd always end up praying for each of my daughters. I did that for every member of my family. My ironing time was my praying time. When permanent press came in, some of my best prayer time went right out the window. I guess I had better find a new way to pray that well."

Do you have a special time of prayer, a special way of keeping the needs of others in front of you? If not, why not look for a way to build prayer into your everyday activities? Why not find a way to use the ordinary events of your day as a vehicle for remembering others to God?

May 15th
Some Time in the Woods

When I was a child, I read a book about George Washington Carver. I was intrigued by him because he developed over 300 uses for the common ordinary peanut. I wondered what gave him all of those ideas and just where he got his inspiration. A few years ago, when reading another biography of Mr. Carver, I read an interview he had with an author by the name of James Childers. Childers asked George Washington Carver for the secret of his success. His response was that every morning he would get up at 4 a.m. to (as Carver put it) "... go into the woods. Once there in the middle of God's woods, I listen to God and to His plan for me." In other words, George Washington Carver knew that if he was to do anything of use to humanity, he had to nourish his soul and his life with a daily dose of deep prayer.

If your life and your soul are to produce a bounty of fruit like that which George Washington Carver's endeavors produced, you too must spend some of your time "in the woods" listening to God and to His plan for your life. This is the best way to nourish your life and your soul.

May 16th
A Net

When the Golden Gate Bridge was being built, it was the longest, highest, widest and most expensive bridge anywhere in the world. Because of the height, there was great danger for the laborers who worked on it. In fact, all the workers were so frightened of falling off the bridge that the work was at least a year behind schedule. Life for those construction workers was terribly scary. Then someone hit on a brilliant idea. Why not build a great safety net under the construction area? Then, if anyone fell, he would not fall to his death, but would be caught in the net. The idea seemed to be a good one, and in no time at all the net was constructed and installed under the work area. Several men fell during the course of the final construction, but no one was seriously injured. Not only was no one injured, but the work proceeded at a much faster pace once the workers had the assurance of the safety net. That safety net proved to be a wonderful idea that truly saved lives.

I believe that this same idea can help us in our everyday lives. Wouldn't it be wonderful if we could have a safety net built under each one of us that would catch us when we made mistakes or slip-ups? Wouldn't it be great if we had the assurance of a "safety net" under us when we had to make rather difficult decisions? In trying out new ideas, wouldn't it be great to know that even if you made a terrible mistake, those who love you would gently catch you and cushion your fall from any spirit-breaking critical remarks that unfeeling people might make about you?

Life today can be very scary. It's not unlike those people who had to build the Golden Gate Bridge without a net. Any slip can mean a horrible fall. In our harsh and critical world, even the slightest mistake or decision we have to make, with which others may not agree, can cost us emotionally. We live in such a hypercritical world where relationships, marriages, families, neighborhoods and even in parishes, a critical spirit can grow and develop among us so that each of us can end up living in an atmosphere of harsh criticism. We can end up living in the fear of being judged or disliked by those around us. That is a horrible way to live.

Jesus came to show us another way. It's His "safety net." He asks us to put away harsh criticism, destructive talk and cruelty. Jesus asks us to live in such a way that our kindness and our willingness to love, understand and accept each other's frailties can create a "safety net of Christian love and compassion." Wouldn't it be great to live in such an atmosphere?

May 17th
Into Your Hands

As the next few months unfold, the Nobel Prize committees will be announcing this year's winners in many fields. Perhaps the best known of the Nobel Prizes is the Nobel Peace Prize. Many distinguished people have been given this award through the years, but no one is better loved than the 1979 winner, Mother Teresa of Calcutta.

When Mother Teresa was nominated for the award, the committee was asked what evidence they had that she was truly working for the cause of peace. The committee responded by saying that as of 1979, 7,500 children were being educated through the schools she had established; some 960,000 patients had been cared for in dispensaries; some 47,000 lepers were tended to in 54 different clinics; some 1,600 orphans were being looked after in 20 of her homes, and some 34,000 dying persons had been ministered to in 23 other facilities. These numbers, the committee said, were the best evidence that Mother Teresa was a woman of peace.

When Mother Teresa was asked what made her a woman of peace, she did not point to her work. She simply said, "Once I abandoned myself to God and to God's will, I became a free woman, filled with peace. Everyday, I give myself totally to God, and He fills me with His love and peace. Then, I have something to share with the people."

If you are looking for peace, perhaps you need to abandon your life to God's love. I've been praying the following prayer for the last few weeks. Perhaps you'd like to pray it each morning as you start your day. Why not clip it out and tape it some place where you will see it often?

Father, I abandon myself into your hands;

Do with me what thy will.
Whatever you may do, I thank you.
I am ready for all; I accept all.
Let only your will be done in me, and in all your creatures;
I wish no more than this, O Lord.

Into your hands I commend my soul;
I offer it to you with all the love of my heart,
For I love you, Lord and so need to give myself,
Reserve and with boundless, confidence,
For you are my Father.

May 18th
A Single Act of Kindness

A very wealthy English family invited some friends to spend some time at their estate. As the adults were gathered on a veranda to talk, the children went for a swim in a nearby lake. All went well until one of the children got into deep water and was drowning. The gardener of the estate heard lots of commotion and ran to see what was happening. He quickly jumped into the water and was able to save the young boy. The boy's parents were so overwhelmed by the thought of almost losing their son, they both cried. When they were assured that their son was safe, they asked the gardener what they could do to show their appreciation for what he had done for them. The gardener simply said, "I have a son, and I know that my wife and I would be devastated if he were ever taken from us in some tragedy. You owe me nothing, I'm just glad I could help."

"We really want to thank you," the boy's father replied. "Tell us, what can we do for your son?"

The gardener hesitated a moment and then said, "Well, my son wants to go to college to become a doctor ..." Before he could finish his sentence, the young boy's father interrupted him and said, "My wife and I would love to pay his way. We will pay all his expenses."

Now it was the gardener's turn to be overwhelmed. "Sir, I cannot thank you enough! My son, Alexander, talks of nothing else but becoming a doctor. Now you have made it possible. Thank you!"

The young boy who had been saved by the gardener that day was Winston Churchill. Many years later when Sir Winston became Prime Minister of England, he became very ill with pneumonia. The illness became quite serious and it looked as if Mr. Churchill would die. The king sent for the best doctor in England, Sir Alexander Fleming, the man who had developed penicillin. He came and administered the drug, and Winston Churchill's life was spared. Dr. Alexander Fleming was the son of the gardener who had saved young Winston's life those many years before.

Upon his recovery, Winston Churchill said, "Rarely has one man owed his life twice to the same person. I wonder how many other lives were saved by that gardener's simple, generous act of bravery so many years ago. That act of kindness is still bearing fruit."

You can never tell what kind of fruit a single generous act of kindness will bear. The saving of one son's life led to another son's medical education; that education led to the development of a new wonder drug; the drug that has saved and continues to save many lives.

Jesus said that you can tell a tree by the fruit it bears. What kind of fruit is your life bearing?

May 19th
Aging – Maintaining Hope

I was going through some old papers the other day when I found some of my notes from a class I had taken on aging. One of the handouts given in that class was an account of Douglas MacArthur's thoughts on aging:

"Nobody grows old by simply living a number of years. People grow old by deserting their ideals. Years can wrinkle the skin, but giving up enthusiasm wrinkles the soul. Worry, doubt, self-distrust, fear and despair ... these are what make the long, long years that bow the head and turn the spirit back to dust. Whether seventy-one or seventeen, there is in every being's heart the love of wonder, the sweet amazement of the stars and the star-like things and thoughts, the undaunted challenge of events, the unfailing childlike appetite for what's next in the game of life. You are as young as your faith, as old as your doubts, as young as your self-confidence, as old as your fears, as young as your hope, as old as your despair."

Take a few moments right now to consider this. According to Douglas MacArthur's definition of aging, how old are you? Have you been able to maintain your ideals throughout the years with the daily struggles that life can bring? Have you been able to cope with the difficulties of life in such a way that you have not lost the joy of living? Are you a person filled with faith and hope, excited about what life can bring? In other words, how old are you?

May 20th
Allow Yourself to Be Shaped By God

A year or two ago, I saw an advertisement in a magazine that made me stop and think. It showed a picture of a plain iron bar with a price tag of $5.00. The next picture was of that same iron bar, but now it had been made into horseshoes with a price tag of $10.50. The next picture showed the same iron bar made into needles with a price tag of $5,000. The final picture showed the iron bar made into balance springs for watches and the price tag this final time was $250,000. The ad went on to say that it's not just the material that makes something valuable, but how it is used or fashioned.

It seems to me that this is also very true of us. We are all human, all valuable in God's eyes. God is the master former and inventor of the universe. He can take simple human beings and fashion us into something wonderful. Sometimes we keep God from transforming us into useful instruments of His glory. We have the great God-given gift of freedom. If we choose to cooperate with God, we will be transformed. If we refuse to be molded and shaped by God, we remain like those simple iron bars – useful but not spectacular.

Put your life in God's hands. Allow Him to shape your life and your future.

May 21st
Am I Wise Enough To Know I Don't Know it All?

I was reading a very interesting article this week about being lost. The article indicated that the worst thing for any man to experience is getting lost. Being lost makes men feel "out of control" and somewhat stupid, and therefore most men cannot admit that they're lost and will not seek directions from anyone until it is absolutely the only solution possible. The author said that this does not seem to be a problem for women because they are more apt to ask for directions at the first sign of being lost. Men, on the other hand, seem to run faster and faster the more they realize that they've lost their way. It's as if going faster will somehow get them where they are supposed to be.

Does your spiritual life feel like that? Do you feel that you are racing faster and faster but ending up nowhere? Maybe it's time to seek direction. This just makes me think of those "wise men," the Magi, who knew enough to know that they didn't know it all. They trusted that God would lead them where they were supposed to be. They followed the star, and it led them to Jesus.

The question we have to ask ourselves today is, "Am I wise enough to know that I don't know it all? Am I wise enough to know that I need others, that I need guidance, and that those around me may have some insight or some wisdom that could lead me to God?" As you think about these things, why not make a resolution to seek Jesus in new places by following the "light" of a trusted friend or confidant?

May 22nd
Light

I think it was St. Francis De Sales who was weeping at the death of a member of his congregation of whom he was very fond when someone asked him, "If you are a great believer in life after death, why are you weeping over the death of this poor man?"

"I'm not weeping because I am sad," St. Francis said, "I'm weeping because my friend has gone to live with the Lord and because he has blessed my life with light. When he was born, there was not much light, but now, because of his life and its influence on me, there is no more darkness – what a blessing God has given me in knowing him!"

Have you ever taken some time to consider those wonderful people God has given to you who have, by their life and influence, brought you light?

May 23rd
Appreciation of Life

This past week I read an article by Art Linkletter about how much he had learned from children throughout the years of his career. "Children have a different and refreshing way of looking at things," he said.

There was one anecdote that Linkletter included in his article which I think can help us realize how richly blessed we are. One time while visiting a class of 8-year-olds who were beginning to study some basic science, he asked what he thought was a basic question. "Boys and girls, what is salt?" he asked. A little girl named Debbie raised her hand and said, "Salt is what ruins the potatoes when you leave it out."

While that may not be a particularly scientific answer, it certainly does express a truth. Debbie's answer became for me something I used in my prayer for the rest of the week. Every day when I began my prayer, I asked myself, "What would ruin my life if I left it out?" I came up with quite a few answers.

First, can you imagine how "ruined" your life would be if you left out a spirit of thankfulness? Wouldn't life be ruined if you "left out" kindness or gentleness or sincerity? Certainly many relationships would be completely ruined if we "left out" empathy, understanding, compassion, and plain old patience.

Sometimes we can assume that there's not much worth to our lives. Little Debbie's comment about salt helped me to realize how rich my life truly is. This week, why not take some time to consider how different your life would be if some aspects were "left out."

May 24th
Watching

In 1800, a number of Native American chiefs and warriors met in council in Battle Creek, New York, to hear some missionaries preach the Gospel of Jesus. The chiefs and warriors were very attentive as the missionary spoke at length about how the Gospel can change lives. After an hour and a half of listening, one of the chiefs, Red Jacket, got up to speak on behalf of all those in attendance.

He said, "Brother, we have been told that you have been telling all our white neighbors about this Jesus just as you have been telling us. We are well-acquainted with our white neighbors. We will wait a little while to see if Jesus, the one you have been telling us about, will have any effect on these neighbors of ours. If we find that this Jesus does them good, makes them honest and less inclined to cheat and belittle us, then we will certainly consider this Jesus. We will be watching them very closely."

If these Native Americans were "watching" you, would they find enough evidence that Jesus has had an effect on your life? There may not be Native Americans watching you, but your children, fellow workers and neighbors certainly are. What kind of witness are you giving for the Gospel of Jesus?

May 25th
Open Doors

In the past week, I have had quite a few conversations with people who are frightened by the prospect of change. Some people are frightened by a change in their health, some by a job change; another person was concerned about changes that necessitate moving a parent into a nursing home. A few were concerned about the changes that come with getting married or having children, and there were even some who told me that they were upset by changes in local parishes. One woman called this week to warn me that if I changed anything in the church or in the parish, she would call the Archbishop and have me transferred! "We don't have such a shortage of priests that we have to put up with someone who wants to make us change!" she screamed into the phone. (She didn't give me a chance to reply, but I wanted to tell her that transferring me would only increase the possibility of change.)

Isn't it amazing how the prospect of change frightens people? I think changes make each of us a bit uncomfortable and that's why we may get angry or overreact to them. When changes begin to get to me, I often think of the symbol that the Chinese have for change. It consists of two symbols that are put next to each other. The first symbol is the character for "danger." It is a reminder that change tends to make us uncomfortable, that it may threaten us, that things never stay the same. The second symbol is the Chinese character that stands for "opportunity." It's a reminder, that while every change might mean some discomfort, it may also be a doorway to new opportunities. Change is a part of life. How we respond to the changes that occur in our life is most often determined by whether we see them as dangerous threats or welcome opportunities.

May 26th
In Heaven We Shall Know

In recent weeks, I have been reading the life of Mother Elizabeth Seton. One aspect of her life is rather striking. She was very well acquainted with death and loss. Her mother died when Elizabeth was three. Her father died of yellow fever. Her husband died when she was only twenty nine, leaving her with five small children. Her sisters-in-law, who had joined her when she founded her religious order, died at a young age. In the following ten years, two of her children to whom she was very close, Anna Maria and Rebecca, both died.

Elizabeth Seton was a woman of great faith and trust who also grieved deeply. She not only experienced the death of many loved ones, she also experienced loss. When she felt called to convert to the Catholic faith, many of her family and friends deserted her. She truly knew what it was to feel loss on many levels. We too experience the death of loved ones, and we know also the pain that various kinds of loss can bring. Mother Seton learned that in every "ending" is an implied "beginning." She also learned that in every "beginning" there is an implied "ending."

One profound truth that Elizabeth Seton can pass on to us is that when we cling too tightly to people and things in our lives, it leaves little room for God's "new beginnings." Only when our cup is empty is it ready to be filled again. As she grieved for her loved ones, Mother Seton said, "In heaven, we shall know each other by a mere glance of the soul." She knew that the "end" of life in this world was truly the "beginning" of life in the next.

May 27th
Enough for Today

I read recently about a woman whose husband was killed in an automobile accident. Her world caved in on her. She felt that she couldn't cope with all that she had to do. She had five kids to take care of, a huge house, two dogs, and a mountain of bills that needed tending. She had to make sure that her kids were "okay" with their father's death and she had to help them cope. Her husband's parents were devastated by the loss of their only son. She felt responsible for helping them too. As she looked ahead in her life, she realized that she was in for some very difficult times. "How will I ever do all of this?" she gasped to herself. For weeks she brooded about it. She didn't sleep, but just lay awake at night wondering what she would do next. She let no one near her. Whenever anyone asked how she was doing, she simply said, "Just fine!"

Then one day a note arrived in the mail. "I've been watching you since the accident," the note began. "It looks to me like you're acting like you're holding your breath under water. Eventually you'll have to come up for air. I've been where you are, and I just want to give you some wisdom my old grandma gave me. Grandma told me that I didn't have to solve all my problems and heal all my wounds all at once. All I had to do was get through one day at a time. All I had to do was to be strong enough, smart enough, and hopeful enough for one day; and if that was too long, then five or ten minutes were enough. Most people get overwhelmed if they try to take on too much of the future at one time."

The note changed the young woman's life. She knew that she was facing many difficulties, but now she had a way to face them.

Abraham Lincoln once said, "The best thing about the future is that it only comes one day at a time." Realizing this can make all of the difference in how we cope with life. If we entrust our lives to God and live that life as it is given to us – one day at a time – we will be able to overcome life's difficulties.

May 28th
Have You Let Jesus Come Into Your Heart?

There was an Ecumenical Prayer Service a few years back at which a Methodist pastor preached about one of the stained glass windows in his church. The center panel of that particular window about which he preached was a reproduction of William Hunt's famous painting, "The Light of the World." The picture shows Jesus with a crown of thorns on his head, holding a lantern, knocking at a door that has no latch or door-knob on the outside and can be opened only from the inside. The minister said that when he was teaching a Bible lesson to a class of third-graders, one little girl asked him a question.

"Reverend, do you see that picture of Jesus up there in the window?"

"Yes," replied the minister.

"Did they ever let Jesus come into the house?" she asked.

The minister went on to ask the congregation the same question, "Have you ever let Jesus in your house, in your heart?"

So ... let me ask you. Have you ever let Jesus in your house or your heart? Are you Jesus' friend in name or in fact?

May 29th
Not Heard

In January of 1992, a letter was sent to a resident of South Carolina from the Health and Human Services Department of Greenville County containing the following message:

"Your food stamps will be stopped effective March, 1992 because we have received notice that you have passed away. You may re-apply to the food stamp program should your circumstances change."

There is nothing quite as frustrating as trying to get a government agency to listen to you and respond appropriately. Many people find that this is also true of health insurance companies, hospitals, and universities as well. Almost everyone has had their own exercise in futility when dealing with these institutions. But it's not only institutions that can frustrate us with their lack of listening. Individuals can do that too!

When was the last time you felt that someone you love has not really listened to you? It was probably rather recently, wasn't it? A recent survey of married couples showed that the number one problem in their communication was that they often feel that their partner does not listen to them. Teenagers complained that their parents don't listen to them, either. Poor listening is not only a problem for married couples and families. Many corporations are beginning to offer courses in good listening skills to improve the effectiveness of their work force.

How do we get those around us to listen to us? Probably the best way to get listened to is to do what the Bible tells us to do – "Do unto others as you want them to do unto you." (Matthew 7:12). If you want to be listened to, be a good listener. We may never be able to solve all of the communication problems of large government agencies or insurance companies, but we can make a difference in the level of good listening in our family relationships by being good listeners ourselves.

How do we become good listeners? We learn as much as we can about the art of listening and then model that art for our loved ones. If we learn to be good listeners, we may, unlike that poor food stamp recipient whose "circumstances" are not likely to change, find that the condition of our relationships will certainly improve.

May 30th
Finding Light Where You Can

In the 1980s a group of ranchers joined together to set a bounty on wolves. They did so because they were losing large numbers of their livestock to the hungry wolves. Thus, they set a bounty of $2500 for each wolf brought in. Two "fortune hunters" named Sam and Jared went on a hunt for wolves, scouring both mountains and forests in search of their prey.

After about three weeks without much luck in finding any wolves, the disappointed hunters were exhausted. One night as they fell into a very deep sleep, they awoke to find that they were surrounded by about 60 growling wolves with fiery eyes and bared teeth. Sam cried out, "Oh God, we're dead men!" Jared replied, "Sam, we're not dead men, look around you ... we're rich men!"

Did you ever find yourself in a situation like Sam and Jared, feeling like you are surrounded by a bunch of hungry wolves? No matter what the situation, we can choose to see it the way Sam did ("Oh God, we're dead men!") or we can see it the way Jared did, as a great opportunity. It's up to us.

May 31st
Judging Others

A woman who had been called for jury duty was explaining to the presiding judge that she didn't feel qualified to be on a jury for a particular trial because she did not believe in capital punishment. The judge interrupted her and said, "Madam, you don't understand. This is a civil case, not a criminal case. This case is about a man who spent $10,000 of his wife's money on gambling and other women. It's not a capital case." "Well," said the woman eagerly, "I'll be glad to serve on THAT jury, your honor, and I've changed my mind about capital punishment!"

If you were the man on trial in this case, how would you feel if this woman was on your jury? She doesn't sound very impartial, does she? Fortunately our judicial system depends upon people who can be impartial and make their judgment based solely on the facts. But the legal system is only as fair and impartial as the individual jury members choose to be. If you were asked to sit on a jury, could you render a truly fair and impartial verdict?

I bring this up because I think that even though most of us are not called to serve on juries very often, all of us are called to sit on a kind of jury every day. We are asked to sit on a jury with regard to how we see each other, how we treat each other, and how well we can accept each other. Many members of our society suffer a great deal from the rash judgments that are made about them.

How fair are you with your family members or co-workers in the judgments that you make about them? It is so easy for us to jump to conclusions about people without knowing all the facts. Yet, wouldn't it be horrible to be judged unfairly by all those around you? Isn't it interesting how our convictions about particular people can change when, like the woman in the story above, we put ourselves in someone else's shoes?

Jesus taught us to be careful not to lay judgments on others, because those judgments would only come back on us. Jesus calls us to be people who look at others with the eyes of compassion and understanding. I think that this is one of the reasons our Lord tells us to love others as we love ourselves. Let us make sure that in the "court" of life, we will be truly fair and impartial jurors.

June 1st
Are You All That You Could Be?

While he was on vacation, an artist was traveling through a small town in New England when he noticed an area on the town square where artists could offer their work for sale. Since he did not have any of his work with him, he decided that he would set up his easel and offer to do portraits for anyone passing by. It wasn't long before he had a big crowd gathered around him watching him draw and paint portraits. Many people sat for him and were delighted with the results of his work.

One man who was watching was a heavy drug user; he was quite dirty and unshaven, and hadn't had a bath in over six months. He lived on the streets and was known to be a thief. He offered the artist ten dollars to do his portrait. The artist agreed, but said that he would only charge the man two dollars for his work. After the artist had worked much longer than he had on any of the other portraits that day, he picked up the canvas and presented the finished work to the man. The man looked at it and said, "What is this? This isn't me!"

The people in the crowd who had been watching looked over the man's shoulder to get a peek at the portrait. They too were astonished because the man in the portrait was very dignified, smiling and well dressed. In addition, the man looked to be very much at peace with himself.

"I won't give you two dollars for that! It just isn't me!" the man said. The artist looked at him and said, "You can keep this, I won't charge you anything."

"But it just isn't me!" the man repeated.

"But it's the man you could be," the artist replied. "I see something in you than you are not able to see in yourself right now. Take this with you, and I'll bet that over the next few weeks you'll begin to see that this really IS you. Please take it as my gift." The man took the portrait and walked off muttering to himself, "Could this ever be me? It just doesn't look like me!"

God is very much like that artist – able to see beneath the surface to what we really are capable of becoming. Jesus, the Master Artist, came to paint us a picture of what we truly are called to be. The problem is that we spend most of our time thinking that we couldn't be any more than we are now – that it "just doesn't look like me!"

If Jesus were to show you a portrait of what He wants you to be, would you recognize yourself? Are you all that you could be? Are you willing to become the person Jesus wants you to be? It's something for all of us to think about.

June 2nd
Criticism Kills Healthy Relationships

Something to ponder: A tree surgeon was giving a lecture in which he was explaining to a group of visitors to the forest just what had killed a giant oak tree. "It wasn't the many long, bitter cold winters, even though that does kill many trees. It wasn't the terrifically heavy snowstorms, the lightning, or the intense heat of the summer. It wasn't even the near-drought conditions of the past several years that killed this tree. It was simply the millions of bites of these little beetles that finally toppled this great oak. Tiny little beetles literally bugged this tree to death!"

As you consider the relationships of your life, are you slowly killing healthy relationships with constant criticism, nagging or bugging those whom you love? As you notice all of the trees coming to life this spring, pay attention to those you love and be sure not to kill their spirit.

June 3rd
Don't Be Afraid to Learn New Things

During a retreat with some college seniors, I asked the students to tell about some of the important things that they had learned about life since they had entered college. One comment that I remember was from a young man who said that he learned the most valuable lesson of his college career during his freshman year.

He recalled a day when most of his friends in the dorm were going bowling. They invited him to go, but he refused. The harder they tried to get him to go, the harder he resisted. Finally, they left without him. He said that the reason he refused to go was that he had never bowled before and he didn't really know how to do it. He explained that because he was an excellent athlete – he played football, baseball, basketball and ran track – he felt that he had to appear to be good in all sports. He felt he had an image to maintain and he was afraid to look stupid or to look like a geek. For that reason, he just didn't get involved and missed out on a lot of fun. He concluded by saying that what he learned was that if you want to really enjoy life, you have to be willing to be a learner or a beginner. He said, "If you look like a geek, that means you're just a learner. You don't have to be perfect or accomplished. All you have to be is someone who enjoys learning."

Have you ever felt like that college student felt in his freshman year? Have you missed out on life because you were afraid to admit you didn't know what you were doing? One of the laws of the spiritual life is that you must first be a disciple before you can really be a follower. You can't start out being an expert if you don't take the time to learn the basics. Another way to say it is that you must first learn to crawl before you learn to walk.

This is a good time for us to learn or even "re-learn" some of the basics of our faith and of the spiritual life. Why not take a few minutes each day to read a few verses of the Gospel? Being in touch with Jesus in the Gospel passages can be a great way to draw closer to Him and to become a true follower.

June 4th
God Provides Safety Nets

Recently I read an old National Geographic article about mountain goats which I found quite interesting. According to the scientist who wrote the article, mother mountain goats care for their young in a rather unique way. As soon as their young are born and they begin to walk around on the top of the mountains, mother goats stand downhill from their babies. Why? They do this because baby goats, like all other baby animals, love to run, jump and play. On level ground that's fine, but on the narrow tops of mountains, this can be very dangerous. Mother goats always stand downhill below their young so that they can block their falls. They know that the young goats are unsteady on their feet. Sure-footed mother goats literally become safety nets for their kids.

There's a message for us here. Isn't it marvelous how the God who provides sure-footed mother goats to protect all those baby goats, also provides "sure-footed" people for us to "block our falls?" If you think back over your own life, I'll bet there have been some pretty "sure-footed" people who have been a safety net for you.

Give thanks to God for such a great gift, and better yet, why not give thanks to God by becoming a "sure-footed" person for someone else?

June 5th
Attitude

Have you ever heard this prayer?

"Dear God, so far today, I've done all right. I haven't gossiped, I haven't lost my temper; I haven't been greedy, grumpy, nasty, selfish, or self-indulgent. I am very thankful for that. But in a few minutes, God, I am going to get out of bed. And from then on, I'm probably going to need more help. Amen."

That's a great prayer! Have you ever wondered how to keep yourself from becoming greedy, grumpy and nasty, and all the rest? It was St. Francis of Assisi who said that the best way to keep a good Christian outlook towards life is to keep an attitude of gratitude. He taught his followers to look for an opportunity to give thanks to God no matter what the situation. Francis believed that in a heart filled with gratitude, there was no room for discouragement, greed, grouchiness, selfishness or any other ill humor.

This week, let us all take time to recall how blessed we are. Like Saint Francis, let us fill our hearts so full of gratitude that there will be no room for ill-humor.

June 6th
Spiritual Health

How much time do you spend making doctor's appointments, waiting in a doctor's office, running after prescriptions, and taking care of your physical health? Probably a lot more time than you really want to. I read an article the other day that indicated that many people spend one-fifth of their time trying to maintain their health. They not only spend a lot of time, but they also spend a lot of money. This makes sense. After all, as most sick people will tell you, you are truly wealthy only if you have your health. We are all becoming aware of the need to take good care of our bodies. That's why you see so many people joining health spas and fitness clubs – prevention is the best medicine. We all know that the better we take care of ourselves, the less time, energy and money we will have to spend on doctors.

How much time do you spend tending to your spiritual health? When was the last time you had a spiritual checkup? Have you developed a routine of spiritual exercises that keep you spiritually fit? If you haven't, might I make a suggestion or two?

How about taking some extra time for prayer? The Holy Hour practice that many parishes have is an excellent way to improve your spiritual health. Seven days a week, one hour each day, members of a parish join together for prayer before the Blessed Sacrament. An hour of quiet with the Lord can do wonders to soothe tired, worn-out souls! When was the last time you went to Confession, or sought the spiritual insight of a trusted friend? When was the last time you prayed the Rosary, read the Scriptures, or went to a talk on spiritual matters? Why not make up your mind to begin doing something about your spiritual health?

June 7th
The Earliest Age

It's that season again! Whether it's kindergarten, grade school, high school, college or graduate school, this is the graduation season. It's the time we set aside to celebrate learning and to honor the academic achievements of family and friends.

Last Sunday I was talking with a high school senior who was looking forward to his graduation. "Finally," he said, "I can stop having to study and learn stuff!" A comment like that would probably make his former teachers die of embarrassment. What amazed me most about that senior's comment was that he was confused by my reaction. He was unsure as to why I laughed when he said it. "What's so funny? What are you laughing at?" he asked.

"The reason I'm laughing," I explained, "is that the whole purpose of going to school in the first place is to teach you how to observe and learn from life. Your diploma is a kind of license for learning. Learning is not supposed to end when you leave school, but graduation is when learning is supposed to really begin."

I'm pretty sure that my comments were lost on that guy, but the conversation did serve to reaffirm my attitude about learning. I am always impressed by many of the older members of our parish who have continued learning and growing throughout their lives – they are almost always happy, positive and enthusiastic people. They remind me of the famous Roman scholar, Cato, who began to study Greek when he was over 80 years old. Someone asked him why he bothered to learn something as difficult as Greek at his age. Cato replied, "It's the earliest age I have left." He never stopped learning when his formal training stopped. He realized that schooling serves to show us how to spend the rest of our life learning.

This is the season to celebrate academic achievements. May it also be the season that reminds us that our learning is never complete, and that we are never too young or too old to learn.

June 8th
Not Insignificant

A young nursing student was quite surprised that during her second month of nursing school, her professor gave a pop quiz. Because the nursing student was very dedicated to her studies, she did not find the quiz to be very difficult, and thought that she would ace the test. That is, until she got to the final question. The question was: "What is the name of the woman you've seen mopping the floors every day as you came to class?"

She knew she had seen that woman almost every day, and she could describe the woman, but she certainly never took the time to learn her name. That nursing student was not the only one in her class who could not name the cleaning lady. Not one student could do so.

When one student asked the professor if the last question on the quiz would count towards the grade, the professor replied, "Absolutely! In your careers as nurses, you will meet many people. Some of them will be important people, but not one of the people you will meet will be insignificant. Every person deserves your attention, your care, and most importantly, the best you have to offer."

Jesus poured out His life for you, for me, for everyone – and none of us is insignificant in His eyes. When God sent His Son, He sent the very best, and Jesus gave the best He had to offer to you.

June 9th
Gatekeepers

Several years ago, I had the great experience of traveling through China. One of my favorite memories is that of walking along the Great Wall. The wall was built in answer to the many armies from the north, who were constantly invading and attacking Chinese villages. The emperor who had the wall built wanted it to be absolutely impenetrable, so he ordered it to be too high to climb over, too thick to break through, and too long to go around. The wall is 30 feet high, 18 feet thick and 1500 miles long!

As impressive as the wall is, it was not as strong as the emperor had hoped. Three times invading armies were able to get through the wall – not by going over it, not by going around it, and not by digging under it. The armies got through the wall by bribing the gatekeeper! The wall itself was only as strong as the moral principals of those who controlled its gates.

The Great Wall of China can serve as a good lesson for us. Our family, our community, and our nation are only as strong as the moral character of each individual. Each of us is important, and the strength of character or lack of it has a powerful effect on everyone. It is important for each of us to remember that we are all "gatekeepers" for one another.

June 10th
Holy Amish Folk

An Amish man stopped his farm work one day to watch a new neighbor move in. He marveled at the many items that were being delivered to the new neighbor's home. There was a wonderful high tech refrigerator and ice cube maker, a state of the art computer-driven entertainment system with a big screen TV, VCR and DVD player, ultra high-tech sound systems, and lots of other electronic equipment. There seemed to be no end to the luxuries.

The next day, the Amish man and his wife and children paid a visit to their new neighbors. They took them some homemade bread and jam. After the usual greetings and conversation, the Amish man concluded with the words, "… and if anything would ever go wrong with any of your new appliances or equipment, please don't hesitate to call on me."

"Thank you!" the new neighbor replied, "that is very generous of you. I'm surprised that you Amish would know how to fix such things."

"Oh, I doubt if I could FIX any of it! But I could teach you how to live without all of them."

In the Gospels, Jesus is tempted by the Devil. The purpose of those temptations was to distract Jesus from his true mission. We, too, are very often being tempted to abandon our true mission in life. Concerns about acquiring "things" or of having more and more possessions can easily distract us from what is truly important in life. Perhaps we could all use a good Amish neighbor to show us to live without all of those things that might distract us from our real mission in life, to love more deeply.

June 11th
Parents

Here we are in the middle of graduation season! It's a time for us to recognize the hard work, discipline and academic achievements of both students and teachers. We give the graduates gifts and we congratulate them for completing another level of their education. Many kind words and some platitudes are expressed to the graduates because, in a sense, they are heroes. This is all well and good, as far as it goes, but more needs to be said.

Just as with most heroes, when it comes to our academic heroes, there are some "behind the scenes" people who deserve some credit at this time of year – parents. As we recognize the discipline, hard work and academic achievement of our graduates, let us remember that no one is born disciplined or inclined towards hard work. This has to be taught, encouraged, and fostered. It takes a special kind of person, namely a loving parent, to stick with a kid to make him or her do the homework which is much less appealing than playing football in the street or talking with a friend on the telephone for hours at a time. It takes a loving parent with the patience of Job to spend hours helping a child to better understand the complexities of algebra, the intricacies of a classic novel, the causes of the American Civil War, or maybe just the fact that two plus two equals four!

If you are a parent and your child is graduating, congratulate him or her, but don't forget to take a bow yourself. You are a big part of your child's success.

June 12th
On Fear and Making a New You

A young college student on retreat came to an insight into his life when he realized that he had been treating his family terribly. When he spoke with the priest who had been leading the retreat about what to do to change the situation, the priest advised him to find one simple thing to do that might start the process of healing for his family. The young man thought about it for quite a while and concluded that when he returned home he would make a first step by saying "thank you" whenever his parents did something for him. After he had done this twice, his father looked up at him when they were at the table, smirked, and said, "Oh, so a few days away on retreat, and now you're holy." The young man was so embarrassed by his father's sarcastic words, he immediately gave up his resolution, feeling like a real fool for having made it in the first place.

Has this ever happened to you? Have you made a resolution to treat your family or friends differently only to have them react in such a negative or disbelieving way that you felt foolish for even trying? Or again, have you ever been like this young man's father who reacted poorly to someone you love who attempts to change their behavior? If so, read on…

That young college student grew so despondent over his family's reaction to his simple first step in treating people better, that he sought out the priest who had led the retreat. "Why did my father try to make such a fool of me?" he asked the priest.

"I can tell you this much," replied the priest, "your father is afraid. He knows how to deal with the old you; he may not be too certain how to deal with the 'new' you. He may need some time. The only way you will ever be able to bring about a great healing is for you not to run from this. You must not be derailed in your attempt to be a better person. Make more room in your heart for your dad. Give him the space and time he needs to see that you are really trying to change. Don't let fear – your father's or your own – keep you from doing what needs to be done."

The young man went back to his plan. He simply began saying "thank you" whenever his parents or brothers and sisters did anything for him. In six months time, the atmosphere in the family had dramatically changed. One family member's determination to change and not to be intimidated by fear made all of the difference.

One of the greatest gifts we can give to our family or friends is to be someone who fosters their spiritual life. By making room in our hearts for those around us who are trying to take some first steps in changing, by not belittling their attempts to grow, we can give them a whole new lease on life. And who doesn't need that?

June 13th
Pillars of Fire

I watched a film on the life of Yitzhak Rabin, the former prime minister of Israel, who was assassinated in 1995. While the film was rather ordinary and I don't remember most of what was said about Mr. Rabin, I do remember a very striking scene in the documentary in which his granddaughter stood before the crowd gathered for his funeral. Looking over the vast crowd, Noa Ben Artzi spoke about her grandfather and the closeness of their relationship. She said that while he was a leader for the rest of the world, Yitzhak Rabin remained for her simply "grandfather." With eyes full of tears, she said "Grandfather, you were, for me, a pillar of fire ... in front of the camp leading me ... you were my hero."

This is one of the most moving speeches I have heard in a long time. It became part of my meditations this past week, and it caused me to ask myself some questions. Perhaps they might be a part of your meditation this week.

Has there been anyone in your life like Yitzhak Rabin, a "pillar of fire" leading and guiding you? Who are the heroes in your life's story? What impact have they had on you? How has your spouse or your children or your parents been a "pillar of fire?" Have you ever stopped to consider what impact you are having on others? Is it possible that God has called you to be a "pillar of fire" for others?

As you pray this week, take some time to thank God for all of your heroes.

June 14th
From the Heart

When was the last time you stopped to consider the condition of your prayer life? Have you ever evaluated your prayer life and then decided to make some changes to improve it? Perhaps now is the time to do that.

In preparation for my trip to Israel, I did research on the various religious groups that live and pray in Jerusalem. They have a lot to teach us about prayer.

One of the most conservative of all of the Jewish sects is called the Hasidic sect. You can distinguish them by their classic dress, by their use of Hebrew, and their very strict keeping of all of the laws and traditions of Judaism. One of the surprising things about the Hasidic Jews is their attitude about prayer. One might think that they would be very conservative in the kinds and ways of prayer, but they are not. In fact, one of the things that has been handed down to them through tradition is the use of dance in their prayers. The founder of Hasidic Judaism said, "A dance for God is better than any prayer if the dance comes from the heart."

Probably few Jews (and few Christians, for that matter) agree with him, but it certainly is true that a prayer that does not come from the heart is just empty words. This week, take time to consider your prayer. How would you describe your prayer life? Would you say that it is full or rich? Do you feel as close to God as you do to your friends? When was the last time you danced in joy to the Lord? (Remember, King David danced before the Lord.) When was the last time you poured out your heart to God? Do you tell God all of your true feelings when you pray? Having answered all these questions, what is the condition of YOUR prayer life?

June 15th
Jesus' Friends

The famous sculptor Rodin said that the one piece of his work that was his favorite was his sculpture entitled the "Hand of God." It is a huge hand, on the palm of which is etched an image of a man and a woman embracing. In preparation for his work of art, Rodin literally sketched a thousand hands. They were the hands of people he met every day – the hands of people at the market, his personal doctor's hands, the hands of people on the street, the hands of children in a schoolyard, a farmer's hands, a young mother and her child's hands, an elderly couple's hands, and so on. Rodin believed that by making the "Hand of God" a composite of many people's hands, he was telling the world that we come to know God more intimately whenever we use our hands to reach out to each other, to embrace each other, and to use our hands to caress, soothe and heal one another.

Traditionally the Church has held out Lent and Advent as seasons for us to take an inventory of our Christian life. Summer time, too, can be a good time to take a look at the use of our hands and our reaching out to others in God's name. Why not resolve to use some of your vacation time to do good for others. In other words, why not practice the art of being Jesus' friends?

June 16th
New Eyes

Recently a jeweler was strolling through the aisle at the Tucson Gem and Mineral Show when he noticed a blue-violet stone the size and shape of a potato. He liked the stone and picked it up to give it a more thorough inspection. The man selling the stones spoke up first, "Do you like that rock, Mister?"

The jeweler responded, "I do like it. How much are you asking for it?"

"I've been asking $15.00, but if you like it a lot, I'll let you have it for say, $12.00."

The jeweler looked at it again and said, "How about I give you $10.00?"

"Sold!" the vendor shouted.

The jeweler paid his $10.00 and quickly left the gem and mineral show. He wanted to get back to his workshop to test the stone. When he did a few tests, he was certain that what he suspected at the gem show was correct. That $10.00 "rock" turned out to be a 1,905 carat natural star sapphire. It is 800 carats larger than the largest stone of its kind ever discovered. The stone is worth $2.28 million dollars!

It took a jeweler's trained eye to recognize the real beauty and value of the blue-violet stone. This news item reminds me that when God looks at you and me, He sees our real value, our real beauty. To God, each one of us is worth much more than a mere $2.28 million dollar sapphire. Each one of us is worth the life of Jesus, which He willingly gave on our behalf.

How are we to give thanks to God for all He has done on our behalf; how are we to respond? Probably the best way is for us to look at one another with "new eyes." Perhaps we can take some extra time to look at those around us and recognize the goodness that is there in each person. In other words, one of the best ways for us to thank God is to become like that jeweler who looked beyond the surface of the "blue rock" and saw a real gem, a real treasure. Let us take time today to become aware of the "treasures" that the people around us truly are.

June 17th
Gifts

A high school teacher was teaching her class that each person looks at life with a different vision. She said, "If three people stop to look at a tree, each will probably see something different. One might see the tree as so many feet of lumber worth so much money. Another person will look at the tree and see it as a great source of wood for the fireplace that he counts on to keep his family warm in winter. The third person might look at the tree and see it as a masterpiece of God's creation. Each person sees the same tree, but each person sees it differently."

As she finished speaking, one of her students raised her hand and asked, "Even though each person sees the tree differently, shouldn't their response be the same?"

"What do you mean?" asked the teacher.

"Shouldn't all of their ways of looking at the tree be summed up in a response of thanksgiving for the tree itself? After all, even if they see the gift differently, it still is a gift, isn't it?"

No matter how you ordinarily look at things, why not take some time to look at your life through the eyes of gratitude – take some time to be aware of the many gifts you have received in this past year. Pause and give thanks to the One who has provided all of them.

June 18th
Tears

This past week, I read an interesting article about human tears. Researchers have found that while the flow of tears can be caused by any number of things – sorrow, happiness, peeling an onion, and that proverbial "smoke that gets in your eyes," the composition of those tears is different. For example, the make-up of the tears caused by peeling an onion is almost pure water, whereas those tears shed because of joy have an entirely distinct composition, and those tears shed because of smoke are completely unlike the others. One interesting fact is that tears shed because of sorrow are almost entirely composed of what the researchers' term "toxic waste." In other words, when you cry because you are sad or hurt, you really are being cleansed and purified. I guess what science is trying to tell us is that a good cry can do wonders for the body. Scripture tells us that sorrow and tears of repentance can do the same for the soul.

Is there a "toxic waste" dump in your soul? Are there sins in the past that you are sorry about? As we grow in our faith, perhaps its time to shed a few tears of repentance to clean up the toxic effects of sin.

June 19th
The Caregiver

There was a holy man who sat in the lotus position near the highway leading up to the holy city of Jerusalem. Passing before the holy man as he prayed were the destitute, the wounded ones, and the beaten ones of the world. It was a great parade of suffering that passed by him. The holy man saw every kind of suffering – horrible ailments, tragic victims of violence and hatred, victims of abuse of every kind, hollow shells of people dragging themselves toward God's holy city. Seeing all of these, the holy one threw his prayer beads on the ground and cried out to God, "How can you, the loving God who created every beautiful thing, every lovely person, how can you see this wretched mass of people and do nothing to stop this suffering?"

There was a long silence, and then there was the sound of a quiet voice. The voice was gentle and full of kindness. For a moment, the holy man thought that the person speaking had been crying. The voice spoke these words, "I did do something about all of this suffering – I made you. I didn't make you to be an onlooker, but a caregiver. Be what I created you to be!"

June 20th
Squash

A student, tired from studying for exams, saw the college president walking across the campus. The student turned to the president and asked, "Isn't there a shorter, quicker way to get through college? I think it takes entirely too long!"

The president thought for awhile and said, "Well, I suppose that there is a shorter, quicker way through school, but it depends on what you want to be. When God wants to make a mighty oak tree, He takes His time – 100 years or so. If God wants to make a mere squash, then He only takes a few months to do it. Take your time and you'll end up like that mighty oak, or rush through and you'll end up with 'squash' for brains. It's up to you."

Like intellectual greatness, spiritual greatness cannot be rushed. Just as a student gradually assimilates knowledge as he/she grows towards wisdom, so too does a disciple of the Lord gradually assimilate spiritual insight as he/she grows toward an ever-deepening conversion. One of the great gifts that God gives us is the gift of time. Each second of every day is filled with opportunities for growth. If we are to be faithful disciples of the Lord, we need to slow down, to take our time so that we can be nourished by every grace that God sends our way. The spiritual life, like the intellectual life, cannot be rushed, just as we cannot usually see a tree growing except over time. God is doing great things in each of us. Little by little we are being formed by His grace. Be patient – God isn't finished with us yet!

June 21st
Two Different Seas

While on sabbatical in the Middle East, I spent time at Israel's two seas, the Sea of Galilee and the Dead Sea. I learned a great deal about them and about people, too.

Both seas get their waters from the snows and streams of Mount Hermon, but each sea does something different with the water it receives. The Sea of Galilee is a very beautiful deep blue body of water that is teeming with life. Its waters provide drinking water for many villages and cities, its fish feed scores of people, and farmlands are irrigated with its waters. The Sea of Galilee shares what it receives with the world around it through the Jordan River and other streams that fertilize the Jordan Plain.

The Dead Sea, on the other hand, is a different story. It also receives its waters from Mount Hermon, but the Dead Sea has no outlet. The water just stays in the sea basin where the process of evaporation allows the sea's salt content to build up to the point that nothing can live in it. It is completely desolate of life. What water it receives it keeps to itself.

People can be like these two seas. Selfless persons receive many gifts throughout life and share them with others. Selfish persons also receive gifts, but hoard them and keep them to themselves. Therefore, like the Dead Sea, they grow stagnant and eventually suffocate all life within and around them.

If you were a sea, would you be like the Sea of Galilee or would you be like the Dead Sea?

June 22nd
The Tide Always Returns

In one of his many books, Dr. Norman Vincent Peale recalled an old painting a friend of his had hanging in his study. The picture was of a very large rowboat that was three or four times the size of a regular rowboat. Its two oars rested dejectedly in the sand next to it. The tide was out, and the boat was stranded high on the beach.

The sea was far off in the distance. Dr. Peale said that the effect of the picture was somber. He couldn't think of a more hopeless thing than a beached rowboat so far away from the water's edge. Much too heavy to pull or drag, it looked quite stuck.

One day when he was in his friend's study, Dr. Peale asked his friend why he kept such a terribly somber picture hanging in his study. "Doesn't it depress you?" he asked.

His friend smiled and said, "Read the caption under the picture." It read: "The Tide Always Comes Back." The friend went on to explain that when the tide came back, the dejected rowboat would come back to life. It would rise on the shoulders of the sea, it would dance on the waves, it would be filled with life again. The tide always returns.

If you feel like that tired old rowboat so much that you feel that your life may have run aground, it may be that this Summer will bring you something new. Remember, the "tide always returns." Perhaps the summertime will give you new life, the new boost you need to make a new beginning.

The tide always returns ... May God grant you a great Summer!

June 23rd
The Way We Live Our Lives

At a recent author's workshop, participants were asked to write an essay answering the question, "What two books have most influenced my life?" One writer answered the question this way: "I was raised by my grandparents. I think the two books that influenced me the most during those years was my grandmother's cookbook and my grandfather's checkbook!" Another author said it was the Bible and a novel by Flannery O'Connor. There was one author who wrote, "There is one book, not two, that has had the greatest influence on me, and it continues to influence me even to this day. That book is the book of my parent's loving, happy marriage. I go back to the way they loved, understood, honored, respected and truly delighted in each other for so many years. Their relationship is a book that I go back to over and over again as I seek to grow in my relationship with my husband, my family, and my friends."

That author certainly offered a wonderful tribute to her parents' marriage. She also reminds us that each one of us is, in a very real sense, writing a book by the way we live our lives. This leads to a question we might ask ourselves. "What would those who know me and the way I live my life say about the 'book' I have been writing?"

June 24th
Patched Up

A priest explained to his congregation why he thought the time to retire had come. He said, "I woke up the other morning and realized as I was getting ready for my day that I wear two hearing aids, trifocal glasses, false teeth and a brace on my ankle, and sometimes I need a cane to walk around. I think that God is telling me it's time to retire."

After Mass, a silver-haired woman came up to the priest and said, "Father, I think you've got God's message all messed up! He's not telling you that it's time to retire. He's telling you that if you keep going, He'll keep you patched up!"

Have you ever felt like that old priest, ready to "toss in the towel" because you think you've begun to fall apart or have grown weary? One thing that the Bible teaches us is that while we may grow weary from time to time, God does not grow weary of taking care of us. He will always be there for us, to build us up, to help us to hear, to see, to get wherever He wants us to be. One thing is for certain, if you give your life and heart to the Lord, He'll keep you "patched up."

June 25th
In Progress

I've been reading Irving Stone's famous book, *The Agony and the Ecstasy*, which is an account of the life of the great artist Michelangelo. It is a fascinating story. It is believed that during his lifetime, Michelangelo started forty-four huge marble statues but he completed only 14. There is a museum in Italy where you can see his 30 unfinished statues. There are huge blocks of marble with perhaps just an arm or foot completed. Others show the beginnings of a head, and some look like images of people who are stuck in the marble and are struggling to get free. Even though "unfinished," each block of marble is a wonderful work of art.

If you stop to think about it, those blocks of marble are a great image of you and me. Aren't we all a bit "unfinished"? I don't think there would be any of us who could claim that we've got our act together enough to see ourselves as finished works of art. It reminds me of a sign I once saw over a friend's desk, which proclaimed, "Be patient with me. God isn't finished with me yet!"

It is good for us to remember that we are all "works in progress." If we get discouraged because we feel we are not making much progress in our spiritual or personal growth, it would be good for us to consider Michelangelo's unfinished works. If you get discouraged because a child of yours seems to be "going nowhere," just remember those unfinished statues. Your child is an unfinished work of art that God is still working to complete.

June 26th
Thinking

What have you been thinking about lately? When was the last time you stopped to think about what you've been thinking about? Sounds like a stupid question, doesn't it? It may sound stupid, but it really isn't. What we think about has a great effect on how we live and what we do. Think about this: If you were to put a six-inch wide, ten-foot long plank of wood on the ground, you probably wouldn't have too much trouble walking the length of the plank without falling off. Lift the same plank three feet off the ground and most people would not even care to try to walk the length of the plank. The plank is just as wide on the ground as it is three feet in the air, but there is a big difference. The difference is that when it is three feet off the ground, we think about falling rather than walking. And we usually do what we think about! My thinking would have me falling in no time at all!

That's why I ask you what you have been thinking about. What we think about affects what we do. If we spend our time thinking about our problems, we may keep our noses in our own little world and miss the bigger world around us. In the last several weeks, many people have told me about some of the difficulties that they are facing. Some people have had some health crises, others are concerned about their finances, and others are fretting over past hurts or grudges that they may have toward a family member.

If you've been spending your time thinking about such things, I'll bet your family or friends haven't found you to be very good company of late. If you're always thinking about dark, gloomy things, you are probably getting to be a dark and gloomy kind of person.

Perhaps it's time that we all "take five" to think of some good things that are going on around us. Maybe we could think about how to surprise our family or friends with flowers or a special treat, or maybe with just a good joke or a laugh. You might even try getting your friends to walk across a wooden plank without falling off! I tried walking on a curb with my eyes closed this past week and fell right off the dumb thing! It gave my nephew a great big belly laugh. Just thinking about how silly I must have looked gives me a good laugh, too.

Take a few moments right now to consider what you've been thinking about and just remember how much we are affected by what we think.

June 27th
People of Life

There is a story told of a holy man who was captured by a bandit who threatened to kill him. "Would you be good enough to fulfill my dying wish?" the holy man asked.

"What is your wish?" asked the bandit.

"Would you just use your sword to cut off the branch of that tree there?" After one mighty slash of the sword, the tree limb tumbled down to the ground.

"Is there anything else you want before I kill you?" asked the bandit.

The holy man looked at him and said, "Put the branch back again."

"You must be a crazy old fool to think that I or anyone else can do that," grumbled the bandit.

"No, you are the fool to think that you are all powerful simply because you can wound and destroy. That is the wickedness of evil children. Only the holy, the compassionate and the kind know how to create and to heal. It is only Jesus who can bring life back to that which was dead."

Every Sunday we recall the truth that Jesus, the holy and compassionate one, destroyed death and restored life. Pope John Paul II reminded us that while we are people who live in a world that worships death, as Christians, we are people who rejoice in life, the life that Jesus gave us.

June 28th
Spreading the Gospel

A famous artist was once asked to paint a picture of a dying church. It was expected that he would paint a small and humble broken down, dilapidated church building. Instead he painted a magnificent cathedral with beautiful windows, classic statues, fine artworks and a manicured lawn. Near the door of the church, however, was an offering box marked MISSIONS, with the contribution slot blocked by cobwebs. The artist's message was clear – a church that is not spreading its message by sharing its gifts with others is certainly dying, if not already dead.

This month we celebrate the Feast of Saints Peter and Paul. St. Peter, the Apostle to the Jews, and St. Paul, the Apostle to the Gentiles, knew well that they were carrying the greatest gift ever offered to the world – the Gospel of Jesus Christ. Are you aware that you, too, are a missionary who carries within you that same Gospel? There are people alive in the world today who need to hear the Gospel, and you may be the only person who can speak to them in such a way that they can understand and embrace it.

You may never be asked to carry the Gospel all over the world as Peter and Paul did, but you just might be asked to carry the Gospel across the street to your neighbor. Jesus is counting on you and me to share the gift of faith that we have received.

June 29th
Purposeful Pausing

If you watch or listen to the news lately, there is no shortage of frightening news. It seems that all the news has a dire edge to it and lots of anxiety is being generated. Many are becoming more and more unsettled about the future. The future seems a bit bleak especially when it comes to economic difficulties. How are we believers supposed to respond to this?

One of my favorite lines in the Old Testament comes from the Book of Exodus. The line comes from a scene in which the Israelites are complaining to Moses because they are being pursued by Pharaoh. Moses had led them out of Egypt where they had all been very much oppressed, and now Pharaoh, who was incensed, was making good time in catching up to them. The Israelites were terrified. Moses attempts to calm them down, but they will hear none of it. They are so frightened of what the Pharaoh might do to them that they would much rather return to a life of slavery. Moses tells them to stand firm, to "get a grip" and stop being afraid. Then, when the people are silenced, Moses says this line (my favorite): "Fear not … The Lord himself will fight for you; you have only to keep still!"

I love that line because it reminds us about what we can do when we are overcome by fear. It is a way out of the terror that racing thoughts and heart-squeezing worries can cause us if we let them run wild in our imagination. The pathway out of fear is the way of calm, peaceful thoughts. These calm and peaceful thoughts have tremendous power to calm the surging waves of fear. How does one get to calm, peaceful thoughts when your thoughts are racing around in you head? The answer is found in what Moses said to the Israelites that day, "You have only to be still."

By literally stopping ourselves in our own tracks, by turning off the mind for a moment, and by being completely still, we can create a space in which God himself can reach out to us and give us peace. Peace is, after all, the gift that Jesus promised to give, and it is, as Jesus said, a peace that the world cannot give. Purposeful pausing to catch our breath, to stop the racing that's going on in us, and the finding of a point of stillness will open a doorway to God that many have not yet discovered. This week, as you may continue to hear dire news about our economy, the situations of violence around the world, or if there are difficulties in your own family, perhaps it might be a good thing if you were to take a few minutes for some purposeful pausing so that peace can come for you.

June 30th
Changes

A man went to his doctor for his annual checkup. A few days later he visited his doctor to get the results of his physical examination. The doctor looked at his patient and said, "Joe, you're just going to have to face facts. The best thing you can do is give up eating rich foods and to give up drinking."

Joe thought a moment about what the doctor had just advised him and replied, "What you're telling me is that the best thing I can do is give up the food I love and give up drinking as well?"

"That's exactly what I'm telling you," the doctor replied.

Joe paused to think for a few minutes more and then turned to the doctor and said, "What's the second best thing I could do?"

Does Joe sound like anyone you know? Have you ever felt like him? So often we become aware of our need for change, yet we hesitate to make the necessary changes. For example, have you found yourself wanting to lose weight, but unwilling to give up your favorite foods? When you were in school, did you ever want better grades, but just couldn't force yourself to study more? Did you ever want to play the piano, but couldn't find the time to practice? It is very easy for us to dream about becoming better people or about a life of fulfillment and happiness, or to even dream about deepening our relationships with one another. The problem is that much of this will never come to be if we are unwilling to make the changes that this dream might require.

Take some time to examine your life in a kind of spiritual "check-up" to see if there aren't some changes that would improve your life. Why not take advantage of this Summer by deciding actually to make the changes that you know you need to make?

July 1st
Of Course!

In an old National Geographic, I read that during the Apollo missions to the moon, the various space crafts were off course more than 90 percent of the time. I found that to be utterly amazing to think how off course things were. What kept things from completely spiraling out of control was their continual communications with Mission Control. It was Mission Control that tenaciously made the thousands of corrections that got the space crafts back on their right flight plans. It was by staying in touch with home that the astronauts were able to get safely to their destination and back.

It's a bit corny, but as I read that, it occurred to me that our journey through life is pretty much like those Apollo Missions. We are probably off course more often than not, and it is only by staying in touch with God (our "Mission Control") that we could ever find our way safely through it all. This is why prayer is so vitally important for each one of us. If we ever hope to get our lives going in the right direction, we need to stay connected to our true home base.

July 2nd
Where Your Treasure is, There Your Heart Will Be

An old monk was making a pilgrimage through the desert to the holy city of Jerusalem. During the day it was terribly hot, and at night it was horribly cold. Often there were fierce sand storms. About half way through his journey, the old monk stopped at a small inn to spend the night and to regain his strength.

As the monk was eating a meager supper, the innkeeper asked the old fellow how he intended to get all the way to Jerusalem through such miserable conditions. The old monk cheerfully answered, "My heart got there first, so it is easy for the rest of me to follow!"

"What do you mean by that?" asked the innkeeper.

"Do you have children?" The monk asked.

"Yes, I have six children, and oh what a struggle it is to raise them!" the innkeeper replied.

"Has it been difficult to care for them, to guide them and to train them and to provide good things for them?" the monk asked.

"It has been such a difficult struggle for me and my wife, because each of our children is so different. What seems to work in rearing one does not work at all in guiding the other children. Sometimes we are so exasperated that we are ready to give up!" the innkeeper said sadly.

"Ah, but you and your wife haven't given up, have you? And I know the reason you haven't given up your journey with your kids. The reason is that long ago you both gave your heart to each of them, or as I like to put it, your hearts got there first. So, ever since that day, the rest of you just works to catch up with your hearts. Your kids are blessed because of you two."

"Are all 'journeys of the heart' difficult and filled with struggles?" the innkeeper asked.

The old monk thought for just a moment and then said, "Yes. And the struggles you endure are part of the heart's gift. Whenever you give your heart to anyone, you are also giving them your journey to them as a gift as well."

July 3rd
A Good Time

I was in a greenhouse at a plant nursery the other day admiring all of the plants. One section of the greenhouse was set up for the care of young saplings and I was fascinated by the variety of trees being cultivated there. They had a sign posted which got my attention: "The best time to plant a tree was ten years ago. The next best time to plant a tree is right now."

The message of that sign struck me as being a good sentiment for us in our spiritual lives. It reminds me of a conversation I had recently with someone who had wanted to come back to church.

"I have been away a very long time, so long that I am ashamed that I have wasted valuable time worrying about my sins and stuff," the man told me. "I should've come back a long time ago. Do you think it's too late for me? Is it a case of too little, too late, do you think?" he asked me.

I reassured him that it's never too late to come back to God. The Lord never gives up on us and we shouldn't give up on God, either. I suppose it's like that greenhouse sign said: The best time might have been ten years ago, but the next best time is right now.

In your own life, have you ever worried that there are things that you should have tended to a long while ago? Perhaps the sign in the greenhouse has something to teach you too. Right now is a pretty good time.

July 4th
Wandering Thoughts

One of the hermits from the early days of the church approached St. Anthony of the Desert about a problem that plagued him. The hermit said, "Oh holy one, I have great difficulty with my prayer – whenever I sit in my cell to pray, instead of my thoughts focusing on almighty God, my thoughts wander all over the place. I cannot concentrate. I am sure that I must be wicked and there is probably no hope for me if I cannot even keep my thoughts from wandering away from God. Can you help me?"

Saint Anthony answered him, "My brother, please continue to sit in your cell. Do not give up. I want you to do this: Fetch a mother donkey and her young foal. Tie the mother donkey to a rail, but not her foal. Then pay attention. Notice that whereas the mother donkey never leaves because she is tied to the rail, the young foal dances and prances around her. It even runs off quite a distance away. But now, notice what else happens. Even though the young foal wanders around and dances and prances, it always, in time, returns to its mother. It cannot fail to do so because it is only with its mother that it finds the food it needs. This same thing happens when one sits patiently in his cell seeking God. His thoughts may wander but eventually they do return to God because that is where they are fed."

There is probably no one who is serious about their prayer who has not had to deal with the plague of wandering thoughts. I think St. Anthony's advice to the young hermit is certainly advice we can all use. Perhaps this is the time for us to re-commit ourselves to a deeper prayer life. That deeper prayer is possible when we practice the spiritual discipline of sitting patiently seeking God.

July 5th
Contaminated Food

With all of the news in recent weeks about contaminated animal feed, I began thinking about something that I read from the life of Mahatma Gandhi. He used to have long discussions with his friends and he would teach the bits of wisdom that he had learned over the years to the many young students who visited him at his ashram. One of his teachings concerned something that had happened in the early 1940's in South America. According to Gandhi, a rumor of a famine swept through a province of a small country in that part of the world. In actuality though, the crops that year were quite good and they were growing well. In addition, the weather that year was exceptional and all was set for a bumper crop. But because of the rumors, 20,000 small farmers abandoned their small farms and fled to the big cities to find work so that their families would not starve to death when the famine hit. Because of their actions, the crops did fail, thousands did starve, and the rumor of the famine did come true.

Mr. Gandhi concluded the story by saying that we are all very much affected by what we "feed on." If we feed on fear, rumor and negative thinking, we will reap a harvest of destruction. If we feed on truth, compassion, and love, we will reap a harvest of justice and peace. In your life right now, what do you feed on?

July 6th
He Came With the Sun

An elderly woman, Martha McCallum, was feeling sorry for herself one day because her arthritis was slowing her down. She had never been a woman who did anything slowly; she had always been a person on the move. So, when her health began to take its toll on her, Martha would sit at her kitchen table thinking and just kind of staring off into space. She said that on one occasion, on one of those windy days when the sun keeps coming out and going in, she had an experience that blessed her life.

"I was sitting there feeling all my aches and pains, feeling a bit blue, and all of a sudden, a sunbeam crossed my kitchen table and lit up my crystal saltshaker," she said. "There were all kinds of colors and sparkles. It was the most beautiful sight I had ever seen. But you know, that very same saltshaker had been on my kitchen table for fifty years. Surely there must have been other mornings when the sun crossed the table like that, but I was just too busy getting things done. I wonder what else I missed? I then realized what it was that I experienced that sunny morning. It was grace."

Martha McCallum later described that experience as God paying her a visit. She was able to have that experience because her illness had slowed her down. Are you living life slowly enough so that when God comes to visit you, you won't be so busy getting things done that you miss Him?

July 7th
First Steps

I was in the library the other day looking through some books when I came upon a picture of one of Van Gogh's paintings. I liked the painting. It was one I had never seen before and it was entitled, "The First Steps."

In the painting, two young parents are in the middle of a half-planted field. A shovel has been cast aside. The father is kneeling on the ground with his arms open wide, and he appears to be calling his little girl to come to him. Across the field is a doting mother who is standing behind the little girl, helping her to keep her balance as she is in the process of taking her first step. It's a beautiful painting that brings a smile to your face as you look at it, because Van Gogh has brilliantly captured a very human event. Every parent has had the experience of watching their little ones take their first steps. And each of us has experienced our first steps as well.

As I thought about that painting, it dawned on me that each of us lives that painting every day. Everyday we are either taking our "first steps" into some new experience or helping others to take their first steps. Whatever part we play in the process, first steps are very important.

In your life right now, are you facing some new endeavor and are you feeling a bit intimidated? Perhaps this is the time to remember that there are people around you who, like the young father in the painting, are ready to encourage you in your desire to take those first critical steps. Listen to them and accept the gift of their encouraging words. Or again, perhaps there are people, like the young mother in Van Gogh's painting, who are hovering behind you to steady you as you try to keep you balance while you negotiate your way. When God calls us into new adventures, God also provides the people who, with open arms, both invite and catch us as we take those first scary steps.

July 8th
Grace at Work

I was on a retreat a few years ago during which there was a discussion about happiness. The gist of the discussion centered on what it takes to find happiness. Each person present was supposed to give their ideas on how to find happiness. I think the best response to the question I heard that night was from one of our senior priests. He remarked that the happiest people he ever knew all had the same thing in common – they knew how to be grateful, no matter what happened. To illustrate his point he pulled out a little note card from his billfold. He said that one of his favorite quotes was from a 17th century Biblical commentator named Matthew Henry. "Henry," he said "was well known during his day for his sense of gratitude."

According to that senior priest, Matthew Henry kept a diary in which he often wrote about the things that he felt blessed his life. One striking example was the diary entry in which he describes having been violently robbed. The senior priest began to read from his note card, saying: "At the conclusion of the entry, Matthew Henry wrote this, 'In this event as in all others, I find cause for gratitude. I am thankful that during these years I have never been robbed until now. Also, even though they took my money, they did not take my life. And although they took all I had, it was not much. And finally, I am most grateful that it was I who was robbed, not I who robbed.'"

I think what that senior priest was trying to explain was that the way to find happiness is to develop a way to see grace at work in every event of our day. Looking over the events of your day at the end of the day with an eye for discovering how grace has been at work in your day's activities can give you a lot for which to be grateful, and it is gratitude that leads to happiness.

July 9th
Greed

One of the great spiritual teachers among the Desert Fathers spent much of his time forming his disciples in Gospel living. He wanted them to know how much God loved them, and he was concerned that if they lost touch with that love they could be snared by vice. It was said that he often worried that his followers would be trapped by the demands of daily life and would become slaves to one particular sin or fault – greed. Now this was a rather curious fear, because most of his disciples had already given all of their worldly goods to the poor and had made off for desert areas to spend much time in prayer. How could these men and women ever fall victim to the snare of greed?

That great teacher would begin his sermons on greed with this statement, "The greedy one demands all of the figs, while the blessed one tastes all figs in just one." What made that holy man so great was that he truly knew the human heart. He knew, way back in the third century, that the true cause or source of greed is not just wanting things.

It is more than that. The true origin of greed is a very real fear. What fear? It is a fear that we in our own day have as well. It is the fear of being left out. This fear plays itself out in destructive behaviors. When we believe that we are behind others or have less than others, we somehow want more than we need. It produces the belief that if I just get the things I don't have, the job I don't have, the money I don't have, the mate I don't have, then I'll feel whole. Then I will be of some value.

When we are caught in the mindset of greed, no amount of success, no amount of money, no amount of admiration or love will ever be enough. "Greed," that holy desert father would say, "is not being satisfied until we have it all. The truth is that one simple thing received as a gift has the power within it to satisfy your hunger to be loved by everyone. The blessed one can taste and savor all figs in just one because they know the gracious love of God."

July 10th
Unexpected Sermons

Heard any good sermons lately? I am always amazed at the number of sermons I hear just about everyday, and none of them are in a church. I heard one earlier this week.

I was sitting in a restaurant the other day working on a Sudoku puzzle, when an elderly woman at the next table began to cough so violently that I thought she might pass out. As several of us got up to see if she needed help, she motioned to us to go back to our places. Then she began to speak.

"There's one thing I have learned the hard way," she said. "And that is to do something about your bad habits when you're young. If you don't, you'll be sorry."

Before any of us could say anything in reply, she launched into a bit of a speech. She said, "See me here all hooked up to this silly oxygen thing? I regret every cigarette I have ever smoked. They have done me no good at all. Oh, I'd tell myself they were calming me down or helping me to relax. That's a lot of hooey! If I hadn't smoked, I wouldn't be lugging all this fake air around with me everywhere I go. What excuses I made! Oh, let me tell you right here and now, do something about your bad habits today, right now, before they get you! If you don't do something now, those bad habits will suck the life right out of you!"

Having finished her little speech, the woman got up, paid her bill and slowly made her way out of the restaurant. As the cashier was putting the money in the cash register, she looked up at the rest of us and said, "Well now you've all had your sermon for the day. Anyone want any dessert?"

We all laughed. Then we began to talk about what she had said and how all of us probably have some thing or other that controls us. In the end, she left us all thinking.

Have you heard any sermons lately?

July 11th
First Words of the Day

Take a few moments right now to recall yesterday. Think of all that happened yesterday and try to recall all that you did yesterday. Now, try to recall the very first words you spoke yesterday morning. What were they? Can you remember them?

I ask you that question because I have been studying prayer and in the course of my studies I came across a teaching from one of the great rabbis. He taught his disciples that words are very important, especially the very first words of the day since they "open" the creation of your new day. He said that just as Yahweh spoke those first words "Let there be light" and the day was filled with light, so, too, do our words have an effect on the day we speak them.

There is an old Hasidic poem which takes up this idea:

Take special care to guard your tongue before the morning prayer.
Even greeting your fellow, we are told, can be harmful at that hour.
A person who wakes up in the morning is like a new creation.
Begin your day with unkind words, or even trivial matters –
even though you may later turn to prayer, you have not been true

to your Creation.
All of your words each day are related to one another.
All of them are rooted in the first words you speak.

The words we first speak can set the tone for the words we speak the rest of the day. The words we first speak each morning can frame the way we see life the rest of the day. Those first words we speak can even determine how we hear God's voice throughout the day as well.

When it comes to our spiritual lives, the words we speak are very important. So, too, are the words we choose not to say. We are made in God's image. God is the Creator whose words shape the universe. We too are creators whose words can shape our day, our outlook, the relationships we share with others, and even the relationship we have with God. I guess we had better pay closer attention to our words, don't you think?

July 12th
Under the Influence

A great holy man and prophet came to a city to tell all of its inhabitants about the wonderful love of God. In the beginning, many people came and listened attentively to his sermons. Filled with enthusiasm, the holy man continued speaking about God's love. People still listened for a while, but gradually, one by one, they drifted away. Eventually there was not a single one to hear the holy man when he spoke.

One day a traveler who had paused to listen to the holy man said to him, "Why do you go on preaching and, with such enthusiasm, too?"

The holy man replied, "In the beginning I hoped that I could change these people's cool hearts. But now, I continue to speak, talk, preach and even shout, not to change their hearts so much. If I still speak, it is to prevent them from changing me!"

Have you ever stopped to notice the people with whom you spend much of your time? What influence do you think they are having over you? Have they changed your views, or the way you see yourself? Have your attitudes, disposition and convictions changed since you have first been with these people? What do you think? Has the time you've spent with them been good for you or not so good?

Have you ever stopped to consider how you may be influencing the lives of those with whom you spend a great deal of time? Has the time that they have been with you been good for them or not so good? What do you think?

We are all living "under the influence" of one another. Just what kind of influence it may be is yet to be seen.

July 13th
Feeding the Right Dog

I recently read an account of a Native American Tribal Chief who was teaching the young people of his tribe about how to be a good person. When the chief had finished his talk, one of the young men in the group asked him if he could describe his own troubles with trying to be a good person. The chief replied by saying, "In my own life I have come to discover that there are two dogs inside me. One of the dogs is mean as hell and very evil. The other dog is very good. The mean dog fights the good dog all of the time."

Someone in the crowd asked him which dog usually wins the fight. After a moment or two of reflection, the chief answered, "I suppose it's the one that I feed the most. Being a good person is a matter of feeding the right dog."

Does that tribal leader's description of the struggle to lead a good life ring true to you? I've been using his description in my prayer these last couple of weeks and I have found it to be a good way to pay attention to the choices I make. I have been simply asking myself, "If I choose to say or do that, which dog would I be feeding?"

If you were to ask yourself that question about the choices you have been making with your family and friends or at work or school, which dog have you been feeding?

July 14th
At the Top of the List

There are many graces we ought to pray to receive, but there is no grace we each need more than the grace of forgiveness. I'm not talking about the grace of BEING forgiven, though we do need that too. I'm talking about that grace which helps us to forgive those who have wounded us.

Whenever I read Jesus' parable about the rich man and that poor man who used to eat the scraps that came from the rich man's table, I remember those terrible words spoken by Abraham to the rich man after he has died and is in the torments of hell. Abraham says, "There is fixed between us, a great abyss or chasm that keeps us from crossing over to each other." How well those words illustrate what happens to us when we are unable to find a way to forgive each other. I'm sure there are untold numbers of people who are estranged from family and friends because they are unable to find within themselves the ability to let go of past hurts.

Samuel Johnson once wrote that, "A wise man will make haste to forgive, because he knows the true value of time, and will not suffer it to pass away in unnecessary pain." Now when I first read those words, I began to think of the many times in these past few months and years when I have been with various families at the time of a funeral. Inevitably, in every one of those situations, someone remarked about relatives who have not spoken to each other for years. The conclusion of those conversations is always the same – how much time we have wasted and really lost in not being with each other. Every person regrets time lost, time that could have been spent enjoying one another's company. I am certain that of all the graces we ought to pray for, the graces of being able to let go of past hurts and the ability to forgive the past are right at the top of the list.

July 15th
You Are Good

There is an old story about a man who was so holy that even the angels in heaven marveled at how holy and truly good he was. The thing that amazed the angels was that the good man had no notion whatsoever that he was holy. He just walked through life, going about his business spreading good wherever he went. The world was a better place because he was in it, and heaven itself rejoiced that he was so good.

He was able to be so holy because of a special gift that enabled him to forget each person's past and he would only see them as they were now. In addition, he was able to look into each person's heart and soul and see there the innocence that had been there from birth. Thus, he was able to love and to forgive each person he met. He didn't see himself as anyone too extraordinary because this was just his way of looking at people, that's all.

One day God sent an angel to the man to inform him that God was well pleased with him and that God was granting him a special gift. The holy man could ask God for anything, and God would give it to him. So, the angel began by asking the holy man a series of questions:

"Would you like to have the gift of healing?"

"No," said the holy man. "I'd rather God did the healing himself."

"Well then," said the angel, "would you like to bring sinners back to the path of goodness?"

"No, that's not for me; touching human hearts is the work of the angels," came the reply. "I am not worthy of such business."

The angel thought for a moment and then asked, "Would you like to be such a model of holiness and virtue that everyone will want to imitate you?"

"Absolutely not," answered the holy man, "for that would make me the center of attention and that is something I surely do not want."

"Tell me then what is it you wish for?" the angel asked.

"I simply want the grace of God with me," the saintly man said. "If I have that, I will have all that I'll ever wish for or need."

"I'm quite sorry, sir, but I am told that you must ask for some miracle or one will be imposed on you," the angel informed him.

"If that be the case," the man said, "then I shall ask that much good be done in and through me, but that without me ever being aware of it."

And so it was decreed by God that the holy man's shadow would be endowed with healing properties so that wherever his shadow fell, the sick were healed, the land it fell on would be fertile, and fresh springs of water would well up. The man's shadow would lift the burden of those on which it fell, goodness would abound everywhere the man went, all the while the holy one would be unaware of his influence.

I love that story because it reminds me of the truly good people I have met over my years as a priest. In almost every case, the truly good and holy people I have met were completely unaware of the goodness they bring to others. They seemed completely unaware of just how good they were. I am sure that you, too, are filled with goodness, and I am equally as certain that you are probably unaware of just how much your life has blessed those who know you. It is important for you to know just how much God is at work in you and that He is using you daily to spread goodness throughout His Kingdom.

July 16th
Respecting Christians

The comedian Rodney Dangerfield is famous for his complaint, "I don't get no respect!"

With that line he told many jokes about how he had been mistreated throughout his life. Millions have laughed at the ideas and jokes he came up with at his own expense. He once said that he thought he appealed to most people because most people feel that they too "don't get no respect." He said that respect in our culture seems to be in short supply.

When I read Rodney Dangerfield's comments about respect, I recalled something I read by William Barclay.

William Barclay was a rather famous Scottish New Testament scholar who served not only as a University professor but also as a pastor of a local church. He used to tell his students about one of his favorite teachers from his youth. According to Barclay, before the beginning of each class, his teacher would stand before his class and make a very profound and reverent bow to his students. Then the teacher would stand up straight, close his eyes, take in a deep breath, sigh a bit, and then utter these words, "One never knows."

One day, someone asked that teacher why he did this. The teacher replied that he made the profound bow because he didn't know how any of his students might "turn out," but that he was certain that some of them would be great people who would make a profound difference in the world. "Each of you," he said, "is God's handiwork, a bundle of possibilities. So, I bow in reverence of the Creator's handiwork. One never really knows whom God has placed among us."

William Barclay recalled that his teacher really did reverence his students. "He always made you feel worthy of respect, and so we all found ourselves being respectful to each other and most especially to our teacher. The great thing that teacher taught us was that everyone deserves to be respected, and even reverenced, since each of us is a reflection of God."

William Barclay also preached about respect. He used to tell his congregation that the true measure of a Christian was the reverence they gave to others. A good question we all have to ask ourselves then is, when it comes to reverencing others, do we measure up as good Christians?

July 17th
Encouragement

The other day I was reading about Mary Lincoln, the granddaughter of Abraham Lincoln. One of her most precious possessions was a small box in which she kept the contents of her famous grandfather's pockets from the night he was assassinated at Ford's Theater. When Mary died, the box and its contents were given to the Library of Congress. One of the items that Abraham Lincoln carried in his pocket was a copy of a letter to the editor praising Lincoln for his singleness of purpose and that he had never given up his mission. A spokesman for the Library of Congress commented on the letter by saying, "I guess this goes to show us that even a president as great as Abraham Lincoln needs encouragement."

When I read that article, I immediately thought of all of the people I know who go at their life with a similar singleness of purpose as Lincoln did. I think of parents who tirelessly take care of their infant children and those who will go to great lengths to keep open communication with their adolescent children especially when it would be so easy to cut off communication altogether. I think of the many spouses who with singleness of purpose work at their relationships to build and keep a loving marriage together. I think, too, of the many among us who with such loving care minister to their mates who are chronically or terminally ill.

Then again, I think of so many of our youth who with a singleness of purpose work to keep their grades up, or those who dedicate so much of their time, talent and hard work to a sport, to music or drama or whatever interests they may have. I am reminded of the many grandparents, aunts and uncles among us who pitch in and contribute so much to the growth and formation of their grandchildren, nieces and nephews. There are so many among us who with a singleness of purpose strive to make our world a better place by reaching out and caring for others, and everyone of them, like Abraham Lincoln, needs encouragement.

If you are one who is worn out by your hard work and your own singleness of purpose, by caring for and worrying about others, let this brief article be for you what that letter to the editor was to President Lincoln. Let it be a sign that there is at least one person somewhere who truly appreciates all of your efforts and knows that you are truly a blessing for our world.

July 18th
A Hole to China

Every one of us finds ourselves rushing from one place to another in our day-to-day activities, but have you ever stopped to look around at what you might be missing in your rush to get to your next destination? Let me explain.

At the library earlier this week, I came upon this bit of wisdom: "It's in the traveling, in making the trip itself, not in the destination, that life is truly lived." As I began thinking about it, I recalled a little story someone had shared with me just last week.

According to the story, two small boys were digging a deep hole behind their house. Several older boys stopped to find out what the boys were up to. Finally they asked the younger ones what they were doing.

"We are going to dig a hole clear through the earth," one of them said.

"We plan to come out on the other end just about in the middle of China!"

The older boys began laughing, "You can't dig all that way through the earth. That's impossible!"

There was a long period of silence, after which one of the smaller boys picked up a jar that was next to the hole. It was filled to the brim with spiders, worms and other curious looking insects and slugs. He removed the lid, showed the older boys the wonderful creatures swarming around in the jar.

"Even if we don't get there," the younger boy said, "look at all the great stuff we found already in this hole. Just think what great other gross stuff we'll find!"

We may not be thrilled to have a jar filled with spiders, worms, slugs and other "gross stuff," but that young boy made a great point. Some of the most wonderful things in life are often discovered and enjoyed while we are on our way to some other place. As we are "digging a hole to China," we may see things we may have never been able to discover had we not paused as we made the trip. Unfortunately we often think we are too busy and we can miss out on some of the best parts of life if we are in too much of a hurry to get where we are going. Some "purposeful pausing" can do wonders for us.

Why not take some time this week to slow down enough to discover some really "great stuff" along your way?

July 19th
How Was Your Trip

As we are entering into the deep days of Summer, many of us are heading out on vacation travels. Traveling with its new sights, sounds and experiences and the meeting of new people and the making of new friends can be an exciting and rewarding experience. But, as one spiritual master put it, if we have no real home to return to where someone will ask us "How was your trip?" we might be a lot less eager to travel.

Taking a trip is a lot more enjoyable when we travel with the eyes and ears of those who love us. Let me explain. Haven't you ever been in an incredible place and said to yourself, "Wow, I wish my husband or my mom, or best friend was here to see this!" This is what the real journey of life is all about – receiving gifts from God and then sharing them with those we love. The important thing to remember, however, is that if we are moving too quickly through life, if we are so busy and so over-scheduled that we can hardly breathe, we will miss what God wants us to have.

I think that life is very much like traveling. I believe that when God created us, he lovingly sent us on a trip and he wants us to experience everything along the way at a deliberately slow pace. If we travel slowly enough, and if we go with the eyes and ears of the God who sent us, we will experience wonderful, incredible things. We will see spectacular sights, hear wonderfully beautiful music, meet interesting people, make life-long friends and be amazingly happy to come back home again. I also believe that God is waiting for us at the end of our journey of life. He will welcome us and say, "Welcome home! How was your trip? You have to tell me all about it!"

July 20th
Survivor

I believe it was Charles Dickens who told the story of a sole survivor of a shipwreck. According to the story, a survivor had washed upon an uninhabited island and spent the days hunting for food and building a simple shelter. He spent his evenings praying that God would send him rescuers. Days turned into weeks and weeks turned into months, still no one came to save him.

Finally, after a particularly difficult and rather long day of hunting and gathering, the survivor made his way toward his little hut. As he neared the hut he was horrified to see his little home was engulfed in flames. All he had worked so hard for was lost. The absolute worst had happened and he was plunged into a deep depression. All hope was lost and he spent the night praying for death.

Early the next day a ship drew near, dropped anchor and sent a landing crew to rescue the man. "How did you know I was here?" he asked the crew.

"First we saw the smoke, then we saw your signal fire and we made straight for this island." It was at this moment that the survivor realized that it was in losing everything he had that made his rescue possible.

Have you ever had your whole world collapse around you so you fell into a deep, dark depression? Have you ever felt despair? Are present difficulties leading you to lose hope? Perhaps Dickens' story can be of help to you. The story is meant to remind you that though it may not seem so now, your present situation may be the very instrument that will bring along your future rescue. Your prayers do not go unheard. Your salvation is already in the works. God cares for you and will send a crew to rescue you!

July 21st
A Spiritual Revolution

It is said that one day St. Francis of Assisi was walking through the fields just thinking about life when he came upon one of Assisi's leaders, a nobleman. That nobleman had been out looking for Francis because the town leader was upset with the evil and corruption he found in government leaders, in church leaders, in his fellow nobles and in the peasants as well. The nobleman was inconsolable and felt that there was no reason for hope.

Francis told the man that there was every reason for hope because there was a very simple solution, a true remedy for these terrible problems, a kind of revolution. The nobleman wondered what kind of remedy there could be for such evil. Francis replied, "Kind sir, it is quite simple what must be done to counter the effects of such worldly evils. You and I must first work to become what we ought to be; then we shall have brought forth an inner healing. Then, let each person do the same and in no time the world will be reformed and transformed. If we are sincere and truly want to follow Jesus, we can never spend our time trying to reform others. Our best efforts must be directed at meeting head-on the chaos and scandals that are within our own hearts. Talking about reforming others leads nowhere. Working to change your own heart leads to a spiritual revolution."

Are you being called to lead a "spiritual revolution?"

July 22nd
It's Revolutionary

I'd like to offer you a chance to participate in a revolution, a revolution in your thinking, in your seeing. I'd like to offer you a chance to experience a spiritual revolution that will set you free and give you peace. Let me explain:

It might be good for us to stop to consider how we might not be as free as we think. We can be held captive by many things, but there is no stronger prison on earth than time.

We have an expression to describe what happens when someone is sent to prison – we say that they are "doing time," or "serving time in prison." The truth is, however, that convicted felons are not the only ones who are imprisoned by time. Everyone of us who says, "There just isn't enough time in the day" or "I can't believe how time flies by" is also a prisoner.

Anyone who spends time worrying about the past which they cannot change, or fearful of the future they cannot know, is a prisoner of time as well. So, how do we get out of such a jail?

All the great mystics of all of the major religions teach the same thing – the way out of time's prison is to cultivate peace in your heart. They teach that if we make cultivating peace our goal or first priority, we will soon find ourselves living in the present moment. When we live only in the moment, in this present moment, we will discover that we are not alone. We are in God's presence. When we come into God's presence, time is irrelevant because we know what it is to be loved unconditionally. Jesus himself told us that the Kingdom of God, the place where we know that we are loved unconditionally and are called to love others unconditionally, is very near. It is at hand. It is in the present moment. It is now.

Albert Einstein spoke once about how we experience time in different ways. He said, "A day spent with a beautiful woman we love with all our heart seems like a moment, yet an hour spent at a job we hate seems like an eternity." When we take off our watches and put away our schedules, when we leave the past in the past and leave the future to tomorrow, a gentle peace settles in us and around us. We are invited to "rest a while," and in the resting, we are set free. The freedom that comes from living in the present will cause a very subtle yet very profound revolution in your spiritual life. It will allow you to be in the presence of God, and that experience, I can assure you, will change you forever!

July 23rd
Out There

St. Anthony the Great once told his disciples a story about a woman who was a close friend of his. Anthony described his friend as a rather devout and pious woman who was filled with love for God. Each morning she would walk to church for prayer and Mass. On her way to church each day, children from the neighborhood would call out to her, beggars and street folk too would come up to speak with her and ask her help. Because she felt that these people were disturbing her recollection and making it impossible for her to be ready to meet God in Mass, the woman would try alternate routes to the church. This worked for a day or two, but soon it seemed not to matter what road she took, people always found her.

One day she walked to church in her usual way and arrived at church on time for Mass. She pushed on the door, but it did not open. She pushed again, and again, but the door would not move. The door was locked.

She was very upset at the thought that she was going to miss attending Mass for the first time in many years. She began to sob, and as she wiped the tears from her eyes she noticed a note with her name on it pinned to the door. She read the note: "Anna, don't look for me here. I'm out there among all of those people you have been avoiding. I'll meet you out there!"

St. Anthony used that story to teach his disciples an important lesson. This is how he explained it: "You certainly will have much difficulty seeing God at Mass if you have difficulty seeing Him out there in the streets. If you want to see and experience God at Mass, you must first go into the streets and look for Him there."

July 24th
Finding the Artichokes

An art student once asked the French artist Henri Matisse about how he was able to maintain his creativity. The famous artist thought about it for a moment and then said, "My friend, the key to life and to creativity is rather simple and rather easy to come to. You must take time. You must take time to find the artichokes in your life."

These words confused the art student, so Matisse then took the young student outside to his garden. They wandered around the garden until they came to a patch of artichokes. Matisse stopped, took a deep breath and said, "Look, artichokes! Let's just pause here for a moment and be still. Try to drink in what is in front of us. I have painted over 200 canvases and in each of them I try to discover new combinations of color and pattern. When I come to look at my artichokes here in the garden, I let no one disturb me. Standing here in front of my artichokes, I find relaxation, inspiration, new ideas and a whole new perspective on things. I recommend it to you. It can make all the difference – my friend, you must find the artichokes in your life! Do that and you'll never be without inspiration."

Henri Matisse taught that young art student more than art; he taught him the first steps of contemplation. Contemplation is a doorway to God. This week, why not take a few minutes to find the artichokes in your life? I can assure you that if you do, you will be opening a door to God Himself.

July 25th
Bulls and Lions

In one of his letters, St. Peter warns his readers to beware of the Devil who prowls around like a lion seeking someone to devour. Whenever I read or hear those words, I often think of one of Aesop's Fables. It's a fable that tells of three bulls that would feed together everyday in great peace and safety. A lion had long watched them in the hope that one or all of them might become his food, but the lion found little chance of it because the bulls were always together. He therefore began to secretly spread evil and slanderous reports of one bull against another. Slowly, over time and many whisperings, a jealousy and anger began to be fermented which grew into a distrust among the bulls. Soon they began to avoid each other and took to feeding alone. This gave the lion the opportunity it had longed for, and one by one, the bulls were killed by the lion.

What happened to the bulls is something that can happen to us in our families or neighborhoods, among our friends, in our churches or cities and nations. When we speak ill of each other or hurt one another with our words, the harmony that is meant to exist among us begins to disintegrate and we create an atmosphere of suspicion and fear that leads to a deadly isolation. St. Peter knew well what he was talking about; there is a lion out there that is just waiting to devour us!

July 26th
All Day Long

As I was paying bills the other day, I came to realize that the month of July is just about over; and with that thought I was reminded of how time seems to just fly by. Don't you find it that way? Later that same day I came upon a biography of Pope Paul VI and as I flipped through the book, I came to one of the last chapters in which the last few months of the Pope's life were described. Those were difficult months, filled with much physical pain and a great deal of worry, anxiety and mental suffering.

Those last months were probably the worst days of Pope Paul's life. When he was asked about what he was going through, the Pope said that he had been spending his quiet times reflecting on time itself. When he was asked what he had concluded in his meditations on time, here is what Pope Paul VI said: "When I was young days flew by and a year was long. Now that I am old, it's the years that fly by and a single day is very long." Then he added, "A long day is often a lonely day."

Those words ring true, don't they? When we are young, years seem like an eternity and we long for them to pass quickly so we can get to the things we long for in the future. Yet, when we are older, and perhaps enduring some kind of pain or hardship, the years seem to run away from us, while a single day can feel like a lifetime.

If you are at a point in your life in which the days seem endless because they are filled with suffering, pain, worry, or loss, it might be good to recall the words of Jesus – "I am with you always." One way to ease the burden of a long day is to not spend it alone. All of the great spiritual guides teach that burdens can be cut in half if we share them with another person. They also teach that when we reach out to help another person to carry their load, we lessen our own. A day need not be long or lonely if we remember to treasure both people and the time we spend with them.

The truth of the matter, however, is that no matter how long or short a day may seem, each day is still just 24 hours long. It's what we do with each day that makes all the difference.

July 27th
Tis a Gift to be Simple

I was reading a sermon by a great rabbi in which he begged his congregation to take some time out to be simple. He pleaded with his people to set some time aside to notice simple things and not to read all kinds of hidden meanings and complicated explanations to the simple beauty of God's creation. "Go look at some birds and simply marvel at their gracefulness of flight or the beauty of their colored feathers," he said

As I was reading this I remembered a true story about a group of literary critics who had formed a poetry club and had gathered together to discuss the poetry of the great Robert Frost. For hours and hours they discussed the deep metaphysical symbolism and dark meaning of these famous lines:

> *"The woods are lonely, dark and deep, But I have promises to keep,*
> *And miles to go before I sleep."*

After many hours of heated discussions with no real conclusion, the group decided to pay a call on Robert Frost himself. In a rather point-blank way they asked the poet what he really had in mind when he wrote those few lines. Frost said this to them: "Shucks, all I meant was I was tired and I wanted to get on home and go to bed."

Isn't it amazing how we can complicate life by looking for dark, hidden meanings in things that aren't really there? The rabbi who begged his congregation to take time to be simple was on to a great spiritual insight. He knew, as the old Shaker Hymn put it, that "'Tis a gift to be simple, 'tis a gift to be free!"

As you enjoy these Summer weeks, take time to be simple!

July 28th
If I Have to Tell You ...

The other day I was reading some periodicals in the library when I came across an article in a magazine dedicated to international diplomacy. The article was about power and how it can affect world leaders. Many well-known world leaders were quoted, but the one quote I found particularly interesting was one from former British Prime Minister Margaret Thatcher. She had been asked what it was like to be one of the most powerful women in the world. She said, "Being powerful is like being a lady—if you have to tell people you are, you aren't."

Margaret Thatcher's quote made me laugh, but it also made me think. If we applied her idea to ourselves, what conclusions could we draw from it? If we have to tell people how good we are, maybe we aren't. If we have to tell people how kind we are or how humble we are, maybe we aren't. Again, if we have to tell people we are Christians, maybe we aren't.

Jesus promised to send us the Holy Spirit, who would empower us to share the Good News. The question we have to ask ourselves is, is that power evident in the way we live our lives?

July 29th
You Have the Power

I spent some time in the library this past week reading about life during the Communist era of the Soviet Union. Part of the material I read was about how people who were held as prisoners in Siberia managed to survive their ordeal. One former prisoner who was quoted was Alexander Solzhenitsyn, a dissident who was often horribly mistreated at the hands of some very sadistic guards. At one point, Solzhenitsyn was so physically weak, so discouraged and so fully spent after years of inhumane treatment that he hoped for immediate death. In fact, one day, knowing that if he stopped working, a guard would attack him so savagely that he might be killed, he simply quit digging and just stood there leaning on his shovel.

That was his plan – he would just stop working and allow the Soviet guard to come beat him to death. But when he stopped, a fellow Christian reached over with his shovel and quickly drew a cross at the feet of Solzhenitsyn, and then just as quickly erased it before the guard could see it. It was a simple gesture, but very effective.

Years after that experience, Solzhenitsyn recalled that at that moment his entire being had been filled with a kind of hot energy that changed everything. He said that the simple kind gesture from a fellow believer gave him courage to face anything because it filled him with hope. He concluded by saying, "It was the most important gesture of encouragement that I ever received in my whole life. It taught me that every one of us can be an agent of hope if we would simply take the time to offer some gesture of encouragement to those around us."

July 30th
Keeping Your Edges Sharp

I recently finished reading a new biography of Abraham Lincoln. The author of that book included many anecdotes that Lincoln used to tell both when he was a practicing lawyer and when he was President. One of my favorites is one that Lincoln told about his own childhood. Lincoln said that when he was a boy, he often went for long hikes in the woods. On one such occasion he came across a man who was vigorously chopping down a tree with a very dull ax. As Lincoln watched, he noticed that the man was making very little progress except in building up a big sweat. Lincoln asked the man why he didn't stop and sharpen his ax. "I don't have time to stop and sharpen this ax!" the man said. "I've got to chop down twenty more trees after this one!"

Lincoln said that he had learned a very valuable lesson from his encounter with that woodsman. He learned that if you are going to do an important task, it's wise to make the proper preparations for that task; otherwise we will simply sweat a lot and accomplish very little.

In your own life right now, do you find yourself "sweating a lot" over something and wearing yourself out without accomplishing much? Perhaps you have not made some important "ax-sharpening" preparations like taking time for prayer to ask for God's guidance and help. By spending a bit of time with God, you may discover what first needs sharpening in your life, and then you will be ready to take the next steps in your life's journey.

July 31st
Winding Our Clocks

Years ago, before World War I, in a remote village of Poland, a priest gave a sermon one Sunday morning which helped people to change the way they lived their faith. In his sermon the priest told of his hometown which had not been visited by a clockmaker for many years. After a while, the clocks in the village were all telling different times. Most villagers gave up even winding their clocks because they seemed useless to them. Finally, a wandering clockmaker did show up. The villagers ran to the man with their clocks to have them repaired and set to the proper time. But their clocks had rusted and corroded from long years of disuse – except for one clock, whose owner had wound it each day. Even though he knew it was not telling the exact time, he had remained hopeful that a clockmaker one day would come to the village. The clockmaker made a few minor adjustments, and then set the clock to the right time.

When the priest finished telling his congregation about his hometown and its clocks, he turned to his people and said, "The faithful disciple of Jesus is often like that one man who kept winding his clock. The faithful follower of Jesus continues his/her daily routine of prayer and devotion, even though all of those around have stopped doing so. The faithful one knows that even though he/she may fail in minor ways, one day the Lord, like that clockmaker, will come back. When He does, the doors of the heart of that faithful follower will not have rusted shut, but will swing open wide in welcome."

The priest then paused and in a soft whisper concluded his sermon by saying, "Let each of us daily wind the clock of our hearts with love for God and for one another. May we all continue to 'tick' with faithful devotion to Our Lord. Amen."

August 1st
What Other Folks Carry

Some years ago I was at a conference at which Steven Covey spoke. In the middle of his presentation he told of an unusual experience that he had on a New York subway. He said he was doing some work as the subway traveled along, and as he worked he thought of how peaceful the ride was since hardly anyone was speaking. Just as he was thinking about the quiet, the subway made it to its next stop. A man entered the subway car with his four overactive, noisy children. The once quiet subway car was now a place of utter chaos and commotion. The children's inappropriate behavior was obvious to everyone but their father. The children's father just sat there with his eyes closed and sighed a few times. After about 15 minutes of utter chaos, Covey said he could stand it no longer, so he got up and went over and confronted the man.

Steven Covey said that the man opened his eyes and seemed to be evaluating the situation as if he was not aware at all as to what his children had been doing. The man finally cleared his throat, and then spoke just a few words. "I'm so sorry; I guess I should have done something to keep them quiet. But you see, we just came from the hospital, where their mother died about an hour ago and I just don't know what to do. I guess these kids just don't know how to handle this yet." Steven Covey said that he was so embarrassed and ashamed of having burdened the poor man that he just went and sat down and hung his head.

As I listened to Steven Covey tell that story, the woman sitting next to me leaned near me and said, "I know that this man is the big expert and all, but what he took a half hour to say, my grandmother told me in just a few words. She would say, 'Now Gracie, always remember that you don't know what hidden burdens people are carrying around inside them. Always be kind – that way you won't wound people who are already hurting terribly. Being kind is so important.'"

Gracie's grandmother summed it up perfectly. Kindness truly is important. We really never know just how much other people are burdened. Simple acts of kindness can go a long way to lighten the load that other folks carry.

August 2nd
Discovering New Worlds

The Polynesians have an interesting way of describing how the world and much of creation came to be. They tell their children that when the Creator, whom they call Taaora, woke up one day, he found himself growing inside a great shell. As he awoke, he stretched and broke the shell, and the Earth was created. Then Taaora continued to grow and after awhile he found himself inside another shell. Again he stretched and broke that shell, and when it broke the moon was created. Taaora continued to grow even more and when he found himself within another shell he did as he had done before and stretched. This time all of the stars in the heavens were created.

That Polynesian creation story can serve as a great teacher for each of us about true growth. For us, true growth does not happen unless we are able to "stretch" our thinking, our ideas of ourselves and even our love enough so that we can break free from the "shell (s)" that hem us in.

Often people refuse to grow and to change because they are afraid to leave behind that which is comfortable. It can be a frightening thing to step out into unknown territory, to try new things, to reach beyond what we know.

In the work I have done over the years with addicts, I have come to learn that real growth and real change only come when we are willing to break out of our old shells, our old way of doing things, our old ways of seeing things. Only when we shed the "shell" of bad choices or bad behaviors can we come to live life in a new way. Jesus taught us this.

Another example of "shell shedding" is when we set off to college or when we start a new career. It can be a frightening, even a shocking thing to step out into a whole new world of people, ideas, and experiences. It can be difficult, but this is what life is all about ... growth.

Growth always brings with it a whole series of change. Remember how different the world was the day you first fell in love? Think of how your life changed the day you got married. Think of how your world view changed when you became a parent. At every step of our lives we are forced to shed an old shell and move into a new and bigger universe. This is the pattern that God has established for us – we are always being led to the next new world. Always we are given the opportunity to discover something new, something deeper, something even more wonderful. Will this cycle ever end? I don't think so. I think it will go on and on in this life and even into the next. Isn't God the Creator wonderful?

August 3rd
Feeding Sheep

One of the most remarkable scenes in the Gospels is an event that took place after the resurrection of Jesus. Jesus comes to Peter and asks him three times, "Do you love me?" Some scholars say that this is Jesus' way of allowing and encouraging Peter to forgive himself for his three denials. In other words, Peter can now make amends for having allowed his fear to overwhelm his love.

This is an important scene for each one of us because none of us can claim a perfect record when it comes to love. Everyone fails in their efforts to love whole-heartedly. We can even betray a loved one inadvertently. This is one of the worst pains that can be associated with love, yet we can not afford to be paralyzed by our past failures. Jesus comes to each of us, as He came to St. Peter, to call us to love again and again. He is with us so that we will not allow our fear to overwhelm our love.

"Do you love me?" Jesus asked Peter. "Do you love me?" Jesus asks us as well.

St. Peter's response was a resounding "Yes!"

Jesus' response to Peter was quite simple, "Feed my Sheep." Peter spent the rest of his life doing just that.

When you experience your own failings in love, Jesus will come to you and ask you the same questions. Will you respond as St. Peter did?

August 4th
Into the Darkness

Flipping through the channels this past week I happened on a news program in which elderly people were being asked to share their wisdom. One man, named Henry, had just celebrated his 100th birthday, so he became the focus of many of the questions. The one thing he talked about that made an impression on me was his experience as a sailor in the South Pacific way back in 1915. He spoke about having to be rescued in the midst of a terrible storm. He said that his ship was bouncing and pitching all over the place as it was swamped by huge waves and terrible winds. Visibility was near zero – and this was before the use of radar. He could barely make out the rescue ship which had managed to pull along side his ship.

He said, "I had only one chance to jump and I couldn't see much at all; I was pretty scared because I had no idea if I would end up on the deck of that other ship or in the drink! I just told God that He had to point my feet in the right direction and that I was counting on Him. Well, I'm here, so God must have known what He was doing!"

The interviewer asked him if he had any wisdom he wanted to pass on to people. The man thought a few moments and then said, "I guess I would tell them not to be afraid to trust God enough to take a few blind leaps in your life. As I think of jumping in the middle of that storm, I can't help but think of all of the other times in my hundred years that I had to take some blind leaps in the dark. Leaps like when I decided to go ahead and ask my sweetie to marry me, or the time I quit one job to take another, or when we decided to pull up stakes and move clear across the country. Those were all pretty scary leaps. They all turned out pretty well. I guess I'd tell people to trust God to point your feet in the right direction and not be afraid."

That sounded like some pretty good advice to me.

August 5th
Are You Wealthy?

Do you consider yourself a wealthy person? Most folks would not call themselves wealthy because they think wealth consists of having huge amounts of money and possessions. We think of the billionaires and millionaires who have vast holdings and estates around the world and since we do not have these things, we certainly are not wealthy by any means. Yet it is quite possible that we are far wealthier than we realize.

Did you know that many of our native cultures measure wealth not by what a person possesses, but by what one is comfortable giving away? It is true. The amount of things one owns is not the true measure of wealth for these peoples. Wealth is measured by the ability to give away freely the best that they own. These native peoples celebrate what they call potlatch. It is a kind of great giveaway feast. They purposely choose the finest of their possessions to give away to others. They do not give from their surplus; they do not give leftovers, castoffs, or worthless trinkets. They do not give the kinds of things that we might give to St. Vincent de Paul or the Salvation Army or some other thrift store. No, they give the things that they love the most, their beautiful things, and their precious things. They believe that by sharing their best, they are truly giving themselves away and they believe that this is the only gift worth giving to another human being or to God.

Freely giving yourself away to others is what makes a person wealthy in those cultures. They call it big-hearted giving. It's not how much a person owns but how big-hearted they are in their giving that constitutes true wealth. Thus, a person living in a tiny hut can be wealthy if they are big-hearted in their giving. In the same way, a billionaire living in a grand estate, but who is not big-hearted in their giving, may truly be the poorest person in the world. Wealth is a matter of giving, not having.

So, by the standards of those native peoples, are you a wealthy person?

August 6th
Who We Are

I recently came across a Taoist story the other day that I think can serve as a reminder to us. According to the story, a carpenter and his apprentice are walking through a forest looking for some wood for one of their projects. After a short walk, they come upon a very tall, huge and gnarled old oak tree. As they pause to look at it, the apprentice remarks that the tree is the most beautiful tree he has seen in years. The carpenter agrees. Then the carpenter asks his apprentice, "Do you know why this tree is so tall, so huge, so gnarled, old and beautiful?"

The apprentice looked at the carpenter and says, "No ... why?"

"Well," the carpenter replies, "because it is useless. If it had been useful, it would have been cut down years ago to make tables and chairs and benches and other useful things. But now, because it has been useless, it could grow to be so tall, gnarled, old, and, yes, quite beautiful. Now many people can come and sit in its shade and relax. Birds can make nests in its branches."

The Taoist masters use this story to remind their students that our worth does not come from how "useful" we are, or how much talent we have, or how much money or property we own. Our worth does not come from what we produce, but from whom we are.

Jesus asked his disciples to "look at the birds of the sky" and know that you are worth more than a whole flock of birds to Our Heavenly Father. Or again he says "consider the lilies of the field" and "seek first the Kingdom of God, for it has pleased the Father to give you the kingdom."

We are all God's children, we belong to Him, and our worth does not come from what we produce, what we own, or what we can or cannot do. Our worth comes from the fact that we are God's own children and brothers and sisters to one another.

August 7th
Training

A few days ago while reading in the public library, I came across a collection of letters written by Mark Twain. In one of those letters he writes about an experience he had on a train bound for Washington, D.C.

According to his story, Mark Twain was quietly reading a newspaper when the conductor came down the aisle collecting passenger tickets. When the conductor collected the first two tickets, he noticed that those people were on the wrong train. A few seats later, as the conductor collected more tickets, he noticed that these people were on the wrong train as well. "It's a bit strange that so many of you got on the wrong train," the conductor said as he continued taking tickets.

When the conductor got to the back of the railroad car he realized what had happened. Everyone had gotten on the wrong train! Then it began to slowly dawn on him – it was he who was on the wrong train.

Mark Twain concluded his letter by saying that sometimes life is just that way – we assume everyone else is going in the wrong direction only to discover that in reality we are the ones who are on the wrong train.

As we take our first few steps on today's travels, it might be good to check to see if we have boarded the "right train."

August 8th
Wings

One of the most famous classical musicians today is Itzak Perlman. I was struck by what he said at an awards show that was on TV. I remember him saying that there were two things that happened to him very early in his life that shaped his life forever. He said that when he was only four years old he contracted polio. The disease changed everything for him. He said it forced him to live life differently from other kids; it forced him to move through his life differently. The second event from his young life was that he once heard a recording of the famous violinist Jascha Heifetz. Perlman said that once he heard that beautiful music, he knew his life would be about creating such beauty. As he put it, "Although polio had stolen my legs, it was Heifetz's music that gave me wings!"

If you were to look back over your life, is there anyone who has given you "wings?" Is there someone in your past who has inspired you to do good and great things? Is there anyone now who gives you "wings" by calling the best out of you? And then again, is there anyone in your life that God is asking you to give "wings?" One of the most valuable gifts we can give to one another is the gift of "wings" – which is, in reality, the gift that helps us to see great possibilities and to do great things. Do you have "wings?" Have you given anyone else "wings?"

August 9th
What God Wants Us to Be

A man in his early fifties went to seek advice from a famous Zen spiritual master. As the man poured out his tale of woe, the Zen master listened attentively. "I have had three marriages," the man complained, "and every one of them has failed. My wives have never understood me – they only find fault with me and put me down. My career is a mess; no one I work with has the insights I have, so they don't listen to me. My talents are never really put to good use at my company. I have few friends, and I am lonely most of the time."

"Have you sought the help of counselors or therapists?" the Zen Master asked.

"No, I don't hold much stock with those folks. I think they are just after money," the man replied. "Besides they never really help anyone."

The Zen Master then paused to gather his thoughts. Finally he spoke:

"An ancient Zen saying goes something like this, 'When the gentleman archer shoots his arrow and misses the target, he looks inward.'"

The man thought for a minute or two and then said, "What the hell is that supposed to mean?"

The Zen Master calmly explained, "Its meaning is that when a gentleman archer misses his mark, the target isn't at fault. All true archers know that the way to improve their aim, is to improve themselves. Perhaps this important bit of wisdom has been inadvertently left out of your education. If you want to improve your life, look inward." Perhaps that Zen Master can help us. Those two words, "look inward," are two good words to use as we try to be what God wants us to be.

August 10th
God and You

How are you at accepting gifts? Most folks, I assume, are pretty good at receiving gifts and presents, and I bet you are too. But, I wonder if we can say the same about accepting help? I'll bet most of us who are pretty good at accepting gifts may not be so good about asking for and accepting help when it is offered. For most people, receiving a gift is relatively easy. Allowing someone to help us, or asking for help, well, that may be a different thing altogether.

For many people, this is also true when it comes to their relationship with God. I've had some people tell me that they never ask God for help with their problems because God certainly has more important or more pressing matters to deal with than their little problems or difficulties. I have also noticed over the years that many of these same people are the ones who most often express feelings of hopelessness, depression and even despair. I often wonder if they see the connection between their view of God and their lack of hope.

In recent weeks I was away leading a retreat for the men who were to be ordained priests. While browsing through some of the books at the retreat house library, I came upon some of the writings of the novelist Evelyn Underhill. I was so struck by one particular passage that I wrote it down. Here's part of what she wrote,

"God never says, 'I've had enough of you.' He never says 'Your timing is bad ... I'm rather tired ... Come back when I am not so busy with other more important things, or other more important people ...' Above all, God never dismisses us as 'hopeless cases,' unworthy of further attention. God is always coming to us, always entering to refresh and enhance our lives. He is always with us giving hope, sustaining hope, building on our hope. No one is more important. No one has a greater claim to his gifts than we. But we must make room for hope. We must keep the entryway open ... The creative life of God, the source of hope, is not there just for the asking. It is ours just for the accepting."

If you are at a point in your life that you feel twinges of hopelessness or are feeling a bit blue or depressed, perhaps you've lost touch with the truth of who God really is. As an old Spiritual song once put it, "God has His eye on the sparrow and God has His eye on you!" You are God's own child, there is a place in God's heart that only you can fill. There is every reason to have hope because God's love is unconditional and it is eternal and it is there for you. It is not there just for the asking, it is there just for the accepting.

August 11th
Living the Life You Are Living

I read an article a few weeks ago about some of the conversations that Ronald Reagan and Mikhail Gorbachev had when they were trying to bring an end to the Cold War. One of the ways in which they were able to build bridges to each other was through humor.

While Ronald Reagan was quick with a joke, Gorbachev was also quick-witted. He loved to tell the story of a time when two diplomats, one British, the other Russian, were having a discussion about the value of newspapers. The Russian diplomat said that he wanted to explain the difference between the newspapers of Great Britain and those of the Soviet Union. Here is how he explained it:

"Suppose you and I had a race, and you came in first. Your British newspapers would report it this way: 'Soviet and British ambassadors had a race yesterday. The British Ambassador won.' In our newspapers the report would perhaps read this way: 'A race took place yesterday between ambassadors. The Soviet Ambassador came in second. The British Ambassador came in slightly in front of the last man in the race.'"

Both Gorbachev and Reagan had a great laugh over that story, but it also reminded them of the importance of honesty and of seeking the truth. They both came to realize that if their negotiations were to come to anything, they had to be based on dealing honestly with each other and they resolved to do just that. They had learned that honesty was the best foundation for their relationship.

All of the great spiritual masters teach that honesty is the key to all relationships, and it is especially so when it comes to our relationship with God. I think it was St. Francis of Assisi who spoke of this one day when he was asked to preach to a group of pilgrims who were seeking to be close to God.

He began by saying that the way to being close to God is to learn to be honest. Then he paused and said, "It is especially important to be honest with yourself about just why you are living the life you are living. Do you really want to be close to God? Then, you must ask yourself honestly, 'Am

I living in such a way that will allow me to be close to God and God to be close to me?' Honesty is the key to opening your heart to God."

In your life right now, do you want to be closer to God? Perhaps it is time to take an honest look at your life and to ask yourself that same question: "Am I living my life in such a way that will allow me to be close to God and God to be close to me?"

August 12th
Is it Time for a Coffee Break?

A renowned psychologist was asked to give a keynote address for a convention of psychologists. He had been asked to deliver a lecture on the most effective therapies available to treat people who are overwhelmed by the difficulties that life can bring. He thought long and hard for months on which therapy he might recommend to the group, but could not settle on just one. Finally he sat and spoke with his wife and asked her what she thought he ought to talk about. She thought for a moment and then advised, "You should tell them what you have seen over the years that has done the most good for people."

When he rose to speak at the convention, this is what that psychologist said to his colleagues: "In the more than thirty-two years I have been practicing, I have discovered one particular therapy that provides more profound healing to the patient than any other. I have come to believe that the best therapeutic work is accomplished between good friends over cups of coffee at ten o'clock in the morning. It is better than a day spent in my office. In short, the best medicine when your world falls apart is a good long talk with a good friend. There's nothing better."

At the conclusion of that convention, the doctors who had attended were asked to evaluate the week's program. The results were unanimous: "the most helpful lecture was the one on the value of a good friend."

In your world right now, you may feel like things are falling apart. Why not seek out a friend for a good cup of coffee and a talk? Or again, perhaps there is someone among your friends who is going through a rough period of time. This might be a good time for you to share some coffee and a good ear with them.

And finally, don't forget that good friend who is always ready to listen — Jesus.

August 13th
More Than Appearances

I read an article about something that happened in Italy in 1990. According to the Italian press, in April of 1989 a mandatory seat belt law went into effect throughout all of Italy. Many people protested that this was an infringement on their rights and that the government shouldn't be telling them what to do. Dr. Claudio Ciaravolo decided to make some money on the issue by designing a T-shirt with a black horizontal stripe that made it look like the driver who wore it was actually buckled up when he or she wasn't. The shirts sold so well that stores couldn't keep them in stock.

In 1990, a year after the mandatory seatbelt law went into effect; one of Dr. Ciaravolo's best friends was involved in a terrible accident. He had been speeding and lost control of the car. The car struck a tree, and the driver was thrown from the car and instantly killed. He was not wearing a seatbelt. He was however, wearing one of the famous T-shirts. It failed to protect him.

Obviously, just looking like you are wearing a seatbelt won't keep you safe. Only wearing the real thing can protect you from harm. In the same way, just looking like a Christian doesn't really make you one; there has to be more to our faith than that.

Jesus invites us into a real relationship with Him. He takes us seriously and wants us to take Him seriously too.

August 14th
How About a Nice Prune?

If you were to choose a word that best describes life today, what one word would you choose to sum it all up? I read a survey which asked that question of six different focus groups. The focus groups were: 25

parents of young children, 25 CEOs, 25 teachers, 25 college students, a high school football team, and 25 grade school aged kids. The results of the survey said that close to 90 percent of the respondents used the same word to describe their life today. What was that word? It was a simple four letter word – busy.

It seems that so many of us see ourselves as way too busy. No one seems to have any free time. It appears that just about everyone has schedules that are booked up weeks in advance, and still we try to cram in more and more things to do. This is not good for us and we ought to do something about it.

I was thinking about this very thing the other night when I met a neighbor in the parking lot. He was standing looking at some apple trees. He began to tell me a lot more about apple trees than I really cared to know, but it was rather interesting nonetheless. One thing he told me was that he always enjoyed watching his apple trees grow. "Each year," he said, "my apple trees sprout new branches without even being asked to do so, they just do it. You might think that those new branches might increase the health and yield of my trees, but this is not so. It's only when I prune away unnecessary growth that those trees really flourish."

As that apple-tree guy continued telling me about his trees, my mind began to wander away. I began to think that when my life gets too hectic, when I want to add new activities, or agree to another committee job in the diocese, or agree to take on more work, I ought to think of that man's apple trees. If he doesn't prune them, they won't flourish.

In everyone's life there are always new things to do. There are always new meetings, committees, children's activities, dinners, parties, concerts, sporting events, classes, volunteering opportunities, work-related events and more. We seem to keep adding things without taking away anything else we are doing.

So, one activity that ought to be a part of all of our lives is a periodic schedule prune. Think about it: When was the last time you took an activity off of your schedule? Perhaps it's time for all of us to take a few moments to look at what might need to be "pruned" from our lives. If we prune it away, we will give ourselves room to breathe, room for real growth. And, one more thing, when we prune, that is not a license to add more activities to your life. It's an invitation to do less and to not be so darned busy!

August 15th
Being Moses at Mass

Very often in the course of conversation people will say something like this to me: "I go to Mass every Sunday, but I just don't get anything out of it. Why do you think I never seem to get much out of it?" My response to that question when it inevitably comes up is always the same. "It's not going to Mass that is important. It's truly 'being' at Mass that is important." Let me explain what I mean.

In the Book of Exodus, God calls Moses to come up on Mt. Sinai. In the ancient texts this is how God says it: "Come up to me on the mountain and be there, and then I will give you the stone tablets with the teaching and the commandments." So Moses set out with Joshua, his aide, and went up to the mountain. (Ex 24:12)

Now when you read or hear those words it seems that all Moses has to do is go up on the mountain and God will give him those tablets. However, a famous Hasidic teacher and master reminded his students to notice that God also says three important words to Moses – "and be there." That Hasidic teacher said that God was telling Moses with those three words that he was not just to be physically present on the mountain, but he was to be there fully present in the moment - mentally, spiritually, and emotionally. Moses' true deep relationship with God will only be realized when ALL of Moses shows up. He must be more than just physically present. Moses has to be there fully alert and attentive. When all of Moses shows up, God will speak to him "heart to heart." A kind of union with God will take place. This is why God tells Moses to "Come up to me on the mountain and BE THERE."

What God asked of Moses on Mount Sinai, God also asks of each one of us at Mass. God invites us to "come and to be there." When people ask me why they do not get anything out of Mass, I usually tell them that it may be that while they are physically present for Mass, the rest of them may have been left at home or elsewhere. I believe that God wants us to be Moses at Mass – to be just as alert and attentive to God as Moses was on Mount Sinai. If we approach Mass like that, something wonderful is bound to happen in and for us at Mass.

As you get ready to come to church this weekend, recall the words God spoke to Moses: "Come up to me on the mountain and be there."

August 16th
The Eggs Are Teaching the Chickens

Probably during your college days you were required to read some of the classics of literature. One of the classics that I was required to read as a history major was Tolstoy's, *War and Peace*. Although it was far too long for my tastes, I did like the book. I happened to come across that book in the library this past week, and as I flipped through the pages I came across one scene that caught my attention.

The scene is 1812 and Napoleon is marching on Moscow. Because the city is doomed to fall, the wealthy people of the city are busy packing all of their possessions onto carts so that they can evacuate the city. One of the wealthy Russian counts has more than 30 carts crammed with his possessions. He is looking for even more carts to allow him to take even more things with him.

All over the city there are hundreds of carts loaded down with things. But also all over the city, lining all of the streets and courtyards, are wounded soldiers who know what awaits them as Napoleon's forces enter the city – they will be killed.

Suddenly that wealthy Russian count's daughter sees it - possessions on the carts ready to be saved from destruction, wounded people left on the ground to die. Crying, she runs to her father and begs him to put the wounded on the carts and the things on the ground.

The Count, whom Tolstoy describes as "tender-hearted," sees the situation and feels ashamed. He begins to cry, hugs his daughter and says: "The eggs are teaching the chickens." Then he quickly tells the servants to take his possessions off and put the wounded on the carts. The wounded are saved, the possessions are left behind.

I had forgotten that scene, but I found it to be a good source for meditation. That little vignette from *War and Peace* can raise some interesting questions. Questions like, "What is on the 'carts' of our hearts – possessions, things, or wounded people?" or "Who are the 'wounded soldiers' that lay on the streets of our lives?" or again "Are there things or possessions that are sucking all of our time and attention away from the people or situations that need us?"

August 17th
Is Anything Happening Here?

Recently I was walking through a greenhouse when I noticed some bamboo plants for sale. As I was looking at the plants, one of the workers who was busy setting up some equipment saw me and started to tell me more than I ever really wanted to know about bamboo. Some of what he told me in the course of a 45 minute impromptu mini-lecture on the love and care of bamboo, was rather interesting. For example, it takes five years for the seed of a bamboo tree to show any growth above ground. Once the above ground growth does appear, well, then it really takes off. In just six weeks the tree can grow to a height of 90 feet! I thought that was pretty interesting.

The bamboo tree could serve as a good image of our spiritual life. Those five years of the apparent absence of any growth are actually five very productive years of building a root system that will sustain life through any storm. I have often spoken with people who were about to give up on their prayer or spiritual disciplines, because, as they put it, "it seems like nothing is happening." It has been my experience that real growth only happens after very long periods of quietly going about seeking sources of nourishment and strength. Then, after our "roots" are deep enough to sustain the growth, God calls us out of the darkness into the light which produces new life and new growth.

If you are at such a place in your spiritual development that you feel that "nothing is happening," perhaps God is going about getting you more "rooted" so that you will be able to sustain the growth that He has planned for your future.

August 18th
Hey, Where Are You Going?

Saint Anthony of the Desert told a story about himself. He said that when he first went into the desert as a result of God's call, he felt true peace and solace because he felt God's presence. Then, as time went on, he became aware more and more of himself and of all of his faults and sins and weaknesses. He wrestled with his own weaknesses and was then overwhelmed with terrible temptations. So, he decided to abandon his cave and go somewhere else where these temptations would not bother him.

After packing up his few belongings, he began putting on his sandals so that he could get away. As he was doing this, he saw another monk who looked very much like himself who was also putting on his sandals.

Anthony called out to the man, "Who are you, sir? You look so familiar to me I'm sure I must know you – who are you?"

"Why, I am your self," was the reply. "And if it is on my account that you are packing up and leaving this place, I want you to know – and I guess I warn you, too – that no matter where you go I shall go with you. I suggest you stay put."

"Why should I stay put in this terrible place that I need to run away from?" St. Anthony asked.

"Because both what you run away from and what you yearn for is found within you. Stay where you are and you will see this as clearly as you see me."

Saint Anthony unpacked his few belongings, took off his sandals and realized that he, like Moses, was on holy ground, where God is to be discovered.

I think that every one of us has gone through times when we wanted to run away, thinking that a change of scenery will bring about some kind of a cure or change in us. Most spiritual masters are quick to remind their disciples that "geographic cures" seldom work. Staying put, looking more deeply at our situation, often produces the realization that we too are on holy ground, where God is to be found.

If you are at a time in your life where you feel like running away, don't be so hasty. Why not stick around and see if you too are not on holy ground right where you are.

August 19th
Awesome God

The other day I spoke with a college student who is trying to deepen his relationship with God. I have been teaching him some basic ways to pray and as a part of that, I tried to give him a better sense of just who God is so that he can better focus his prayer. As we spoke he paused and asked me if I knew about the Christian hymn called "Awesome God." He was happy to hear that I love that song, but he wanted me to explain what it means to say that God is awesome. I gave him the following paragraph to read:

"If you are going just to begin to get a glimpse of the sheer awesomeness of God, consider the universe and all of its mysteries. Centuries ago, Ptolemy could count no more than one thousand and twenty-two stars. Centuries later, Galileo said he could see five thousand stars through his telescope. In our own time, scientists have estimated that there might be three hundred billion stars. It wasn't long after that when a new group of scientists declared that the figure should be more like eight times that amount of stars in the universe. Today they speak of galaxies and meta-galaxies until the mind boggles. They tell us that our own galaxy is 100,000 times six trillion miles wide, and yet we know that it is but a tiny part of a much larger, unknown star-system!"

"All of this, which we are only now beginning to get a true sense of, is but a part of what God has created. In other words, all of the things described above are just one of God's creations! We have an awesome God, who has created an awesome universe whose dimensions are so vast we cannot even imagine them, yet as tiny as we are in the midst of this vast universe, God knows us as individuals, loves each of us, and knows even the number of hairs on our head! God is an awesome God!"

August 20th
Are You Proud?

Do you think you take pride in who you are and what you are doing with your life right now? I asked a group of high school students that question and almost every one of them said "no" in very definite terms. In fact, they said that they had never really felt too good about who they were at the present time but felt much better about what they might be in the future.

I had asked them that question because of a passage in a book I recently read about the Taft family. According to the book, the Taft family had a rule that every child should always appreciate and compliment every other family member's accomplishments. When young Martha Taft went to grade school she was asked to introduce herself to her class. She began by saying, "Hello, I am Martha Bowers Taft. My great-grandfather was the president of the United States of America and he was a good president too. My grandfather was a Senator of the United States of America. He is a good senator too. My daddy is ambassador to Ireland for the United States of America. He is the bestest ambassador they ever had. And I am a Brownie!"

Do you take pride in who you are and what you are doing with your life right now? Can you recognize the goodness of each member of your family and take pride in the things that they are doing with their lives? When Mother Teresa was asked if she took pride in the work she had done, she replied by saying, "I don't take pride in the work that I have done but in the reason I have done this great work. I have done it out of love for Jesus. When we do anything out of love for Jesus, we elevate that work to the heights. Even the smallest thing done out of love for Jesus can become the greatest act any one of us could ever do. I invite everyone to take true pride in what you are doing by doing whatever you are doing out of love for Him."

Can you take true pride in who you are and in the work that you are doing?

August 21st
Soul Music

This past week, I took a few early morning hours to give myself a little mini retreat. As part of that time, I listened to a tape about discipleship. The speaker challenged her listeners to think about what discipleship means. As I spent time thinking about it, I remembered something I had read years ago when I was reading up on China in anticipation of traveling there.

There is a legend, which is said to be a true story. It begins that years ago in Old China there was a man who became a member of the emperor's orchestra. That doesn't sound very unusual except that the man could not play a note or even read music. He got the highly paid position as a flute player by bribing the orchestra leader. Whenever the royal musicians were called to perform for the emperor, he simply held the flute to his lips and pretended to be playing the music. In fact, he never even dared to blow into the instrument for fear that the slightest sound would somehow throw the whole orchestra off. The ruse worked. For many years the man was able to earn a decent living and live a rather comfortable life. He was quite content to live his life in this way. Then one day the emperor decided that he wanted to have soft music played as he ate his lunch. Since he felt that the whole orchestra would be far too loud, the emperor commanded that each member of the orchestra would be called on to give a solo performance for him once a month.

The flutist was terrified at the prospect of being found out, so he pretended to be ill. This bought him some time, but the emperor was not one who could be put off for long. The emperor sent his own personal physician to tend to the flutist's health problems. When the doctor reported that the flutist was perfectly cured, the emperor ordered the flutist to be ready to play the flute on the following day. On the morning of his scheduled solo, the flutist drank poison and died rather than face the music. This is said to be the origin of the old Chinese saying, "He dared not face the music."

That legendary story made me think that each one of us who claims to be Christian is at some time or other going to be called to "face the music."

When Jesus called us, He called us to be people of integrity who would not just go through the motions of being disciples, but would truly be His own. Just doing external actions without connecting them to our hearts is not enough. Jesus calls us to live what we say we believe, to love as we are called to love, to forgive as we want to be forgiven, and to be true instruments of peace. It's one thing to say that we are a Christian, it's quite another thing actually to be a Christian. To be a disciple is no small thing. It is a great calling that requires real courage. Each one of us must be ready and willing to "face the music." This is a great question for each one of us to take to our meditation – If Jesus called you to give a solo performance, could you "face the music" of authentic discipleship?

August 22nd

It's a Jungle Out There!

A local governor wanted to be the best governor possible and he knew that he needed God's help, so he asked a local priest who was well-known for his holiness to come and teach him how to pray. The priest did come and began to instruct the governor. A problem arose, however, quite soon after the priest began his teaching. Every minute or so, someone would come into the room and interrupt the lesson in order to ask some permission or some question of the governor. The governor would take whatever time it took to reply to the intruder. This went on every minute or two for the entire lesson. Finally, at the end of the lesson, the priest got up to leave. As the governor and the priest walked to the door, the governor said that he suddenly realized that he was entirely too busy for prayer. He thanked the priest for his time and then said, "Father, I think it best that you not come back since I am so busy. I guess I am just in such an important job that I can't really take the time out to pray; it wouldn't be fair to the people."

The priest thought about this for a time, and then replied, "You remind me of a man walking blindfolded into a dangerous jungle – who said that he was far too busy finding his way through that dangerous place to take time to take the blindfold off. It's a mistake to think you cannot take time for prayer because of a lack of time. The real reason is that you have an agitated mind and an unsettled heart. These can not be fixed by spending more time fretting; they can only be calmed by resting in Him."

Life can be a "jungle" – are you going into your daily jungle blindfolded?

August 23rd
Holding Hands

While sitting in a hospital waiting room the other day, I flipped through some magazines that were three or four years old. One of the oldest ones was from November a few years ago. The cover story for that issue was an article about celebrating Thanksgiving with children. The article told of a teacher who asked her class of first graders to draw a picture of something they were thankful for. Those first graders were all from inner-city Baltimore and they were from the poorest of the poor of the city so that their teacher wondered what those little ones would have for which to be grateful. As it turned out, most of those little students drew pictures of food, turkeys, and some drew pictures of their mother. The teacher was very surprised when one of the little ones drew a simple picture of a human hand.

The teacher asked the little boy whose hand it was that he had drawn. Before he could answer, the other students started to shout out whose hand they thought it was. One little girl shouted –"I think it's God's hand, 'cause he gives us everything!" Another student thought it was the hand of the guy who raised the turkeys. Still another kid thought it was the hand of the one who bought the turkey. Finally, when everyone had guessed whose hand the little boy had drawn, the teacher asked him whose hand it actually was that he drew. "It's your hand, Mrs. Sullivan," the little boy mumbled.

"Why did you draw my hand?" she asked him.

"Don't you remember when I cut my knee on the playground you put a bandage on it? Also, whenever we go out for our nature walks you make all of us hold hands, but almost always you hold my hand. I like it when you hold my hand."

This past week, many started back to school. Although it is not yet Thanksgiving, it's not too soon to take a few minutes to give thanks for all that going back to school provides for us. Perhaps this is a good time for us to recall that for every one of us there is someone who has been there to "hold our hand" in times of need, or simply to guide us. Maybe this is a good time for us to give thanks, too, for the opportunities that may come our way this year to offer guidance, comfort and yes, maybe even to "hold someone's hand."

August 24th
Just in Case

A philosophy professor was well known at the university as an outstanding teacher. His lectures were so popular that there was a waiting list for those anxious to sign up for every one of his classes. The most popular class was his Philosophy of Religion seminar. One facet of that seminar was a debate in which the professor took on the whole class to prove that belief in God was an utterly preposterous idea. Year after year, the professor won the debate with stunning arguments that completely destroyed his opponent's positions.

While driving home alone one evening he switched off the radio and continued on his way in complete silence, thinking about the debate he had just completed. When he came to a stop sign and brought the car to a complete stop, he heard a voice say clearly, "Why are you fighting me? I want to make you one of my best spokesmen, someone who will help to change people's lives, to save them and not destroy them."

The voice so frightened the professor that he stomped on the gas pedal and sped away from that spot as fast as he could. As he was racing down the road, he checked to see if he had really turned the radio off. He looked in the mirror to see if anyone was playing a joke on him from the back seat. Finally he pulled over to the side of the road and began going though the car to see if he could find the source of the voice. There was no one else in the car and there was no trick or practical joke. He was sure he had actually heard that voice with his own ears.

The following week his Philosophy of Religion seminar met again. With great enthusiasm, he told his students about his experience. Then he said, "I am here to tell you all that I was wrong. There truly is a God. He is real. I have heard his voice. He has spoken to me!"

What happened next was almost as remarkable to him as his own experience had been. His students listened to him for a short time. Then one by one, they stood and with amazingly sharp arguments, many of which were the professor's own past arguments, they pointed out that it was not probable that he had actually heard God's voice. Using psychological reasons, they explained away his experience as a kind of mental "episode" brought on by stress. They said that he had had a kind of auditory hallucination.

As the professor listened to his students' reasoning, he concluded that they were probably right, and that he had been under a lot of stress. In the end, the professor thanked his students for helping him. After class the professor made his way to the car, got in and started it. He sat for a moment in silence. Before he put the car in gear, he turned on the radio and turned the volume up as loud as his ears could stand. Just in case.

Have you ever "heard" God's voice? Have people tried to talk you out of your experience? Have you ever "turned the volume up" as loud as your ears could stand it, just in case God might speak again?

August 25th
Are You Ready?

A woman who worked in town would ride the bus each day to and from work. Because she enjoyed reading the Bible, she often carried it in her purse and sometimes would read it as the bus made its way through town.

One day as she was reading her Bible, the man sitting next to her tapped her on the shoulder and asked, "Do you actually believe all the stupid junk that's in that book?" The woman was a bit taken back by the question, and because she was a very shy person she said in a quiet voice, "I am a Christian and I guess I do believe what is here in the Bible."

"If you believe everything in the Bible, then explain to me how Jonah lived for three days inside the belly of a whale!" The woman timidly explained that she had no idea how that was possible, but that since it is in the Bible, it must be true and that she did, in fact believe it. The man became a little more belligerent and said, "Lady, you should know what you believe and be able to explain it – why can't you tell me?" The woman stated again that she wasn't sure how it was possible for Jonah to survive those three days in the belly of a whale, but that she would be sure to ask Jonah once she got to heaven. Then the man said in a rather angry voice, "Well what if Jonah didn't make it to heaven?"

She smiled and replied, "Well, then you can ask him."

Have you ever been in a situation similar to the one above in which someone begins to harass you about your faith? Or again, have you ever been afraid to share your faith because someone might question you or treat you badly? Have you ever been reluctant to defend your faith because it may not be popular or because people might talk about you behind your back? These are all reasons often given by people for not speaking about the Lord. Yet, did Jesus call us to be disciples and give us the Gospel just to keep it to ourselves? If all of us stayed quiet about the Lord, how would the Gospel ever get preached?

I think it was Mother Teresa who said, "Every day we are either called to be a missionary or we are in need of one." I think these words are so true, yet are we willing to be a missionary? This week you may find yourself in a situation which calls for a missionary to speak the truth about God's love. Will you be ready to be that missionary?

August 26th
They're Jesus to Us

A Princeton University alumnus, now a retired corporate executive, remembers his college days fondly and he often uses his experiences from those days when he is asked to give presentations. In one of his speeches, he recalls the time when he had been appointed as Resident Advisor (RA) in one of the freshmen dorms.

The dean of students had met with all of the newly appointed advisors and reminded them that the university was counting on them to take full responsibility for the good of the institution. Immediately after that meeting, the newly appointed Resident Advisor was rushing toward the campus library when he saw a crew of maintenance men raking and hauling autumn leaves. There were five men in the crew, but only four of them seemed to be doing the work. The fifth man appeared to be just standing there looking at the others and making comments to them.

"That guy is slacking off," he told himself as he walked over to the men. He then proceeded to tell the idle man to get to work and to start earning his pay. Feeling proud of himself, the new RA (resident advisor) walked away and went straight to the Dean of Students, who was at that moment walking across the campus, and said to him, "I just told that old guy over there to get to work and to start earning his pay."

"Oh, do you mean the old man with the grey hair?" the dean asked.

"Yes, that's him!" the student advisor replied. "He seems really lazy and not very smart either."

The dean cleared his throat and said in a serious tone, "I suppose I ought to tell you who it is that you just sent to rake leaves. The 'old' guy whom you thought was rather slow witted who is over there raking leaves with those workmen is Albert Einstein."

That retired executive said that he always concludes that story by saying "It's best to assume that everyone you meet might be an Einstein or a Picasso and they deserve your respect." Mother Teresa put it much differently: "Always show reverence and respect to everyone you meet," she said "Because to us Christians, every man, every woman and every little child we meet at any time truly is Jesus to us."

August 27th
We Are All God's Artists

I recently read a story from ancient India about a sculptor who was known far and wide for his life-sized statues of magnificent elephants. These elephant sculptures were so realistic that when anyone first came upon them, they believed that they were real elephants. One day a king who had heard of these wonderful works of art came to commission some sculptures for his royal palace. As the king walked around the elephant statues, he marveled that the artist had captured the true essence of elephants and he wondered how he could create such masterpieces. The king finally approached the artist and asked him the secret of his fabulous talent.

The artist thought about the question for quite some time, and then replied:

"Your majesty, with the help of many, many men I go out and quarry a gigantic piece of granite. You must know that stone is a living thing, which must be respected. So, when we have quarried the stone, I have it set here in my courtyard. I let it set there for a very long time, and every day I study it from every angle. I sit quietly in front of it, and allow no one to disturb my concentration. It may take days, or weeks, or even longer periods of time, but I do not proceed with the work, until I see something stirring within it. I begin to feel a 'presentment' in the stone that seems to want to come forward. That presentment becomes an outline and perhaps even a shape that makes itself known to me. It grows stronger and stronger until, Oh God, I can see it! It's a wild elephant, held captive much too long. Now it wants out. I then know that God has sent me, with chisel, hammer and mallet, to set it free. At that moment, I know that I am God's artist.

"This is just the beginning of my work, for the elephant has no life in it. From the moment I start to carve, I must breathe some of my life, my heart, and my soul into it – and when the work is finished, it is alive and it has the power to enthrall anyone who looks at it. This is the secret of my work as an artist."

Isn't that a wonderful story? It reminds us that we are all artists whom God has entrusted with chisels and hammers and mallets to set others free and to bring out the best that's in them. Imagine what kind of artist you are as a parent, tending to your children? Imagine breathing your life, soul and heart into them. Imagine what kind of artist you can be at work, school, among your friends or even with any person you meet, with every situation you encounter. Perhaps one of the secrets of life is that whether we know it or not, we are all God's artists.

August 28th
Stepping Away From Blame

Did you ever hear the story of what happened at a Japanese university when people started to mistrust one another? It is an interesting story in that what happened at that university can happen among any group of people. It was a case of people making assumptions about each other, of making judgments, and then finding themselves filled with anger, mistrust and suspicion.

At a small university in Japan, a period of unrest culminated with students going on strike, gathering in large groups and rioting. The groups began to throw stones at passing cars, to smash car windshields, to uproot signposts, and to burn tires in the streets. These students even built barricades across busy intersections, snarling traffic. Police had to be summoned, and much thought was given to calling out the army to restore order. The professors were not only afraid to teach class, but many would not even walk across the campus, so terrified had they become. There seemed to be no end to the unrest in sight.

Suddenly, in the midst of quite an uproar, the main door of the administration building opened. Out came the president of the university. Without any fear at all he walked right up to a very large crowd of angry students. He climbed on top of a wrecked car and began to speak in a calm, soft voice. At first, no one could hear him or even understand anything he was saying, but then those closest to him began to shout for everyone to be quiet. In a short time, silence fell and everyone turned to look at the president.

"Brother and sisters," said the university president, "our university is in utter chaos. Things here are in dreadful shape. Things are not going well at all. Somebody must be at fault. Somebody must be to blame for this!"

At this point in his speech, he produced a thin bamboo rod from his pocket and began to beat himself on his left hand so hard that his hand began to bleed. The bleeding increased as he continued talking.

The students at first were stunned and looked on in silence. They could not understand what was happening. As the president's blood began to flow more and more profusely, they began to protest. They shouted at him to stop. "You are not the only one at fault!" they shouted. They realized that he was not the only one at fault and that he was by no means the worst. They begged him to stop so that they could all talk things over.

The president stopped his attack on himself and said, "Brothers and sisters, if we would only come to know a simple truth. That truth is this: as long as we absolve ourselves of blame and simply accuse others for the chaos in our world, nothing will ever change. And this would be a great pity because when we do this we are adding to the world's chaos. Let us resolve to take responsibility for the wrongs we have done, to the chaos we have caused, and finally to change any of our bad behaviors. Also, let us remember that no people can live together in peace and good will if each person does not take the responsibility of contributing to the peace and good will of the group. None of us can absolve ourselves of the chaos we cause nor can we absolve ourselves of the duty to be peace makers and not peace breakers."

That Japanese university president has lots to teach us. He can serve as a reminder to us who follow Jesus that we are called to take some steps away from blame and creating chaos in our lives to taking some steps towards being instruments of peace in our families, our neighborhoods, in our parish and in our country.

August 29th
I Was Blind, But Now I See!

This past week, a friend of mine told me of an experience he had while traveling through the Atlanta Airport. He spoke of a rather long wait in the security line, a mad dash for the gate, and finally the relief of settling back in his assigned seat as the plane taxied down the runway. As soon as the plane was in the air, my friend opened a book he had been planning to read on his way to his business meeting only to discover he could not find his glasses. In an instant he recalled where he had left them. He remembered placing them in the container at security, but he did not remember ever picking them up after the container had been scanned. A sense of panic slowly set in. A flight attendant assured him however, that since he would be returning to the Atlanta airport later that day that he could check with security on his return and that they would likely have his lost glasses.

On his return, my friend went directly to security in search of his lost eyewear. The agent at the desk opened the desk drawer and grunted – "Help yer self!" The drawer was crammed with at least fifty pairs of eye glasses! My friend suddenly forgot what his frames looked like as he flipped through the assorted mass of frames. Finding about 10 pairs of glasses that might be his, he sat down and tried on each one to see if they brought his vision into focus. None of those ten pair was his. He said it took him about 45 minutes to finally find his own lost glasses.

If you wear glasses or contacts, you know what it's like to be without them. How much we rely on our corrective lenses to keep our vision good and to help us find our way through so many aspects of each day is truly amazing. Our faith and our relationship with God, like corrective lenses, are vital to our finding our way through life. Most of us are not always aware of how much our faith guides our way through each day. Yet, can you imagine trying to find your way through the maze of parenting, marriage, friendship, work, school, or life in general without God?

The next time you put your glasses on, recall how lost you would be without them but how much more so you'd be lost without the Lord.

August 30th
Will You Accept?

When Andrew Jackson was president, he was asked to give a presidential pardon to a man who had been in prison for 10 years for a very serious crime. Because the man had been an exemplary prisoner and because of some special circumstances, Jackson granted the pardon and ordered the prisoner set free. The problem was that the prisoner would not accept the pardon because he felt he was not pardonable. This raised a tough question for President Jackson, "Is a pardon that has been refused really a pardon?" he asked.

In the end, however, the prisoner continued refusing the pardon and would not leave until he had completed his full sentence. The result was that President Jackson finally withdrew the pardon and sadly let the prisoner have his way.

It's an interesting story isn't it? I can't imagine too many people in prison today refusing a pardon, but I do know lots of folks who have done something quite similar. Maybe even you have too.

Have you ever done something that you just could not forgive yourself for doing? I think many people have an easier time forgiving others than they do forgiving themselves. Again and again throughout Scriptures, God reaches out and forgives those who have sinned, yet we often cannot imagine that God would reach out to us. It is important for each of us to remember that, in His great love, God offers us the pardon, the grace of forgiveness. Yet the question remains, when God offers you pardon, will you accept it?

August 31st
Oaks Not Mushrooms!

Do you ever get impatient with how long some things take? I think we all do, but it is important for us to take some time to realize that important works take time. One of the great philosophers (and I can't remember which one it was) said, "A mushroom grows up over night, but it takes a decade for a great oak tree to fully develop."

Those are good words to keep in mind when you think of raising your children. How much of what you do and of what you teach your children appears to be "falling on deaf ears?" Yet, years from now, when your children are mature, you will see that your work has finally produced its fruit. It takes years for an oak to come to maturity, so too the work you do with your children. This is also true of marriage and close friendships; they take quite a bit of time to develop fully.

Teachers, social workers, counselors, and a host of other laborers cannot always immediately see the results of their work; they must patiently wait for the harvest that is to come. If you are feeling a bit discouraged because you do not see any results from the hard work that you are doing, perhaps it is because you are planting "oaks" and not "mushrooms." Patience ... let the seed you plant today come to its full stature before you make any judgment about the work of your life.

September 1st
Fitting Together

I remember a scene from a play that I saw when I was in college. The main character in that scene is a woman who has been through a lot in her life and has been completely overwhelmed by life's difficulties. The woman is sitting in her garden at a card table, working a jigsaw puzzle. She is very tense. Her hands begin to shake. She bites down on her bottom lip as she tries to force the pieces together. As she struggles, some of the pieces are knocked to the ground. She grows more and more agitated. Finally, she looks up at her daughter and says, "These pieces just don't fit together! The pieces don't fit!"

For so many people, the events of their life simply don't seem to fit together and they grow more and more frustrated and depressed. The play above reminds me of another story I once heard. It concerns a father working at his desk at home, frustrated and unhappy about the way things were going in the world and in his own life. He couldn't believe how unhappy he was and how life had seemingly dealt him an unfair hand. He realized that the world and its concerns and all of his personal problems and worries had left him exhausted and depressed. He felt little hope and was at the point of despair.

His little son was playing with some toys on the floor as his father was working on paying some bills. The young boy asked his dad for something fun to do. The boy's father went to a hall closet and found a small jigsaw puzzle of a beautiful and complicated picture of the earth from outer space. He handed this to his son as he said, "That ought to keep you busy for a while – the world's a mess, see if your little mind can figure out how to put that together!" The man went back to his bills and his worries and his brooding.

In about five minutes, the young boy called out to his dad, "Hey Dad,

I'm finished!"

"Oh come on. How could you be finished so quickly – you had to put the whole world together?" his father asked.

"Look Dad," the young boy said, "On one side is a picture of the world, and on the other side is a picture of a man. I just put the man together and the world fell into place."

All at once it dawned on the man that his son had given him the answers to his life's "puzzle." He knew he could do very little to change the world, but he could do something to change his own life, his heart, his attitudes. He immediately put his bills aside, got down on the floor and began to play with his son. "First things first!" he thought to himself. "If the world is ever going to be better, if I'm ever going to be better, it starts right here with me and my son."

What a wonderful place to begin again!

September 2nd
Come Away

Someone asked me this morning, "How's life in your world?" As I answered the question, I immediately began to think that while we all live on the same world, we all experience a world of our own.

The other day I caught an old rerun on TV of a Bill Cosby special in which he was interviewing little kids about their world and how they see things. So at one point he began to ask several children about their parents. One seven-year old was talking about his family. He was one of eight children. Cosby asked him what he thought his mother did every day. The boy thought for a moment and then said, "she gets us kids to where we are going, she gets dad out the door, she goes to work, she feeds the fish, she washes clothes, she makes us meals or takes us to McDonalds."

"Does she do anything else?" Cosby asked.

"Oh yeah," the boy replied. "She yells a lot!"

When the laughter died down, Bill Cosby asked the child one more question, "Of all the things your mom does, what do you think she wants to do the most?"

The boy's response was immediate: "I think she wants to go back to bed!"

Like that boy's mom, every one of us seems to be pulled in many directions, and also like that boy's mom, every one would love to go back to bed, but very few of us do so.

Precisely because of the unrelentingly hectic lives we lead, now more than ever, it is good for us to take to heart the invitation that Jesus made to his disciples, "Come away and rest for a while." Jesus knew how important rest is to a healthy physical life and for a healthy spiritual life as well. That is why we often find him going off by himself throughout the Gospels. When Jesus wasn't going off by himself for prayer and rest, he was asking his disciples to join him in doing so.

These last summer days that we have been enjoying may offer us a good opportunity to take Jesus' words to heart. Have you taken some time for yourself lately? If you have not yet made plans for a truly peaceful rest, why not do so now? It can make a world of difference both for you and for those you love.

September 3rd
Dangerous

Last Sunday before Mass I was talking with a group of our young people about what they had been doing this summer. What amazed me about them is that they all said the same thing: "Summer time is boring. Nothing ever happens. Everything is the same. There's nothing to do." I could certainly tell that the beginning of a new school year is not too far off. Complacency had set in for some of our young folk. Although that's understandable, it can be dangerous.

Those young people and their comments reminded me of a quote that I had just come across the day before in an article about the life of airline pilots and captains of cruise ships. According to the article, one of the gravest dangers for both groups of people is complacency. Their jobs can be so monotonous that they soon grow bored and finally complacent. They begin not to pay attention to the world and people around them. In fact, this is exactly the time when most accidents happen. Here's how one cruise ship captain put it,

> *"When anyone asks me how I can best describe my experience in nearly 40 years at sea, I merely say, 'uneventful, boring even.' In all my experience I have never been in any accident. I've seen only one vessel in distress in all my years at sea. I never saw a wreck and never have been wrecked nor was I ever in any kind of predicament that threatened to end in a disaster of any sort."*

Those words were written in 1907 by E.J. Smith, who became captain of a ship that was commissioned in 1911; the ship was named the Titanic. Perhaps it was because Captain Smith had never been in an accident, or even been associated with a rescue at sea, that he could not even imagine that anything could ever happen to such a great a ship as the Titanic. For him, life at sea was such a routine that he knew so well that he saw no need to be vigilant. He assumed that because he expected that nothing would happen, nothing could. And we all know how that turned out.

While Captain Smith's inability to foresee the possibility of a disaster or even a minor accident may seem strange to us, many of us are not unlike him. How many people do you know who could never in all of their wildest imaginings see anything ever going wrong in their marriage, only to discover their spouse suing for a divorce? Or how many parents have naively thought that their children certainly wouldn't drink and drive, only to find themselves bailing their child out of jail for DUI?

The truth about us human beings is that we can easily get ourselves into a routine that in a very short amount of time becomes a rut. That "rut" can lead to a sense of complacency or boredom, and that can lead to a disaster in our personal relationships. How easy it is for us to take each other for granted. How easy it is for us to assume that people know that we care for them and so we make too little an effort to express it.

Perhaps this may be a good time for us to realize that these "lazy days of summer" may very well be some very dangerous days indeed and that they require us to sit up and take notice. We must take the opportunity to pay attention to the world and people around us.

September 4th
Cool Clear Water

Recently I read a series of articles and essays by Sister Wendy Beckett, an Anglican contemplative nun, who some years ago hosted a PBS and BBC special TV series on art. Before she entered the convent, Sr. Wendy taught school in South Africa. Prior to the convent she lived a very active life and all of her experiences have shaped her insights.

I was struck by a brief paragraph she wrote about the importance of silence in everyone's life. She said that silence is something that everyone needs. She wrote:

> *Entering into silence is like stepping into cool clear water. The dust and debris are quietly washed away, and we are purified of our triviality. This cleansing takes place whether we are conscious of it or not: the very choice of silence of desiring to be still, washes away the day's grime.*

Isn't that a perfect image of what silence can do? I think that Sister Wendy is on to something. In another article she refers to a daily period of silence as a balm for all the troubles that can circle around us each day. She said that coming into silence and resting there for a while brings one to true peace.

I think it was St. Bernard who said that silence was like walking barefoot in ankle-deep cool water on a very hot day. It calms the mind, heart and soul. It restores us to peace. Do you need God's peace in your life right now? Why not take some time this week to step into the cool waters of silence?

September 5th
Transformation

In the 16th century, a young man named Francis Xavier became a student at the University of Paris. He was a popular guy and was well known as a talented athlete. He wanted to be a track star, to become famous and well connected. These were his simple goals for his life.

One of his friends at the university was an older guy who had been a soldier who had been severely wounded in a war and had not been the same since. This man's goals for his life were a bit different from Francis Xavier's goals. The former soldier had not come to the university easily. He had not had much of an education. In fact, he had no real schooling until he was 34, when he started grammar school. Eventually, he came to Paris in hopes of gaining some credentials so that he could pursue his goal of publicly talking about God.

He didn't wait until he had finished his university training to start talking about God, however. In fact, he talked of God all the time, especially with his friends. The one friend he spoke the most to was his friend Francis Xavier. He knew that Francis was going to do great things in his life because Francis was a man who was consumed by what he loved, sports. He warned his friend that he had to spend his life on something more valuable than a few athletic trophies or he would be lost. Finally he wrote down a verse from the Bible and gave it to Francis and asked him to read it over and over again for several weeks. The verse: "What does it profit a man to gain the whole world only to suffer the loss of his soul?"

Francis did as his friend had asked and it wasn't long before his heart was moved. Francis Xavier's life was never the same. It wasn't long before he was no longer consumed by athletic goals. Soon he was consumed by the Gospel. That one Bible verse brought about a transformation, one that eventually lead him to become the famous Apostle to the Indies and to Asia. He became the great missionary we know as St. Francis Xavier. His soldier friend we now know as St. Ignatius Loyola.

How do you think your life would be transformed if you read that simple Gospel verse over and over again for several weeks?

September 6th
Is it Time to Quit Trying?

Did you ever talk with an addict? In my ministry over the years I have talked to hundreds, I'm sure. A conversation I had with a college student who was addicted to marijuana was very interesting. It was interesting because after years of smoking the stuff, he had finally, as he put it, "lost interest in it." "I'm finally done with it, and I don't think I'll use it anymore," he said.

"How'd you come to this point?" I asked him.

"Well, I'd been smoking pot since I was a freshman in high school just about every day. I would try to quit, but then I'd get nervous or mad at someone and I'd be smoking again. I bet I tried to stop at least 20 times or more – but each time, after a few days, I'd be back at it. Then I got in trouble and had to talk with a counselor. When I told him how hard I had tried to quit pot, and that I could never quite do it, you wouldn't believe what he said to me."

"What'd he say to you?" I asked.

"He said, 'if you've been fighting it that long, maybe it's time to just quit trying.'"

"You mean I should keep smoking?" I said.

"No," he said. "Just quit fighting it. Your struggle against pot is keeping it strong in your mind. Rather than fighting what you don't want, why not cultivate what you do want. Meditate, pray, read good books and do good stuff. Be with people who bring out the best in you – do the things that make you really happy. If you screw up and smoke again, love yourself anyway. If smoking is not the best thing for you, it will fall away on its own, once you start doing what's best for you. Don't let smoking weed be such a major issue that it's all you think about."

"So, did you try what he said?" I asked.

"Yeah, I did, and I must admit that all I thought about at first was not smoking, so, guess what, I smoked! But after a while, I began to think about what that counselor had said. I began to concentrate on what I wanted out of life, rather than what I don't want. I kind of thought more positively and now I am done with pot."

As we continued to talk, I was impressed with how much wisdom that college senior had. It is true that sometimes the more we fight something, the stronger it seems to get. Jesus taught us that the best way for us to overcome darkness was not to dwell on the darkness, but to live in the light. In your own life, do you ever find yourself losing the battle in trying to overcome some addiction, bad habit or sin? Maybe, like that college student, it's time you just quit fighting the bad. Maybe it's time to cultivate what's good, and then there won't be room for what's been beating you.

September 7th

How Precious?

At a retreat a few years ago, I heard a monk describe our relationship with God as a newborn baby. He said, "If you were carrying a newborn in your arms, that baby would have your full attention. If you ran into someone on the street that needed a favor from you, you wouldn't just drop the baby on the sidewalk and do the person the favor they requested. If your car broke down, you wouldn't abandon the baby and walk off to find help. In each of these cases, you would have to solve the problem by taking the baby with you. The infant who is a precious little one would have your attention and you would give your heart to it, or it would never survive. In the same way, your relationship with God is precious, and you must protect it as you would a tender infant. You must give your heart to it or it will never survive."

Do you know what God said about you through the Prophet Isaiah? God said to each of us: "You are precious in my eyes and I love you!"

It is true – you are precious in God's eyes. If you examine the way you have been living your life, what answer would you give to this question: Is God precious in your eyes?

September 8th
Your Teachers

In a biography of Mother Teresa that I read some time ago, I came upon the story that the author said made a big impression on Mother Teresa herself.

According to the story, Mother Teresa and her Missionaries of Charity opened a home for children with disabilities. They asked the parents of children with autism, cerebral palsy, Down's syndrome and many other disabilities if they would like their children to live in the new home where these children would be loved and cared for. Because many of these parents could hardly feed their children and could only give them minimal shelter, most of them were overjoyed at the prospect of their children being well cared for. One mother, however was not pleased at all by the question. When she was asked if she wanted the Missionaries of Charity to take her child and to care for her, she looked at them in horror. She shook her head back and forth and said rather loudly, "NO! How could I ever give you this child of mine?" Then she went to Mother Teresa and said in a very calm whisper, "Oh Mother, I could never give you this child of mine – you see, she is my teacher of love. She calls out the love that's in me."

Perhaps in your life there is someone or some situation which is a big challenge to you, and maybe it is even overwhelming. Is it possible that maybe that very person or situation could be your teacher of love?

September 9th
Got Onions?

This week, while I was at the public library, I came across a little parable by the famous author Fydor Dostoevski. The story is entitled, *The Onion.*

Once upon a time there was a peasant woman, and a very wicked woman she was. One day she died leaving not one single good deed behind. The demons caught hold of her and plunged her into the Lake of Hades. Her guardian angel stood by and wondered what good deed of hers he could remember to tell God about. The angel mentioned, "Why, she once pulled up an onion from her garden and gave it to a beggar woman."

And God replied, "You can take the onion then, hold it out to her in the lake, and let her take hold of it and be pulled out by that good deed. If you can pull her out of the Lake of Hades, let her come into Paradise. But if the onion breaks, then the woman must stay where she is."

The angel ran to the woman and held out the onion toward her. "Come and catch hold," cried the angel. "I'll pull you out." And he began cautiously pulling her out. The angel had almost pulled her free when the other sinners in the lake, seeing how she was being saved, began clutching hold of her legs so they, too, could be pulled out. However, she was a very wicked woman so she began kicking at them.

"I'm the one to be pulled out, not you. It's my onion, not yours. Let go!" As soon as she uttered these selfish words, the onion broke. The woman fell back into the fiery lake where she remains today. The angel sat down and wept bitterly.

Dostoevski is said to have concluded the telling of the story by saying, "And so, whenever you are tempted to be selfish or self-centered, think of that onion and how it could have led our peasant friend right into heaven. Your onions too may one day lead you straight through the gates of Paradise."

Are there onions in your life?

September 10th
Finding Rest, Part 1

I read an article recently about a musician/composer, Oscar Castro-Neves, who writes musical scores for movies. He says that music is a very important part of a movie in that the music truly helps to tell the story so that the movie patron knows what's truly important. He says that in a dramatic scene, composers often gradually bring the music to a great crescendo, and then, in an instant, stop–rest–then silence. Castro-Neves explains, "Whatever is spoken on the screen in that silence is heard more clearly, more powerfully; those words are given an additional potency, because they are spoken out of the silence. When you listen to music, be sure to listen for the cadence of the rest."

To better illustrate what he meant, Oscar Castro-Neves closed by saying, "Do you remember Martin Luther King's most famous speech? Do you know why you remember it? You remember it because of the cadence of the rests: 'Free at last. (Rest) Free at last. (Rest) Thank God Almighty, we are free at last!'"

When you imagine Martin Luther King's famous speech, you can truly hear the importance of the "rest" in bringing home the message. If he had spoken those words as if he were reading a grocery list, no one would remember those words today. In a very similar way, "rests" are an important part of the spiritual life. Purposeful pauses throughout the day can help us find a better harmony with the people around us, with nature, and with God. When we pause to catch our breath, when we take a break from the hectic pace of the day, we can discover that silence has a kind of voice. It can speak powerfully. What it has to teach us can be missed if we don't establish a cadence of rests throughout our day.

September 11th

Finding Rest, Part 2

Almost everyone has experienced or at least knows about jet-lag. Doctors sometimes describe it as a psychophysical disorientation caused by traveling rapidly across several time zones. It can leave a person feeling exhausted, listless, confused, numb and "out of it." Another way of describing it is, "moving our bodies much too quickly through time so that when we arrive at our destination, we have to wait for our mind to catch up with us."

One truth about life today is that we all seem to be cramming too much into our days. We experience life at a hectic pace. Because of instant global news communications, instant messaging, cell phones, internet, texting, and ever newer, ever faster technologies, we seem to be pushing ourselves rapidly through time without ever getting on an airliner. As a result, we are not just experiencing jet-lag; we are afflicted with a kind of soul-lag.

I first heard someone use the word soul-lag a few years ago when I had a conversation with a Maryknoll missionary. He said that one of the first things he had learned from the villagers in his African mission was how to "tend to his soul."

He told of one of the women who had advised him that she was worried that he was going to "die on the inside" if he did not take time to tend to his soul. When he asked her what she meant, she went on to tell him that she had observed that he was always busy, always on the move, and always looking to the next task he had to do and not to what he was presently doing. "If you keep doing this," she said, "you will find no joy in life and no joy in your soul. And soon after that, you will inflict your misery on all those around you, draining the joy and life out of them too."

That Maryknoll missionary said that he became very frightened by the woman because she had so quickly seen right through him. He knew she was right. He knew he needed her help.

"Will you teach me how to 'tend to my soul?'" he asked the wise old woman.

Nodding, she told him that the first thing everyone must learn to do, and that he especially must learn to do, is to learn to ask for directions.

"This means you must start each day in silence and you must go outside and look at nature. You must first look up at the sky and see how high it is and how beyond you it is. If you rise before the sun, look at how far away the stars are and perhaps you will realize that the world is much bigger than your mind is. When you see how big the world is, recall that the one who made it is bigger still. Recall also that any of your thoughts and any of your plans are puny compared to the Creator's. Realize also that any worry you may have is tiny compared to the stars, the mountains, or the earth. The Creator who made the sky and the stars and the mountains made you too. The Creator knows you and did not intend you to just wander off on your own; you must ask the Creator for directions."

The missionary asked the woman to tell him more. Her reply was simple: "All you need to know right now is what I have told you, rise each morning in silence, let nature take you to the Creator, ask for directions."

September 12th
Finding Rest, Part 3

Some of my favorite verses from the 23rd Psalm are: "He makes me lie down in green pastures; He leads me beside still waters. He restores my soul." Those few lines from the world's most popular psalm sum up for me why it is so important for each of us to find "rest" throughout each day. Quiet, unhurried, restful time – Sabbath time really – is kind of an incubator for personal peace. The old saying "still waters run deep" is a reminder of why the Shepherd of Psalm 23 leads us to still waters – in order to bring our harried pace to a sudden stop so that we may be still and in that stillness go deep into our heart and soul.

In a sense, each of our days is like a glass of muddy water swirling around. As long as the water is moving and the dirt particles are moving about within it, the water is quite dark. If, on the other hand, you allow the water to quiet down and become very still, in a short period of time, the mud settles to the bottom, and the water becomes crystal clear. We, like that glass of water, are often whirling around with bits of tasks and duties and errands and worries and fears, and countless obligations and deadlines muddying our minds. But what would happen if we took a few minutes in the afternoon to simply stop, to allow all of the baggage of the day to settle to the bottom so that our mind and heart and soul could be crystal clear for those few moments?

I know what we would discover. We would find ourselves experiencing a kind of stillness that is more than just quiet. We would come to a sense of calmness, a feeling of what the Desert Fathers and Mothers describe as a "soothing ointment for the heart." That calming ointment is a true restorative unction that produces a very tiny whisper of peace. That bit of peace has within it a mighty power to change the world because one person carrying that little bit of peace can transform every person he or she meets, change the tenor of every conversation he or she takes part in, and calm the churning troubled waters of everyday life. The words of Psalm 23 are powerful words for us. I encourage you to pray these words right now so that you can begin the process of finding rest every day: "The Lord is my

Shepherd, I shall not want. He makes me lie down in green pastures; He leads me beside still waters. He restores my soul."

September 13th
The Road Ahead

Have you ever sat in a long line of traffic as road crews were making repairs? Who of us has not had that experience! As you think of yourself sitting in a long line of traffic getting more and more frustrated, imagine what it is like for the people who are actually working on the road. I saw a newspaper article a few weeks ago about a man who operates one of those huge graders. He said that it is amazing how angry people get at him and it is even more amazing the number of hand gestures and verbal attacks he has received over the years. To try to calm people down and to help them put life into perspective, that equipment operator had a large sign placed on the back and front of his rig. The sign declares: "The road to happiness is always under construction. Be patient with me, I'm trying to clear a path for you."

That sign made me stop and think. I began to think about where I am today and how I got here. I began to think of how throughout life, every one of us runs into "dead-ends" or "road-blocks" that can keep us from making progress. Then I began to consider how often there have been people in my life who, like that big equipment operator, have been there clearing a way for me. Those people, who I haven't always taken the time to even remember, much less thank, have been a real blessing for me.

Have you ever stopped to consider the number of people in your life who have "cleared the road" for you or even made a path for you to follow? I'm sure your life is filled with people like that. Have you ever stopped to consider that maybe God is calling you to be one of his "big equipment operators" whose job it is to clear the road for others?

September 14th
Polluting the Atmosphere

At a conference a few years ago, a Jesuit priest gave a talk about what he had learned among the Hindus at an Indian Ashram. The one story he told has stuck with me for quite a long time. He said that he had been sitting next to the swami who ran the ashram when a young man walked up and demanded to speak with the swami about conditions in the ashram. "You have some complaints that you would like to tell me?" asked the swami.

"I certainly do," said the young man. "

What concerns you so?" the swami asked.

"You must get rid of my roommate! He is a very heavy smoker and his smoking is polluting the atmosphere in my room. I am sure that someone as vile as he should never be allowed to live in this holy place. I demand that you kick him out of the ashram immediately."

The swami thought about this for a moment and then made this reply: "I will certainly ask your roommate to move out of your room. I will give him a room all by himself. Polluting the atmosphere with foul smoke is surely a most unfortunate offense. However, I must tell you that I am moving him for his sake – not for yours. You see, whereas it is an offense to pollute the air with smoke, it is far worse that you have polluted the atmosphere with your condemning judgment of the poor fellow. I have found it a good practice when I want to condemn someone for polluting the world to make sure that I, myself, am not guilty of some far more damaging pollution. Perhaps this can be a good teaching for you?" With that, the swami shook the young man's hand and sent him on his way.

That Jesuit priest concluded his talk by saying, "Would that all of us would keep tabs on what we put into the atmosphere around us."

So, what are you putting into the atmosphere of your family, among your classmates or among those with whom you work? Sounds like a good question for each of us to ask ourselves, doesn't it?

September 15th
Have You Been to the Dance?

Among the Hasidic Jews a tale is told of how a great rabbi was able to bring a local congregation into the presence of God Almighty. According to the story, this is what happened:

Word was sent to a small village in Russia that a great holy rabbi would be coming to visit them. This was a rare event, for rabbis seldom had the time to visit such a small, out of the way, unimportant little village. The people were very excited and so they all got together to determine what important questions they wanted the rabbi to answer for them. They all knew that the rabbi was said to be so holy that, like Moses, his face radiated the light of God's presence. Each person became quite worried that they may not have questions worthy of such a holy one.

When the holy rabbi finally arrived in the village they met him in the town hall and he could immediately sense the tension in the room as each person worried about their questions. The people were unsettled and were afraid even to look at the rabbi, thinking that their questions were unworthy and that they themselves were unworthy too. The rabbi said nothing at first; he just looked into their eyes, and began slowly to hum a rather haunting melody. It wasn't long before everyone began to hum along with the rabbi. The rabbi started to sing and the people began to sing along with him. Next he began slowly to sway and dance in a very solemn way. The congregation, mesmerized, began to dance along with him. Soon they became so absorbed by the dance, so enthralled by the singing, so caught up in the reverence of the rabbi that they were lost to everything in the world. Nothing that seemed to worry them before seemed so terrible now. Fears felt only a short time before the rabbi had arrived seemed to vanish. Hearts that had been full of division and bitterness were now made whole and filled with awe and peace. Healing abounded throughout the crowd.

After nearly an hour of dancing, all movement in the room stopped. There was a profound, peaceful silence. The rabbi looked into their eyes and smiled. All questions had vanished. They realized that the rabbi had danced them into God's presence. Then it dawned on them that the rabbi had actually danced with God. And slowly, slowly each one realized that they too had danced with God.

"What have we done?" they asked the rabbi.

"Prayed," the rabbi whispered.

September 16th
A Few Crumbs

In the Book of Revelation there is a rather famous passage from the third chapter which reads, "Behold, here I stand, knocking at the door. If anyone hears my voice and opens the door, then I will enter his house and dine with him, and he with me."

Most of the times when I hear that verse I am reminded of some of those storefront churches you often see in inner-city areas. They almost always have the same painting in the front window of Jesus knocking at the door. The other day, however, when I came across a little article I had stuck in a book, I thought of that same Bible verse in quite a different way.

The article was written by an 87-year-old woman named Sue Powers, who entitled her essay *"A Knock at the Door Can Mean So Much."* When I read her words, I immediately thought of Jesus knocking at the door. Take a few minutes right now and read her words:

"I remember how I thought of old ladies like me years ago – they were cute!

"In my family there were lots of great-aunts, shrunken and shriveled ladies living by themselves in tiny apartments, neat as a pin, with pretty teacups. They were so happy to see me when I bothered to drop by on my way somewhere else. That's how it was. I gave them the crumbs of my life, five minutes here and there. It never occurred to me that they were once just like me, that I could pull up a chair and get to know them as people, not just porcelain dolls.

"Now I'm a shrunken old lady stuck in my apartment, and I know how those aunts of mine waited and hoped for a visitor to brighten their day. My nieces do come over, but it's once in a blue moon. I never know when. A visitor is like gold. It's too bad we cannot understand this when we're young and can still do something about it."

I had often thought of Jesus knocking at the door, but I had never used that famous passage from the Book of Revelation to see that perhaps God could be calling us to be the one who knocks on the doors of those who may simply be looking for the "gold" of a friendly visit. Is there someone in your life right now who might be wonderfully fed by even a few "crumbs" of your life?

September 17th
Consider the Worm

I try to dedicate a part of each day to reading. I have found this practice to be not only an enjoyable way to relax, but it is also very enriching and I have learned so much over the years by doing so. Very often I come across some rather interesting wisdom that I jot down in a small notebook that I keep near me when I read. It was in the midst of my reading just yesterday that I came across a bit of wisdom in the form of a saying from ancient China. I've been turning it over and over in my mind ever since. Here's that saying: "Consider the worm; his day is just two feet long."

Ancient Chinese teachers used that expression to remind their students that every living creature has some very real limitations. These limitations are there for a purpose, and real wisdom lies in living within those limitations. They also taught that living as if one has few or no limitations is a short path to destruction. This got me thinking about the many people I have spoken with who are really distraught, frazzled and without any peace in their lives at all. Often these people will say things like, "I don't know why I am so restless, anxious, and unable to relax or get the sleep I need." More often than not, when they take a long, hard look at their lives they discover that they are not living within their natural limitations. We were not made to go at full speed 24/7. God made us to live differently.

I shared that Chinese saying with someone the other day. She had just come from her psychiatrist's office with a prescription for a new medication that was supposed to help her calm down. "So you are telling me that I am only supposed to live a 'two feet day'"? She asked.

"No," I said. "It's a worm that has a two-foot day. You are not a worm, so you have different limitations. Maybe your lack of calmness in your life is the result of trying to make your day too long. So, maybe those ancient Chinese teachers had something to offer you when they said, 'consider the worm.'"

If you step back and look at how you are living your life, are you trying to do too much? If you were to consider that the worm's day is only two feet long, how long should your day be if you want to live a peaceful, serene life?

September 18th
Looking for a Parking Space

Well, here we are already in the middle of September with most students back in school, and most families back in the old school-year routine of hectic comings and goings, meetings, activities. With vacation season over, most of us are back to the daily grind and on the run from one thing to the next. I've already seen people who look totally exhausted, and we've only just started! This set me thinking.

A few weeks ago I went to visit someone at Good Sam Hospital here in Cincinnati. As I looked for a parking space in the garage there, I had to go all the way to the very top of that building, and still no space. There was simply no space available. I even prayed to St. Anthony, who always finds me a spot, but to no avail. There was simply no space available at all. So, I circled all the way back down to the bottom of the garage and out onto the street.

As I went to find a parking place on the street, I began to think of those lines from Luke's Gospel, "And there was no room for them in the inn..." Once I found a place and began walking up to the hospital, I began to think of another quote about there being no room or space. It is a quote I have used often when giving retreats. It is from Anne Morrow Lindbergh's book, *Gift from the Sea*. It's a quote I use to remind people of the importance of allowing for some "open spaces" in your life, spaces that God can use to get close to us. Here's what she wrote:

> *"My life in Connecticut ... there is so little empty space. There are so few empty pages in my engagement pad, or empty hours in the day, or empty rooms in my life in which to stand alone and find myself. Too many activities, and people, and things. Too many worthy activities, valuable things, and interesting people. For it is not merely the trivial which clutters our lives, but the important as well."*

Our lives are so full of some important stuff, and some rather unimportant stuff as well. Perhaps this is a good time for each one of us, at the beginnings of a new school year, at the beginnings of a Fall season, to stop and make room, to find some open spaces, free from clutter, just for God and us to be together. Who knows, maybe God will come looking for a "parking place" in your life and you have just the spot ready for him.

September 19th
Call Waiting?

I got to thinking the other day about a prayer service I attended at the Cathedral years ago. All of the elements of that prayer service came flooding back to me in such vivid detail that I was really intrigued by it. It came to me in the middle of my prayer after communion at the 6:30 a.m. Mass one day this week. In the midst of that prayer, a very striking image of the burning bush surfaced in my mind's eye. As I was contemplating that image of the burning bush, I recalled the sermon given by a rabbi at that prayer service.

He had just read the account of Moses' experience of the burning bush, and the rabbi said that the burning bush was God's wake-up call to Moses. God had something he wanted Moses to do – so God used a bit of pyrotechnics to get his attention. After that, the rabbi told us, God and Moses got to know each other very well. Finally, the rabbi reminded us that we should all be aware of the fact that God sends a "burning bush" of some kind to each of us whenever he wants us to "wake up." Then, after a dramatic pause, he said, "I am standing here in your Cathedral, a rabbi, speaking to

Christians. Perhaps, I am your 'burning bush.' Perhaps I am your 'wake-up call.'"

Even now I can hear the echo of his voice as he spoke those words. They made a big impression on me. As those striking words came back to me this week, I renewed my own desire to be aware of God's call each day.

This week I want to encourage you to be aware of the "burning bushes" in your life. Is God sending you a wake-up call? Is there something that God is calling you to do? How will you respond?

In my continuing meditation on the burning bush/wake up call idea, I had another image – that of an alarm clock that keeps ringing to wake us up and we keep hitting the snooze button. That alarm clock, however, like God, is nothing if not persistent with its returning alarms. It keeps sounding until we respond. The good news is that when we do respond, like Moses, we and God will get to know each other very well.

September 20th

Losing a Job, Finding a Life

The other day I spent some time with several people who have lost their jobs. They spoke of the things they were doing to cope with the situation and also about how they were going about finding a new job. As we spoke about the emotional toll that such a loss can have, I began to think of something I had read about the famous American author, Nathaniel Hawthorne.

Just like the folks I had been meeting with, Hawthorne lost his job. He had worked for years in a customhouse which provided a good income for his family. One day he went into work only to discover that he was fired. He was at a loss and didn't know which way to turn. He was afraid to go home to tell his wife, Sophia, because he didn't want her to see him as a failure. Finally, he got up his courage and made his way home.

When he arrived, there was Sophia taking care of some correspondence. She knew as soon as she saw him that something was terribly wrong. She got up and went to him. He didn't know how to tell her so he just blurted it out – "I've lost my job. What are we to do?" He began to sob.

Sophia surprised him with, as he put it, "an exclamation of joy." She said, "Well, well, now you can do the one thing you should have done years ago – you can write your book!"

"That all sounds well and good," said Hawthorne, "and what shall we live on while I am writing it?"

To his amazement, she opened a drawer and pulled out a substantial amount of money.

"Where on earth did you get that?" he asked.

"I've always known you were a man of genius, and I knew that one day you would need the time to write your book. So, I have been saving money for years. There is enough money here for us to live on for maybe even a year."

Nathaniel Hawthorne did spend the next year writing. At the end of that year he published one of the great American novels, *The Scarlet Letter.*

Whenever he spoke of the day he lost his job, Nathaniel Hawthorne would always speak of the power of love and the encouragement it often gives. He would conclude by saying the greatest gift we can give each other is a word of encouragement.

How true that is! Is there someone in your life right now who needs a word of encouragement from you?

September 21st
Are You in a Hurry?

Researchers are discovering that one of the greatest threats to our lives and maybe even to society itself is speed. I don't think they are just referring to driving too fast; I think they mean much more than that. I think what they mean is that our world seems to be automatically increasing the speed at which we live life. It is as if we are all running on a treadmill that spins faster and faster. Or, as one reporter put it, "We've become a country of out-of-breath-red-faced folks, racing around with our hair permanently blowing back."

It appears that we all like going fast, and almost everyone hates to wait. But have you noticed lately how much we are increasing the pace at which we choose to live? The world is going faster and faster and we, in turn, are going faster and faster as well. The question we have to ask ourselves is, "How fast is too fast?"

Do you think there is a "speed limit" for life? Is there a point at which the pace of life becomes destructive? Well, researchers are beginning to think so. They indicate that we are moving too fast and doing too many things so that we can hardly take any of it in.

I read an article about just this thing a few weeks ago in which the author, Elizabeth Berg, wrote about how we hurry about and we force our kids to hurry about, too. She described going to a parent/teacher conference at her daughter's school. She explained, "We parents were asked to go to the auditorium to hear the school band play some Mozart before we met the teachers. The musical director was careful to point out that the piece would take only two minutes. I looked at the expectant kids seated behind him, waiting to entertain us with their very best. The director said what he did because he could see us tight-lipped parents looking at our watches. I was deeply ashamed, and I said to myself, "If we don't have time for children playing Mozart, what do we have time for?"

When speed and busyness are cranked up too much, we may well be exceeding life's speed limit. And what is the result of such a violation? It can be summed up in one word – fatigue. We are simply exhausted. We are afflicted with a kind of "hurry sickness" that keeps us filling our schedules with more and more things to do, and we insist on doing them at a frenzied pace.

What's the answer to all of this? I think one of the great prophets from the Old Testament has something to say that may help us to begin to get a grasp on it. Isaiah said this: "They that wait upon the Lord will renew their strength, and they will soar as with eagles' wings. They will run and not grow weary; they will walk and not grow faint."

I use that quote myself when I feel fatigued. I use it because I once read a commentary on it by a crusty old Baptist pastor who explained what he thought it meant. "It means," he said, "that you must ruthlessly eliminate hurry from your life. There is nothing else."

September 22nd
What a Blessing That Is

I saw a quote the other day that was very timely. I had just spent some time with someone who was contemplating ending his life. He had been very articulate in speaking about how unfair life seemed, about how he thought the world would not even be aware of his absence if he would bring his life to an early end, and about how he had never felt of use to anyone. I must say that our conversation was marked by great sadness. He was not at all happy, not at all able to feel any purpose or peace. He said he felt hollow, not only alone, but quite lonely.

We spoke at length and at the end of our conversation we agreed to meet again. Then, a day or two later, I just sort of stumbled on a little passage, a bit of writing from Mister Rogers, of all people. Here's what he wrote:

"If we're really honest with ourselves, there are probably times when we think, 'What possible use can I be in this world? What need is there for somebody like me to fill?' That's one of the deeper mysteries. Then God's grace comes to us in the form of another person who tells us we have been of help, and what a blessing that is."

As soon as I read that quotation, I had to send it in an e-mail to that sad man with whom I had spoken. He really appreciated it and said that he was going to post it on his refrigerator so that he could read it often. "I guess that's the kind of grace I need right now," he said.

I have spoken to that sad young man since then, and he is making slow and steady progress. We've spoken of the graces God is sending to each of us on a daily basis. "I hope I keep my eyes and ears open each day so that I don't miss any!" he said at the end of our last conversation.

"Me, too!" I said. "I need all I can get!"

Do you feel the need of God's grace? In your life right now, are you alert enough to be aware of the special graces that God may be sending your way through others? Then again, you may not only be someone who is given graces, you may be the one God uses to send graces to others. If you are awake enough to notice, what a blessing that will be for you, for those around you, and for all of us. As Mister Rogers put it, "What a blessing that is."

September 23rd
Boiling Waters

I was standing at the stove making a poached egg the other day when I thought of a diary I had read years ago of a young woman who had spent time living in Pakistan as a missionary.

One of the events she wrote about was the death of their six month old little baby boy. As she told of her deep sorrow, she recalled how kind the people in the village where they were living had been to them. She said that there was a kind old Punjabi who had heard about their loss and came to visit them. He told her that she and her husband must be very careful with how they handle this terrible tragedy. He said, "This kind of difficulty is just like being plunged into boiling water. If you are an egg, your affliction will make you hard-boiled, and unresponsive to others needs. If you are a potato, you will emerge soft and pliable, resilient."

I remember the prayer the young mother wrote in her diary – "Oh Lord, I am so overwhelmed by all that has happened to me, please let me be a potato!"

Are the things that are happening in your life making you hard-boiled or are you becoming a potato?

September 24th
Do You Have an Airman's Attitude?

I was talking with one of the students at St. Gabe's a few weeks ago. We were talking about school work and how sometimes it gets to be a bit overwhelming. The student finally summed things up by saying, "You know, sometimes I have so much school work to do, my mom has to do some of it for me."

When I asked her how often "sometimes" is, she said "Oh, about once or twice a week."

"Do you think that's a good thing for your mom to be doing?" I asked.

"Well, if she didn't, I would never get an education," the student replied.

As I recall that conversation, I am reminded of a truth that the Desert Fathers taught their disciples – you cannot be a disciple of the Lord by proxy. You have to put your own heart and soul into it. I remember a sign I once saw on the wall at a swim-meet which read: "There is no such thing as a correspondence course for swimming. If you want to learn to swim, you must get in the pool. Swimming requires getting wet."

Our walk with the Lord requires our full, active participation. C. S. Lewis said that before his conversion to true faith, his view of God was skewed. "I regarded God as an airman regards his parachute; it's there for emergencies, but he hopes he'll never have to use it." After his conversion, he walked every day in God's presence.

We all have to take some time to consider our own walk with the Lord, our own attitudes toward our faith life, and whether or not our view of God is like an airman's attitude toward his parachute.

September 25th
Best Friend

One of my friends, who is a missionary, told me about an experience he witnessed in one of the villages he had served in Africa. He said that in that particular village there was one village leader who refused to be baptized. Many of his family members had been baptized, and some of his friends and co-workers were baptized as well; but he refused it. No one could understand why he was so adamant about not being baptized. He was, after all, a very kind, caring and loving individual who said that he believed in Jesus.

After two or three years, the man came to one of the missioners and asked for baptism. The priest was surprised, to say the least, but he made all of the arrangements. On the day of the man's baptism, the priest asked him why he waited so long to be baptized.

"When my family and some of my friends and fellow workers began to be baptized, I was amazed at their enthusiasm," the man said. "But I wondered if baptism would make any difference in their lives, so I decided to hold back, just to see. Today I want to tell you that I want what they have. They seem to be best friends of Jesus and they act the way I think Jesus' friends ought to act. If baptism did that to them, then I, too, want to be baptized. I, too, want Jesus as my best friend."

How would you describe your relationship with Jesus? Is He your best friend? Are you His?

September 26th
To See the Way You See

A couple of weeks ago I was flipping through some TV stations looking for something to watch when I happened upon one of those talk shows that seem to be on every station. I can't even remember who the host was, but there was a remarkable man being interviewed. The man was 90 years old and had been blind from birth. What struck me about the man was the smile that seemed to never leave his face. The man said that he considered himself to be one of the luckiest people alive. He went on to recount the various blessings he had received in life and how they had made his life really full. As the host was bringing the interview to a close, he asked one final question, "Do you regret having had to live your life as a blind person?"

"Oh, no way!" the blind man replied. "I have had a wonderful life, and I don't really feel that my physical blindness has caused me to miss a thing. On the other hand, I know many sighted people who are as "blind as bats" when it comes to truly seeing life as it is. My physical blindness has made me develop a whole new way of 'seeing.' I see by listening. I listen when people speak not just to what they are saying, but I, because I am not distracted by physical sight, can listen for what they are not saying. I am 'tuned in' to various changes in the voice, and slight modifications in tone that help me to hear and to see them in ways that sighted people cannot. I am blessed with an ability to truly hear what people are saying. No, I don't for one minute regret that I am not physically sighted. I may not be able to see the way you do, but I can surely see in completely other ways. My 90 years of life have been very full. And one more thing, do you know what really gives me hope and makes me excited?"

"What gives you hope and makes you excited?" the host asked.

"Hope for me is contained in this truth: When I finally close my eyes in death, and then once I'm on 'the other side' I open them again, do you know who I will be looking at when these old eyes are made new? Why, the first person I will see is Jesus himself! And that fact gives me all the hope and joy that ninety years of life could never contain. Yep, when these old eyes are finally opened, it will be Jesus looking back at me. Doesn't that thought just get you excited?"

The host of that talk show concluded by saying, "Wouldn't it be great if we would all see the way you do!"

September 27th

More Than a Few Words

There are many stories that come from our country's pioneer days. One such story comes from a journal a young man of those days kept about his adventures.

According to that journal, in one of the small settlements, a family lost all of their possessions to a fire. Their modest little house and all its contents were completely consumed by the flames. In response to this tragedy, the people, who were quite religious, called for a prayer meeting in behalf of the stricken family. As the people gathered and began to pray, a young boy rode up driving a team of horses pulling a wagon full of supplies – there were canned goods, staples, building materials, clothing, seed, animal feed and lots of other needed goods. The boy said, "My father said he could not make the meeting and that he wasn't very good at praying, so he sent this load of 'prayers' and he hopes this will be of some help."

The young man who kept the journal made one comment as he concluded the story. He wrote: "I guess prayer involves more than saying a few words."

September 28th
Some Day

Henry Kissinger, the Secretary of State during the Nixon Administration, was part of a panel discussion at Harvard University when he was asked to speak on what he had learned about life from his many years in public service. He had replied that he never stopped being amazed at the surprises that life brings each day – new challenges and new opportunities. The students listened to his response, then there was a pause while everyone seemed to be considering Mr. Kissinger's remarks. Finally, one student rose and asked the Secretary of State, "Sir, among all of the 'surprises' that life has brought you, what has been the biggest surprise so far?"

Henry Kissinger laughed and without too much hesitation said, "What has most surprised me about life is how much too quickly it passes. It is as if it slips through your fingers and is gone."

How true those words are. Perhaps, a good exercise might be to take a few minutes to actually do the good, thoughtful things we plan to get around to some day.

Why not let today be that "some day"? Life passes much too quickly to put it off any longer.

September 29th
Stupid Bears

"Don't Feed the Bears."

If you have ever been out to one of the National Parks you have probably seen signs like that quite often. I always assumed that the signs are posted to protect us tourists from being mauled by the big animals, but this is not necessarily the case. I was out West last year giving a retreat near one of our National Parks, where I had a conversation with a park ranger about bears. She told me that the "do not feed the bears" signs were posted more to protect the bears than they are to protect humans.

"Do you mean that the food tourists feed to the bears harms the bears?" I asked.

"No, that's not the reason," she replied. "It's like this. Each Fall, when the feeding tourists have long since departed, the park service has to spend a great deal of time carrying off the remains of dead bears who had become so dependent on tourists for their food that they no longer were able to gather food for themselves. When tourists continually feed the bears, they can, ironically, starve the bears to death. A bear too lazy to bother to search for food soon grows weaker and weaker until it finally dies."

I was thinking of my conversation with that park ranger one day this past week when I was told by a family member that he doesn't go to Mass because he doesn't "get anything out of it." I asked him if he had ever seen those "Don't feed the bears" signs. Then I went on to explain that he couldn't expect to have a deep relationship with God if all he ever did to develop it was to go to church, arrive late, sit in the back, not sing, not really listen and then leave early complaining all the while that he doesn't get anything out of it. "Like the bears," I said, "you'll starve to death if you just hang around waiting for someone to hand you spiritual food. If you put nothing into it, you'll get nothing out of it."

Smiling, he looked at me and said, "That makes way too much sense. I think I would prefer you just to tell me I'll go to hell if I skip Mass!" Then he added, "Stupid bears!"

September 30th
True Serenity

I was struck on how the news of the death of Pope John Paul II was being reported.

Many of the news commentators were surprised that the Pope was so serene as he faced death. In fact, one reporter asked one of the cardinals why he thought the Pope could be so serene as death approached. The cardinal didn't hesitate to respond. He simply said, "I have known the Pope for many years. He was serene about life. As he approached life he knew that it was all in God's hands, and he had placed his whole life in God's hands. So, he was serene, not just about life, but about death too. It is all in God's hands and what better hands can there be?"

This reminded me of something I had read written by a French soldier by the name of Nicholas Herman. He had seen much of the ugly side of humanity and it had led him to search for God. Eventually his search for God convinced him to leave the military life for the life of a Carmelite monastery. After years in that monastery, many years spent in deep prayer, he wrote a book. In his book, that soldier, who was now called Brother Lawrence, wrote about how anyone can find God's presence anywhere, and in so doing one can enter into a great serene tranquility.

Brother Lawrence, the once-great soldier, had been assigned to the kitchen at his Carmelite monastery. Because the work of the kitchen was so demanding, he often was unable to join the rest of the monks in the church for prayer. His abbot asked him how he maintained his prayer-life. Brother Lawrence replied, "The monastery kitchen is my Cathedral. With me, the time of business does not differ at all from the time of prayer, and in the midst of the noise and clatter of my kitchen, amidst all of the heat and steam, amidst all of the pots and pans, and while several people are at the same time calling out for different things, in the midst of all of this – God comes and possesses me with such a great tranquility and serenity that I feel as if I am on my knees before the Blessed Sacrament amidst a cloud of incense."

I think Pope John Paul II discovered the same thing that Brother Lawrence had discovered way back in 1666, namely, how near God is to each of us. Awareness of God's nearness leads to serenity. My prayer for you is that you become more and more aware of God's nearness and thus come to experience true serenity.

October 1st
Let Go and Let God Take Care of Us

A man had a conversation with God one day, and in the course of that conversation, the man asked, "Lord God, how long is a thousand years to you?"

The Lord answered without even blinking His eyes and said "To Me, a thousand years is just a second."

Well, Lord God," the man asked, "how much is a million dollars to you?"

The Lord God just shrugged His shoulders and said, "Oh, I'd say just about a penny."

With an idea in his mind, a gleam in his eye and a broad smile across his face, the man asked one more question of God. "Lord God, can I have ... well, uh ... how about giving me one of your 'pennies'?"

To that question, the Lord God replied with a grin on His face, "I'll give it to you in just one of my seconds!"

Have you ever prayed for something, only to find that you seem to be waiting an eternity for God to respond? Waiting for God to act can be a difficult thing for us. We pray and we pray and it seems like God doesn't hear us. But God does hear us. The Bible teaches us that God's time and our time are not always the same. We have to put our lives completely in God's hands and trust that He will take care of us. The problem for us very often is that we can't wait that long. Like the story above, it feels like "a million years" have to elapse before God acts.

Jesus promised his apostles that after He returned to the Father, He would send the Holy Spirit to them. I'll bet those days of waiting seemed like an eternity to them, but Jesus did send the Holy Spirit, and the Church was born. Jesus promised also to be with us in all our trials and tribulations. It may seem like an eternity, but God does care for us, and God does respond.

October 2nd
Jesus Gives Peace That the World Cannot Give

I was at a wedding reception recently when a man I had known since I was first ordained began to talk to me about how successful he had been investing in the stock market. He told me that he had never imagined that he would be as wealthy as he is today. I asked him if his success had changed his life in any way. He told me that in the past, he had spent a lot of his time just "hanging out" with friends, but now he spends most of his free time on the Internet checking the market, looking for new investment opportunities. That was the end of our conversation, as other people joined us at the table and changed the subject. On my way home, I recalled our conversation, and it reminded me of a story I had read some years ago. It went like this:

There was a man named Jeremy, who most people thought was a rather selfish, self-centered person. He realized one day that he could greatly increase his income if he took some time to study the stock market. So every day he spent hour after hour studying the financial pages of the newspaper, sought the advice of experts, and became completely engrossed in the financial markets.

One day, as he was reading the newspaper, he said aloud to himself, "What I wouldn't give to see next year's edition of this newspaper right now! Then I'd make a real killing!" The words were no sooner out of his mouth than there was a large explosion, and a puff of smoke filled the room. As he looked up, he saw a genie walking toward him who handed him a newspaper and then disappeared. As soon as he got over the shock of the explosion, he realized that his wish had been granted. When he looked at the newspaper, he saw that it was dated exactly one year hence. He quickly turned to the financial pages to see how his stocks would be doing in a year. He also noticed which stocks he needed to buy immediately and which he needed to sell.

He was overjoyed because he knew that he could end up a millionaire, so he went out into the New York streets, hailed a taxi, and set off for his stockbroker's office. As he was riding along reading the newspaper, he came to page three and saw a photograph, right at the top of column one. It was his photograph, and beneath that photograph was his obituary. Suddenly the prospect of growing rich lost all of its appeal, for what good is millions of dollars to a dead man?

In the Gospels, Jesus tells us to render to Caesar what is Caesar's, and to God what is God's. The most important part of us, our heart and soul, is meant to belong to God. What Jeremy teaches us in this little story is how easy it is for us to give our heart and soul to that which cannot give us true happiness in this life, and neither can it assure us happiness in the next. We belong to Jesus, and only a life lived for and in Him will bring us true peace of heart, and real happiness.

October 3rd
Is God "Locked Out" of Your Life?

I wonder if this has ever happened to you. I was driving down Glenway Avenue running some errands when I remembered that I had forgotten my billfold. I turned around and headed back home, parked the car in front of the rectory, locked my car doors, went to open the front door of the rectory and then I realized that I had left my keys in the car – in the LOCKED car! I thought, "No problem, I always keep an extra key in my billfold in case I lock myself out of the car." Then I realized I didn't have my billfold! I was locked out of my car, locked out of the rectory, the secretaries had gone home for the day, and no one was answering the door. To top it off, it was raining as it did in Noah's time. Being locked out is a terrible feeling. It forces you to simply wait for help, and waiting isn't always easy.

Have you ever felt "locked out" by God? Have you ever felt that you were banging on God's door and He didn't answer? I have. I can think of many times when I've been praying for someone and it seemed as if God had locked the doors and left me on the outside, looking in. I'm sure you can think of times in your life when you've felt this way as well. It is a terrible feeling.

I was thinking about that this past week when it dawned on me that God probably feels that way about us at times. I'm sure that there have been times in my life when I was so busy or so preoccupied with things that there was no room even for God! Sometimes I might even purposely lock God out because things are not working out the way I want them to work out. At other times, I might lock God out because I'm simply too tired.

It's usually around the time that I've locked God out of my life that a particular Bible verse comes to mind. It's found in the Book of Revelation, and it always brings me back to reality: "Here I am! I stand at the door and knock. If anyone hears My voice and opens the door, I will go in and eat with him and he with Me." (Rev. 3:20). When I read that verse, I realize that God must be hungry and wants to eat supper with me. I'd better open up!

Do you think that God ever feels "locked out" of your life? If you've locked God out, you can be pretty certain that it won't be long before you hear a knock at the door of your heart, and a gentle invitation to supper. Why not take God up on the invitation?

October 4th
How Do You Respond to Difficulties?

I read recently about twin boys who were raised in the home of a father who was both an alcoholic and a drug addict. As they grew up, the boys went their own ways to start their families and begin their careers. At about this time a university began to study the effects of alcoholism and drug addiction on their families, and so the two brothers were interviewed by a research team of the university. The research team made an interesting discovery. The team discovered that one boy had become an alcoholic; the other brother didn't drink at all. The research investigator asked the first brother, "Why do you think you became an alcoholic?" Then he asked the second brother, "Why do you think you are a teetotaler?" To the researcher's surprise, both brothers gave exactly the same answer, "What else would you expect when you've had a father like mine?"

Each of us has the opportunity to choose how we are going to respond to the difficulties or problems that life sets before us. We can choose to respond in a negative way or in a positive way. It's really up to us.

I am reminded of a billboard that the Knights of Columbus sponsored which shows Jesus hanging on the cross, giving His life. At the bottom of the image are three simple words, "IT'S YOUR MOVE." How will you choose to respond to the love of Jesus?

October 5th
Happiness Comes From Helping Others

What would it take to make you happy? Pause right now and give yourself a few moments to answer that question. Consider what has made you happy in the past and then consider what makes you happy now. Is there a difference in your answers? Has your life experience changed your opinion of what brings true happiness?

I was in the library this past week browsing through a book about George Burns. Part of the book was an interview with George when he was 95 years old. He was asked if he was happy. Without hesitation he said "yes" and then went on to say:

> *"If you were to go around asking people what would make them happy, you'd get answers like 'a new car, a bigger house, a raise in pay, winning a lottery, a facelift, more kids, less kids, a new restaurant to go to'—probably not one in a hundred would say 'a chance to help people'; and yet that may bring the most happiness of all. I don't know Dr. Jonas Salk, but after what he's done for us with his polio vaccine, if he isn't happy, he should have his brilliant head examined. Of course, none of us can do what he did. I know that I can't do what he did, he beat me to it! But, the point is, it doesn't have to be anything extraordinary. It can be working for a worthy cause, performing a needed service, or just doing something that helps another person. That's happiness."*

So, after having read George Burns's comments on happiness, what would it take to make you happier? While many people might begin by listing all kinds of material things, most of us know that things don't make us happy. Life experience teaches us that it is being willing to take the chance to help people, to risk reaching out beyond our comfortable limits that makes us truly happy. Whether we are Dr. Salk, George Burns or a less well-known person, each one of us has many opportunities each day to reach out to others and thereby discover true happiness.

I remember one of my professors in the seminary saying with a broad grin, "You should do something every day to make other people happy, even if it means leaving them the hell alone! But whatever you do, don't let a day go by without some effort to help others."

October 6th
Growth Comes From Taking Risks

Recently I read an article on the life of Will Rogers in which the story was told of the time when Will thought his life was at a crossroads. He was terrified because he knew he had to make some changes and those changes were going to be very difficult. He sought out one of his best friends and had a long talk with him. At the conclusion of their discussion, Will asked his friend why he should "go out on a limb to make all of these changes." His friend thought for a moment and said, "Will, if you are ever going to be truly happy, you have to risk making changes. You have to 'go out on a limb' because that's where the fruit is." Will Rogers said that the advice his friend gave him that day was the best advice he had ever received, and he thanked God for it every day. "The only way to grow," he said, "is to risk making changes. You'll never get to the fruit unless you are willing to crawl all the way out there on that limb!"

The Holy Spirit pours out over each one of us many, many gifts. They are given to us, but we, like Will Rogers, must come to realize that these gifts require us to take some risks. We cannot expect to experience the gift of courage or fortitude or faith if we are not willing to "crawl out on a limb" to take a risk.

Perhaps you, like Will Rogers, are becoming aware of the need to make some changes in your life, to live your life differently. Today is a great opportunity for you to take the risk to begin to make those changes. The Holy Spirit asks two things of us – first, that we be open to the gifts, and second, that we be willing to take the risk of using those gifts.

Are you ready to "crawl out on a limb" to accept the "fruits" of the Holy Spirit?

October 7th
Filling In

A few years ago, nine variously handicapped people climbed Mount Ranier. One of the mountain-climbers had a prosthetic leg, two were deaf, one suffered from severe epilepsy, and five were blind. Although Mount Ranier is 14,000 feet high, these nine people successfully made it to the top and back down again.

Asked how in the world they had been able to do such a thing, one of the blind members of the team said, "We had a lot of help from each other on the trip. No one can conquer a mountain alone."

Another member of the team said, "Once we all admitted that we had some limitations, we each promised to 'fill in' for each other whatever each one needed. With all of us 'filling-in' for each other, we made a great team."

Finally, one of the team members said, "Climbing a mountain or living life—we all need each other because whether you realize it or not, every one of us has limitations and because of that you can't negotiate mountains or life very well on your own."

It seems to me that those mountain climbers have much to teach us. How often have you felt overwhelmed and defeated by life? How much of your being overwhelmed and defeated was due to trying to take on heavy burdens alone? Every one of us faces difficulties, yet we do not have to face them alone. Admitting our limitations and reaching out for help are important steps in overcoming mountain-like difficulties. Sometimes we need others to "fill in for us" and some times we are needed to "fill in" for others, but "filling in" is what levels even the highest of mountains.

October 8th
God Is Always Eager to Take Us Back

There is an artist in China who recently became a Christian. In thanksgiving for the gift of faith, he decided that he would paint a picture for the local church. He went to ask the priest what kind of painting he would like. "Paint a picture that tells us how much God loves us – we all need to know how loved we are," said the priest.

The young artist went away for two weeks of prayer to consider how to best capture God's love in a painting. After these two weeks, the artist set to work. In a relatively short time, he had completed the painting and asked the priest to look at it. When the priest saw the painting, he was pleased. It was a depiction of the parable of the prodigal son. It showed the son far off in the distance and the father running toward him with his arms outstretched to welcome his son back. The priest smiled and said it was a lovely painting, and he would be happy to have it in the church. The painting was placed near the sanctuary of the church where many parishioners admired it and said their prayers before it.

One day, not long after the painting had been placed in the church, the priest noticed an elderly woman standing in front of the painting laughing. He couldn't believe that the painting would evoke laughter, so he went to investigate. "Why are you laughing at such a beautiful painting?" he asked.

"Well, it is so much the way God has been with me throughout my life. Every time I mess up in my life and do such terrible things that no one in their right mind would take me back, God does! Not only that, God always seems to rush in to take me back. Look at this painting – the father in this painting is in such a hurry to go out to meet his son that he has his shoes on the wrong feet! Now that's a true picture of God's love!"

October 9th
Finish the Work That He Began

In 1922, the famous composer of operas Giacomo Puccini was told that he had terminal cancer. He was shaken by the news as he began to realize that his time on earth was drawing to a close. One of his big concerns was that he was in the middle of writing an opera which he called Turandot and he was unsure whether or not he could finish it. So Puccini gathered all of his students together and told them, "I know I am going to die; if I don't finish Turandot, I want you to finish it for me."

When Giacomo Puccini died a short time afterward, his students began studying the opera so that they could fulfill his wish. In 1926, one of his brightest students, Arturo Toscanini, conducted the premiere performance of Turandot. The audience was thrilled to hear such beautiful music and they were held in rapt attention. Then, almost without warning, the music came to an abrupt end. Everyone in the audience sat up straight and looked around asking what could be wrong. Toscanini turned to face them, and with tears running down his face said, "Thus far my Master wrote, but then he died..." There was a gasp from the audience as everyone felt their emotions well up. Silence filled the opera house. Then Toscanini smiled and said, "But we, his students and his friends, have finished the work."

When the opera ended, the audience was on its feet giving thunderous applause.

We Christians know that our Master expects us, His students and His friends, to do what Puccini's students and friends did ... finish the work that He began. Every time we reach out to others, every time we listen to someone who is in need of our love, every time we take care of the "least ones," we complete the work of our Master.

October 10th

Conversations That Lead to God

St. Teresa of Avila taught her sisters that one sure way to deepen your spiritual life and development is to engage in what she called "meaningful conversation" with someone you love or with a dear friend. She said that meaningful conversation has the power to open one's soul so that God becomes almost touchable.

I was thinking about that earlier this week when I came across several quotes from Anne Morrow Lindbergh that say pretty much the same thing. She told a group of women gathered for a conference that "good communication, a good conversation with a friend is as stimulating as a good cup of black coffee and just as hard to sleep after." And in an interview with a journalist, she talked about how she lived for good conversation. She said, "A simple enough pleasure, surely, to have breakfast alone with one's husband, but how seldom do married people achieve it." Lindbergh went on to say that she grew the most in her life whenever she took the time to have deep, meaningful conversations with dear ones.

In your life right now, do you ever take the time to have such conversations with your spouse or with good, close friends? If you do, you already know how enriching such conversation is and how it really does open up a deeper spiritual side of life.

October 11th
Four Words

Each year around this time we get that yearly opportunity to "fall back," to get an "extra" hour of sleep as we turn our clocks back one hour ending Day Light Savings Time.

Every year as I turn my clocks back an hour, I have some recurring thoughts. I think of how wonderful it would be if we could "fall back" more than an hour. Wouldn't it be great if we could "fall back" to a time when we could "un-do" or "do-over-again" some part of our life? For most of us, it is only hindsight that has shown us how often we have missed great opportunities; and "falling back" would be a great way to take advantage of them, wouldn't it?

I recently spoke with a man who works as a college admissions director. Every day he deals with folks who regret the fact that they had put off their college education. To illustrate his point, he told me about one of his high school classmates who told him that now at 55 years of age she wished she had gone to college, but thought it impossible to remedy.

She said, "Joe, I'm 55 years old. Because I work full-time, I'd have to go to school part time and it would probably take me five years to get a degree. Why, I'd be sixty years old by the time I graduate! I feel so stupid to have missed the chance to get an education. My life would have been so much better had I gone to college. But there's nothing I can do about it now."

I asked Joe how he'd responded to her.

"I just asked her one question," Joe said. "I asked her how old she would be in five years if she didn't go back to school. Then I said there were four words I wanted her to post on her refrigerator."

"What words did you ask her to post?" I asked.

"Now is the Time!"

"Why would you want her to do that?" I said.

"Because those four words have kept me from missing important opportunities that have come my way, and I think those four words would help her take the next steps she needed to take," he said.

I don't know if his high school classmate took his advice or not. I don't know if she has enrolled in college yet or not. I do know that those four words are some good words to consider as I turn my clock back an hour. Those words remind me that I need to pay attention to the opportunities that are before me right now. Otherwise, next year at this time I may be wishing to "fall back" further than one hour.

October 12th
Harnessed

Earlier this week I came across a quote which I had scrawled across an old notebook years ago in college. I had written the quote down because I had heard it in a lecture and I didn't want to forget it. The professor giving the lecture was quoting the famous Jesuit priest-scientist, Pierre Teilhard de Chardin. I was so taken by the thought that I jotted it down with a big magic marker. When I read those words again this week, the same enthusiasm for them that had struck me way back in college was with me again. Here are Chardin's own words:

> *"Some day, after mastering the winds, the waves, the tides,*
> *and gravity, we shall harness for God the energies of love,*
> *and then, for the second time in the history of the world,*
> *we will have discovered fire."*

What does it mean to "harness the energies of love?" Well, in my college days, I thought that it meant to go out and do extraordinary things, or to do wildly heroic deeds, all in the name of love. I pictured in my mind the stories told of soldiers in war-time throwing themselves on hand grenades to save their fellow soldiers. If not some brave soldier, I thought harnessing the energies of love had to do with missionaries going off to the deepest jungles of Africa or Asia, or maybe it meant to join up with Mother Teresa in Calcutta. That's what I thought it meant back in my younger days.

Today, however, I think "harnessing the energies of love" means something maybe not as mega-heroic or half way around the world as above, but truly heroic nonetheless and a lot closer to home.

Some of the most important harnessing we do is often neither dramatic nor memorable. Sending a card to someone we know who is a bit down and needs a boost, calling a shut-in who is lonely, offering to baby-sit for parents who need a break, or running someone who can no longer drive to the doctor's, these are all simple, yet rather profound ways of "harnessing love." So is taking the time to tutor or teaching people to read. There are as many ways to "harness love" as there are people who see a need and reach out to meet that need.

At times, the world can seem to be a very dark place, but light does begin to shatter that darkness when, as de Chardin put it, "we harness for God the energies of love."

October 13th
God's Rhythm

One time Louis Armstrong was asked by a college professor of music to write a definition for "rhythm." Mr. Armstrong thought about it for a bit and then said, "Rhythm is what, if you got it, you don't need a definition for it; and if you don't got it, no definition is any good anyway!"

While this may be a bit of an unconventional definition, it sure does express a truth about rhythm. I think that this would also be a good definition for what it is to experience God in your life. Once you have experienced God, you can attempt to explain Him, and you can even give a few adjectives, but they all will fall short of the real experience. Once God takes hold of your life, you are never the same. The most important thing you can do is to be open to God in your life and allow God to move into you. Why not take a few moments right now to pause, to take some time to discover or even to rediscover the great things that God can do for you? Maybe you'll become aware of God's rhythm in your life.

October 14th
Time Well Spent

The apostle Paul was a wise man who counseled many people through his letters. I think it is in his letter to the Ephesians that he gives some very important advice. In that letter he says, "Look carefully, then, how you walk, not as unwise people, but as wise ones, making the most of the time ..."

Perhaps now is a good time for us to ask ourselves whether or not we are making the best use of our time. Because time is such a precious gift we ought to truly treasure it. There is no power on earth that can replace an hour of lost time and thus keeping tabs of our time is important.

Consider how, as a grandparent, you treasure the time you have with your grandchildren. I am reminded of a conversation I had with one of our new grandparents who said that she now considers a day without her granddaughter as a day wasted. She told me she had not realized how much that time with her grandchild meant to her until a brief illness prevented her from being with the child.

In the next few months when holiday times come around we will all be aware of those who cannot be with us, and we will long for the times when we can be together again. It's these times of the year that often make us aware of how precious we are to one another, and how much our time together is limited.

Time spent with loved ones is so precious, yet how much of it gets squandered. Take a look at your own life. Consider how much time you have wasted over the years in not forgiving a loved one. Just think of how much time that you could have been enjoying together has been lost because you were slow to forgive and forget. And again how much time do we all waste in brooding over unimportant slights or incidents among family members?

Our time is so limited it has to be used wisely. That is why St. Paul is so right to encourage us to "look carefully how you walk, making the most of time ..."

October 15th
Nobody Else

While on vacation recently I read an article by a young musician who was overwhelmed by an experience he said that had changed his life because it had changed the way he saw himself. According to this young musician, the event happened during a Masters Class he was taking from the great Yo-Yo Ma.

Here's how that young man described what happened: "Yo-Yo Ma taught us about our instruments. He spoke about the cello as if I had never seen one before. Then he spoke about the piece of music we were about to play, a Brahms cello sonata. He spoke of that music as if it were the only piece of music ever written. Then he spoke to each of us and told us how we were privileged to be playing these instruments and to be playing such wonderful music. Then we were invited to play the piece."

As I was reading the article, I thought to myself, "So where's the life-changing event?" Then I read what happened next.

"Yo-Yo Ma closed his eyes and listened to us play," the young musician wrote. "When we had finished, Yo-Yo Ma looked me in the eyes and with much enthusiasm and respect said, 'Nobody else can make the sound you make!' I was overwhelmed. No one had ever told me that I made a difference. I have not been the same musician since. I have not been the same man since."

When I came to the end of that article, I understood. Perhaps for the first time in his life, that young musician had been reverenced for his art. Yo-Yo Ma had given him the affirmation he needed to become a great musician.

"Nobody else can make the sound you make!" Those powerful words are words that can be addressed to each one of us. Each of us has something truly unique to offer the world. Nobody has the gifts you have in the same way that you have them. Nobody in the world can offer to the world what you can offer. The only way the world will ever get what you have, is if you freely offer it. No one else can. Your gifts are in your hands to do with them as you wish. What was true for that young musician is true for each one of us – Nobody else can make the sound you make!

October 16th
Two or Three Steps Ahead

St. Anthony of the Desert was fond of telling the story of a man who was lost in the desert. Later on, when the man began to tell of his terrible ordeal, his friends immediately asked him how he ever found his way out of such a dangerous, and vast place. "Well," said the man. "I was in a terrible way and I began to panic. So, I quickly fell to my knees and cried out to God – 'Save Me Most Holy One or I shall die here in this wretched place!'"

"And did God answer your prayer?" his friends asked.

"Oh, no way, for you see, before even God could answer me, an explorer rode in on a camel out of nowhere and he gave me water and showed me the way out!"

St. Anthony would conclude the story by reminding people that God is always two or three steps ahead of us in all our needs. "While the poor bumbling man was going about getting lost in the desert, our Gracious One was already sending an explorer to find the poor fellow," St. Anthony would say.

In your life right now, you may be going about getting lost or losing your way. But even now, our Gracious One is way ahead of you, watching over you, and is ready to send you whatever kind of "explorer" you may need to find your way home. How good God is!

October 17th
Fasting From Falsehood

St. Anthony the Great advised that every Christian ought to read the Gospel accounts of the temptation of Jesus. He says that it would be good for us to consider what sin we might be tempted to commit.

I think it was St. John Vianney who said that the greatest temptation we face is to lie – not to lie about just anything, but to lie about ourselves. He said we are either tempted to lie and say that we are no good, or to lie and say that we are nothing but good.

St. John Vianney was an insightful person who was well aware of human frailties. He recommended that the best spiritual discipline or practice for any Christian is to "fast from falsehood." If you begin the day by being honest with yourself, and you are truly honest, you won't be dishonest with anyone else. When we are truly honest with ourselves, real change and real conversion of heart is more than just possible, it's already begun!

October 18th
Shortages

In our time, many people have been very concerned about the huge increases in gas and electric bills brought on because of shortages. The bitterly cold temperatures in recent winters as well as the extreme heat and droughts of some of the most recent summers have made this shortage even more acute, and many people have to cut back in other areas of their lives to accommodate the increased expenses. Shortages can cost us dearly.

In the Gospel passage in which Jesus is at that famous wedding in Cana where there was a shortage of a different kind – there was no more wine! We all know the story. Mary convinces her rather reluctant Son to do something about the situation. After a mild protest, he does something about it. In the end, everyone's needs are met.

This famous wedding at Cana can serve to remind us to take notice as to whether or not there are shortages in our own lives. For example, in your relationship with members of your family, is there an ample supply of patience in your heart so that you give your family members the room they need to grow? Are you fully stocked with communications skills so that you can both understand your loved ones and be understood by them? Is there an ample supply of love, kindness and charity in your heart? How about your health? Are you running short of strength, or are you always tired and irritable because you're not as young as you used to be? Is your marriage being spoiled by a shortage of optimism, joy, and exuberance on your part? Are your children drifting away from you because of a shortage of time spent with them?

If you think about it, the recent energy shortages are a serious concern, but they aren't necessarily the most important ones. Why not take some times this week to do an inventory of your own heart? Are you running short on anything truly important to your life, your marriage, your family, or your relationship with God? Take an inventory and then do whatever you need to do to bring your supplies up to speed.

October 19th
It's Time

A few weeks ago after a wedding, an elderly man handed me a note card and said, "My father used to tell this story at the supper table whenever any of us talked about getting married. He would tell us that he knew the secret of how to make a marriage work. Then he would tell us that the secret was a simple thing that anyone can do." Here's the story:

A couple of months before his wedding day, a young man asked his future father-in-law what advice he could give him to keep his daughter happy in their marriage. The future father-in-law said that he would have to think about it, but that he would let him know sometime before the wedding.

The young groom received his answer in a small package given to him by his father-in-law on the morning of the wedding. A card attached to the little package was inscribed with this message: "This is all you need to know to make your marriage to my daughter work."

Opening the gift, the young groom found a wonderful gold pocket watch. When he flipped open the watch cover, he saw that etched on the inside were the words "Say something nice to Sarah." Thus, every time he would open the pocket watch to check the time, he would be reminded to be kind to his wife, Sarah.

That story can certainly serve as a reminder to each of us of how important it is to show our appreciation for each other in the kind words or compliments we give to each other. One of the greatest threats to any relationship is to take one another for granted. Why not take time right now to say or do something kind for someone you love?

October 20th

The Great Preparation

A few years ago I went to a medical ethics conference on genetic engineering. It was a very interesting conference filled with lots of important information, yet the one thing I remember from those two days was an illustration that one of the scientists used as he began his lecture.

He opened his session by telling all of us how glad he was to see us because he said that he was uniquely aware of how difficult it was to get all of us together. I thought he was talking about the distances that some people had come, the clearing of calendars required and the financial burdens it imposed on some people. That was not what he was talking about. He said, "The next time you are feeling unimportant, try thinking about how you ever got here." (Again, I was thinking of the miles traveled. He was not). He went on to say that there is an undisputable fact that it took two people, your parents, to get you here. He went on to say, "Each of your parents had two parents, so in the generation just prior to your mother and father, there were four people whose pairing off and sharing love contributed to your existence. You are the product of eight great-grandparents, sixteen great-great-grandparents, and thirty-two great-great-great-grandparents. Now, keep on multiplying the number by two. If you figure an average of 25 years between each generation, you will discover that a mere 500 years ago, there were 1,048,576 people on the planet just beginning the production of you!"

The scientist went on to talk about all that is in a person's "gene pool" after so many generations. But while he talked about that, I kept thinking about his illustration and came to a different conclusion. I began to think of the great preparation that God takes to get each one of us here. Doesn't it just boggle your mind to consider how much preparation God put into creating you? You and I are no accident. God has gone to a great deal of trouble to get us here. The question we all have to ask ourselves is, what are we doing with the life we have been given?

October 21st
A Pearl of Great Price

Here is a famous parable which is attributed to the Buddha:

"A man traveling across a field encountered a tiger. When he saw the tiger, he ran away as fast as he could as the wild beast chased after him. Coming to a precipice, he caught hold of the root of a vine and swung himself down over the edge. The tiger growled and sniffed at him from above. Terrified, the man looked down and saw that down below, another tiger was looking up at him, just waiting to eat him. Only the vine sustained him. Just then, two mice one white and one black, started to gnaw little by little at the vine, eating away tiny bits of the vine. At that moment, knowing that his life might be quite short, the man saw a luscious strawberry very near him growing on another vine. With one hand holding onto the root, and the other reaching out, he plucked the strawberry. Popping it in his mouth, he was overwhelmed with how wonderfully sweet it tasted."

The Buddha is said to have taught this parable as a means of teaching his disciple the practice of maranasati, or "death awareness." This practice is a kind of mindfulness of one's own death as a way of enriching and illuminating life.

The practice of maranasati can come about when one has a close call with death, as in a traffic accident. Or it can come about when one gets diagnosed with a serious disease or a terminal illness. These experiences can suddenly shock us into a whole series of questions about life: "What is my life about?" or "What have I done with my life so far?" or "Who and what is most important to me?" Sometimes this experience can lead us to realize how limited time is for us and it can push us to changing the way we live. We might say, "There's so little time left, there is none to waste, and I must drink every bit of it in and savor every experience as a gift to be received."

When we come to know how limited time is, it becomes eminently clear just how precious each day is. Each day, each hour of each day, is a pearl of great price, as Jesus would say. I believe that Jesus wants us to live our lives not by accident, but with a real focus of gratitude that leads us to create a life filled with love, beauty and compassion. The Buddha's parable has much to teach us and it can lead us to rediscover the depths of our own Christian faith.

October 22nd
An Undivided Heart

One of the most famous of all of the saints is St. Francis of Assisi. There are many reasons he is so popular – his deep faith, his care and love for the poor, his love of all of creation, his desire to be a true instrument of peace, and his willingness to befriend everyone. Over the years of his short life, Francis became a living sermon whose whole life pointed to Jesus. He gave his heart to God. One of his contemporaries said that Francis had an "undivided heart" – it all belonged to God.

One of the biographers of Francis, Bonaventure, described Francis' life this way: "Francis was full of love, a love that radiated to others. He lived a simple life. He scarcely allowed himself cooked food, and on the rare occasions when he did so, he either mixed it with ashes or made it tasteless, usually by adding water. This was to help him keep his eyes fixed on Jesus; the bare ground was his bed for his weary body, and he often used to sleep sitting up, with a piece of wood or a stone for a pillow. Clothed in a single poor little tunic, he served the Lord in cold and nakedness. Nothing owned him save Jesus. He spent long, long hours in prayer."

St. Francis searched for God wholeheartedly every day. He loved Him and found Him everywhere. He wrote a little prayer for his followers to use before they prayed. Perhaps you will find it as helpful to your prayer as I have for mine:

> *"With our whole heart, our whole soul, our whole mind, with our whole strength and fortitude, with our whole understanding, with all our powers, with every effort, every affection, every feeling, desire and wish, let us all love the Lord God and come before Him in prayer."*

October 23rd
Rude People

As a man was checking his bags at an airport, he became furious with the way the airport employee was handling his luggage and, in no uncertain terms, he let the baggage handler know it. The young worker stood there enduring every kind of belittling and foul language as the traveler stood with his face a few inches from his continuing the harangue in a very loud voice. Surprisingly, the young worker didn't seem perturbed by the man at all. After the traveler had moved on, a woman approached the baggage handler and said, "I really admire you for the way you handled that situation with that very rude man. You never once lost your cool or returned any insult with another." The baggage handler smiled and said, "the traveler is headed to New York and I just sent his luggage to Australia!"

Do you ever have to put up with rude people? As a Christian, how do you handle the situation? One of the marks of a disciple of Jesus is that we are called to return hatred with love, rudeness with kindness, hostility with peace. If you examine the behavior of the young baggage handler above, even though it is funny, would you say his response was a Christian response? Not really. Although he said he never let anyone control him, he had, in fact, reacted to rude behavior with rude behavior. The rude man had controlled the baggage clerk by eliciting a bad reaction.

Every so often it is good for us to consider whether or not our response to the rude behavior of some of the people we meet throughout the day truly does bear the mark of one who is called to be a disciple of Jesus.

October 24th
Finding True Peace

One of my favorite stories from the days of the great Desert Fathers concerns a particular hermit by the name of Abbot Anastasius. According to the story, Anastasius had a very valuable book which was worth 25 pieces of silver. The book was a collection of the Scriptures, both Old and New Testaments. On one occasion a monk came to see the old Abbot and, seeing the valuable book, made off with it. Later that day, Abbot Anastasius wanted to read something from the Scriptures and went looking for his book. When he could not find it, he knew at once that the visiting monk had taken it. But he did not send for the monk because he feared that if he confronted him with the theft, the scared monk might add the sin of perjury to that of stealing.

Now while the Abbot was considering these things, that visiting monk ran off to the city to try to sell the book. He thought he would sell it for 15 pieces of silver. A prospective buyer looked at the valuable book and said to the monk, "Would you mind if I showed this book to an expert to see if the book is worth that extraordinary amount of silver?" The monk agreed to let the man take the book to be appraised by an expert.

Well, with that the prospective buyer took the book to the only expert he knew, holy Abbot Anastasius! "Father," he said, "Take a look at this book and please tell me if you think it is worth 15 pieces of silver." Abbot Anastasius looked the book over very carefully and said, "Oh yes, this is a very fine book, I used to own one just like this and I know it is very valuable, and at the price of 15 pieces of silver it's a bargain – buy it!" So, the buyer went back to the monk and said, "Here is your money, I very much want to buy your book. I showed it to an expert and he said it was very precious and that I should buy it at once."

Thinking that he might get even more money from the buyer, the monk asked him, "Your expert must really know his stuff, did he tell you that it was worth more than 15 pieces of silver?"

"Oh yes, Abbot Anastasius told me that it was very valuable."

The monk was stunned. "Did you say it was Abbot Anastasius who looked at the book?"

"Yes, he is the only expert on these matters. He knows all there is to know about books. He could tell every book and tell you where it came from."

The monk was worried now, so he said, "Did the Abbot say anything else about this book?"

"Oh no, he just said to be sure to pay the seller well because the book is very valuable."

The monk then said, "I've decided not to sell the book after all." Then he ran back to the Abbot and with many tears begged for forgiveness for stealing the book. The Abbot then forgave the crying monk and said, "Here take this book as a gift from me."

"How can you be so forgiving after I stole your most precious book?" the monk asked.

"Oh, well it is, after all, only a book. The Good Lord sent it to me through a dear friend many years ago, and for years I have enjoyed using it. But, after all, it is only a thing. I do not really possess it and it does not possess me either. It has simply been on loan to me, so to speak. I have always 'held it loosely' so that it may not possess me. I advise you too to take this precious book as a gift from God. It is a kind of loan – hold it loosely. This is the way the Lord wants all of us to view both things and loved ones. They are all on loan to us from above. We must hold each of them loosely. We can own none of them. And we must not let any of them possess us. They are all gifts. Once you know this and live it, you will find true peace."

The story ends with the young monk taking the holy hermit's words to heart. The book was a great help to him in his spiritual journey, and he became a great holy man himself through those wise words from Abbot Anastasius.

This week, why not take an inventory of your life and see if you have many "possessions" that steal your peace. Let them go, and hold all the gifts the Lord pours into you heart loosely.

October 25th
A Healing Each of Us Needs

In the fourth century, the deserts of Egypt were populated by some holy men who were known as the Fathers of the Desert. Most of these men lived as hermits, spending their time in prayer, but some of them had large numbers of followers who would come out to seek their prayer, guidance and sometimes healing. One particularly famous case was of a young woman who was suffering from breast cancer. She was very frightened by the future and worried that the disease would soon take her life, so she made her way to the desert in search of a holy man by the name of Abba Longinus. The woman had been told by many townsfolk that he was a true saint who had the power to heal.

Now as the woman was making her way to the desert, she came upon Abba Longinus himself, who was collecting firewood. She spoke to him and said, "Holy one, can you tell me where to find the monk called Abba Longinus? I know that he is a friend of God."

Abba Longinus said to her, "Why are you looking for that old fraud? Do not go to see him for he will only do you much harm. What is it that makes you want to find him?" She told him of the terrible disease that was threatening to take her life and of her great fear. Abba Longinus then told her to have faith and to trust in God's great love. He then laid his hands on her head and prayed a brief prayer. Then he said to her, "I am very certain that God wants to make you well. In fact, you will be well. Go home now in peace. That old fraud Longinus would have been no help to you at all."

The woman went away. She was healed. The disease left her and she lived another 40 years, quite unaware that it was Abba Longinus himself who had prayed over her.

The disciples of Abba Longinus would often talk together about this healing. They wondered why Abba Longinus never told the woman who he was. One day, one of the disciples worked up the courage to ask Abba Longinus about the healing.

"If I had told the woman who I was, and after I had prayed over her and she was healed, she would have concluded that it was I who had healed her, and she would have spent her whole life in gratitude to me," he explained. "Today she simply thanks God for the healing that came to her through some anonymous monk. This way she may begin to see how much God loves and cherishes her. And even though she was healed of cancer, the real healing she received that day was the knowledge that God does, in fact, love and cherish her. This is a healing that each of us needs."

October 26th

Are You Being Gently Delivered?

In the library the other day I came across a collection of ancient wisdom tales. The tales were written to help pilgrims find their way through life. One of the stories concerned the plight of two men who were walking next to a river toward a town downstream from their home. As they walked along talking about how far they had to walk, a storm broke, and a flash flood washed both of them into the river. One of the men panicked and tried to fight his way back to the shore, but found that the struggle only wore him out. Tired as he was, he continued to struggle against the rushing waters, but at last he succumbed and was drowned. The other man realized that the torrent of water was much stronger than he, so he tried as best he could to control his fears, to relax and to let the waters take him wherever they would. Eventually the storm ended and the waters slowed and the river gently delivered the man on the shores of the town he was headed toward when he had begun his journey.

The moral of the story is that often the very torrents that we are struggling to overcome may be the vehicle that could take us where we want and need to go. Currents that appear to be violent and threatening may truly be forces that can gently deliver us. Sometimes God is trying to come to our aid. Sometimes it is best to let ourselves be carried and gently delivered rather than trying to be in control of everything. In your life right now, are you struggling against the strong current of God?

October 27th

Making Room for the Good Stuff

I was flipping through a magazine a few weeks ago as I sat in a hospital waiting area when I came across a little article about a married couple in Israel who had gone to court to make sure that their marriage of 27 years was still legal. According to the story, a Mr. Benjamin Cohen had married Shoshana Hadad, years ago, but it was discovered that the laws of Israel declared their marriage invalid because Shoshana had a very noble ancestor who in 580 B.C. had married a mere peasant. Because that nobleman had married a commoner, all subsequent marriages in his family line were declared not valid and therefore illegal! How's that for holding on to things and nursing an old wound? "I feel like I'm being punished for something my ancestor did – why is this being held against me thousands of years later?" Shoshana Cohen tearfully asked the court.

I don't know the court's response to Mrs. Cohen's question, but the whole thing got me thinking. Have you ever been punished or mistreated because of something that happened a long, long time ago? I'll bet there are many of us who have either punished ourselves or some one else for some hurt from the past. We have all either held a grudge or been the victim of someone else's grudge and the resulting suffering is unfortunate. It is unfortunate because it is a pain that could all be avoided.

An old mentor of mine once told me that holding on to hurts and nursing old wounds just keeps your heart so full that there is no room in it for the "good stuff" that life can bring you. If your heart is full of sludge, there's no room for peace and love.

He also said that one of the signs that you are holding on to old hurts is feelings of isolation. When there is little or no room in your heart for love, there is only isolation and loneliness left.

Our greatest pain in life is not really the hurtful things that have happened to us in the past, but it is the holding on to those past hurts that creates the greatest suffering. Or to put it another way, it's not what happens to us that is important, it's what we do with what happens to us that makes all the difference.

A grace we all surely need is the grace of letting go of the past. Letting go of past hurts, failures or mistakes can make all the difference in life. It will free up space in your heart for the "good stuff," and it will give you a new sense of the joy of living.

October 28th

More Honey, Please!

One of the greatest spiritual guides in the history of the Church is St. Francis de Sales. He was consulted by people from all walks of life in his own day, and people today still consult his writings as they try to deepen their relationship with the Lord. He often encouraged his friends to take the simplest route to holiness. What did he teach as the simplest route to holiness? He put it this way: "The shortest way to true holiness is to learn to practice gentleness with everyone God entrusts to your care. To be kind and gentle is everything."

That reminds me of one of Aesop's Fables in which there is an argument between the wind and the sun as to which of them is the strongest and the most powerful.

To settle their dispute they decided to test their respective strengths on a man they see walking along down on the earth. The man is wearing an overcoat. It was agreed that whichever of them could get the man to take off his overcoat, that one would be declared the strongest and most powerful.

The wind said that he would try first and that he was sure he could get the man to take off his overcoat. So the wind blew and blew to the strength of a hurricane-force windstorm, but the only reaction from the man was to wrap the coat even tighter around him.

Next, it was the sun's turn to try to get the man to take off the overcoat. The sun didn't actually do anything too spectacular – it just shone in the sky in all its brilliance letting the gentle warmth of its rays reach the man. Within minutes the man removed his coat.

Francis de Sales was famous for teaching his students, "You can catch more flies with a spoonful of honey than with a hundred barrels of vinegar."

He advised his followers to take the simplest road to holiness, dispensing more honey than vinegar to those around you. Being kind and gentle to your family is a sure road to God.

October 29th
Selling the Farm

I read about a farmer who lived on the same farm his entire life. It was a good farm, but he was growing tired of his day-to-day routine, and frankly the farm was looking old to him. He needed something new. Because he longed for a change and for something better, he began to find fault with almost everything about the farm. It wasn't long before he began to hate the farm. He called a friend who worked in real estate and set out to sell the old place.

The real estate agent got to work preparing an advertisement which listed all of the farm's best attributes and advantages: an ideal location, up-to-date equipment, healthy stock, lots of fertile ground and so on. Before placing the ad, the agent sent it to him for approval. When the farmer read the ad, he thought it was a brochure for a farm the agent wanted to sell him. He called the agent right away and said, "This is exactly the kind of farm I have been looking for. Just where is this farm located?"

There was, of course, dead silence on the other end of that phone line. Then the agent spoke very slowly, "You do realize you are reading about your own farm don't you?"

The farmer was a bit embarrassed and then began to laugh. "You know," he said, "my farm is exactly the kind of farm I have been looking for my whole life, and here I've been on it the whole time and didn't know it!"

I like that story because it can remind each of us to take a good look at our lives. We may be living the dream we have always had, and been unaware of it. Think for a moment: Just what are the good things that are happening in your life? Are you appreciative of the blessings that have come your way over the years?

Because of the nature of the world today, and the way news media are always looking for something to criticize, we can easily fall into the trap of seeing what's wrong with things in life rather than realizing what's right with life. Everyone of us is wonderfully blessed each day by a loving God. Why not take a few moments to do a blessings inventory of your life? In how many ways has the "farm you are living on" been a place of blessing for you?

October 30th
What Matters

For Catholics, May and October are months set aside to celebrate Mary, the Mother of God. In the Scriptures, one of the most famous verses concerns what Mary does when she sees so many profound events happening to her son Jesus. The Bible says that she "treasured these things in her heart." She treasured them because she realized that what she was witnessing in the life of Jesus was important.

Treasuring events in our hearts is a very common human experience, and so all parents store up precious memories of their children. These stored family treasures have much to teach us. One of the most profound things that we can learn from our "precious memories" is a lesson we long to be taught. That lesson is simply this: To know what matters and what does not.

In our ever more and more chaotic lives, discovering the lesson of knowing what really does matter is vitally important. How many families have been disrupted by quarreling over unimportant things that really do not matter at all? Yet, much time is wasted on "winning" an argument and many are afflicted with hurtful feelings of rejection as we turn unimportant things into walls that separate.

Knowing what matters and what does not can change your life. Most of us only learn this when some health crisis or accident or even a death of a loved one or some other loss whittles us down to a profound sense of fear. It is then that we come to know what is truly important – the precious people the Lord has entrusted to our care.

As we observe the life of Mary, it is good to remember that just as God chose to entrust Mary with loving and caring for His Son, so too has God chosen to entrust you with those people he has given into your loving care. The people that God has chosen to bring into your life are not there by accident or by some mere happenstance. God has purposefully entrusted them to you. Loving and caring for them with the best of what's in you is what truly matters.

October 31st
Walking Away ...

The children of a man who had been smoking for over 25 years were quite concerned about their dad's health. They told their mother about how worried they were about their dad's smoking habits. "Maybe if you talk to him about it or maybe if you showed him some articles from magazines about how dangerous smoking is for your health, he might decide to quit," the mom said. The children did as their mom suggested and made copies of numerous articles about the dangers of cigarettes and gave them to their dad.

A few weeks later the dad finished reading the articles and then said to his wife, "You know, Ann, I've been reading so many articles about smoking and lung cancer that I've decided to quit reading!"

I'm sure that was not the response the man's children were hoping he would have, but I bet it is fairly typical for most smokers. When we like something so much that it borders on being an addiction, we often choose not to see the truth of its dangers when it is presented to us.

Jesus warned his disciples about this very thing one day when a young man came to him and asked, "Master, what must I do to gain everlasting life?"

Jesus answered him by saying, "If you wish to enter into eternal life, keep the commandments."

The young man replied, "Which ones?"

And Jesus replied, "You shall not kill; you shall not commit adultery; you shall not steal; you shall not bear false witness; honor your father and your mother; and you shall love your neighbor as yourself."

The young man said to him, "I have kept all of these since my youth, what more need I do?"

Jesus looked at him with love and said, "If you wish to be perfect, go sell what you have and give it to the poor, and you will have treasure in heaven. Then come, follow me." When the young man heard this, he went away sad, for he had many possessions." (Matthew 19:16-23)

In your own life right now, are there any "possessions" that could cause you, like the young man above, to walk away from Jesus? Sometimes we can be so consumed and preoccupied by some things that they might tempt us to walk away from Jesus. What we truly need to do is to walk away... but not away from Jesus.

November 1st

God Has Plans

It is said that when St. John Vianney, the patron saint of parish priests, went to visit the dying, he always tried to bring them the gift of hope in the Lord's goodness and to help them be at peace. On one occasion, he went to visit an elderly woman who was in the process of dying. As he approached her, he blessed her saying, "Elizabeth, I've come to be with you and to tell you not to be afraid." As he observed her, he realized that she was indeed unafraid. This was not what he expected, so he asked her what she was feeling.

"Oh, Father, I am not afraid. I am simply awaiting the moment when the wall that separates this life from the next life crumbles away and then I shall simply fall into the arms of the loving God who awaits me. I am not afraid."

John Vianney marveled at her faith and remarked to a friend that this was one time when the dying gave him hope and made him feel at peace. He went on to say, "Oh, how I look forward to the day when the wall crumbles away, and the arms of God stretch out to embrace me, wonderfully embracing me and all loneliness is no more, and happiness beyond all imagining!"

I recalled that incident from the life of St. John Vianney as I was praying and thinking about the two great feast days that we celebrate at the beginning of November, the Feast of All Saints and the Feast of the Poor Souls. These two feasts help us to focus on the future days to come when God calls each of us home. For some people, the prospect of their death is quite a frightening thing and they try to avoid thinking about it. Perhaps you are one of those people. Yet, if we stop to consider our faith, we will soon come to realize that we have nothing to fear in the future. Jesus has told us of the Father's tremendous love for each one of us. He has also told us that He is going to prepare a place for us and then He will come back for us to take us with Him so that "where He is, we also may be."

The two great feast days we celebrate at the beginning of this month are a reminder that God has great plans for us. We need not be afraid. We can be at peace, for we are loved.

November 2nd

Nourishing Words

Very early in the morning of November 2nd of last year, the Feast of All Souls, I spent some quiet time in prayer for all of those who have died. Each year on that feast day, I try to find some time to pray for all of my relatives and friends who have passed away. The bulk of my time in prayer is spent in thanking God for each of the people I am remembering.

This year, as I was praying, an article I read a few months ago came back to me. I remember the article because I found it very comforting as I thought of the many people who have died over the years.

The article was written by the widow of Fred Rogers. You would probably better remember her husband by his TV name – Mister Rogers. In her article, Joanne Rogers had written about some of the things that she treasures, especially since her husband's death. This is how she described it:

"One of my treasures is a photo of a sunset that Fred sent to me, with words from one of his songs on a little note that he put on the back of the picture. Fred had taken the picture himself when he was in Nantucket without me for a bit. He loved to take pictures. That photo and those few words he had put on the back have carried me through a lot these days. In fact I have framed that photo and put his words on a little note in front. I'm still being nourished by his words. That picture and its words are a real treasure."

The words that Fred Rogers had penned on the back of that photo for his wife were these: "When the day turns into night, and you're way beyond my sight, I think of you."

Aren't those comforting words? I'm sure that Joanne Rogers finds great solace in knowing that Fred is thinking about her.

One thought that struck me as I recalled those words is the depth of healing that we can receive from others through their thoughtfully kind words. Those words have the power to change us. Or, as Joanne Rogers put it, "I'm still being nourished by his words."

Words of comfort are certainly a great gift, a gift that we may overlook. Perhaps, later this month as we celebrate Thanksgiving Day by eating a nourishing meal with our families, we might take a few moments to consider how our friends and family members have, over the years, offered us words that still nourish. Perhaps this would be a good time to give thanks both for the words and for those who offered them. Where would we be without nourishing words of comfort spoken in love?

November 3rd
Home With the Lord

Once there was an old man who each day would take long walks with the Lord. On these walks he and the Lord would talk about all kinds of things – about important times in the old man's life, when he met his wife, the birth of each of his children, special friends, moments of great insight, and so on. One day while they were out walking for an especially long time, the Lord looked at the old man and said, "We're a lot closer to my home than we are to yours. Why don't you just come on home with me?" That's just what the old man did; he went home with the Lord.

This week marks two great days in our Church year, the Feast of All Saints and the Feast of All Souls. These days are meant as reminders to us of those who have already "gone home" with the Lord, as well as those who are in the process of "going home with Him." These days are also meant to serve as a reminder to us that each one of us is so deeply loved by the Lord that He has reserved a special place in His home for us.

One day, we will be "closer to His home than to our own," and the Lord will say to us, "Why don't you just come on home with me?"

November 4th
Fearful Dark Nights

It was during a cabinet meeting in one of the darkest times of the Civil War that Abraham Lincoln told his colleagues this story from his youth:

"When I was a small boy, I had a terrible fear of the dark. I always tried to get to sleep before nightfall. One night my father taught me a rather simple lesson that I have not forgotten. We were fixing harnesses in the barn one night and my father asked me to go to the shed to get more supplies. I stood at the barn door frozen in fear of the dark night. My father came up to me and said, "Pick up the lantern. Look. What do you see?"

"I see the oak tree," I answered.

"Is there anything between you and the oak tree?" he asked.

"No," I said.

"Then walk to that oak tree and lift the lantern again," he said. When I got to the oak tree he said, "Now what do you see?"

"I see the mulberry bush," I replied.

Then he said, "Walk to the mulberry and lift the lantern again." By the time I'd gotten to the mulberry bush I had figured out the procedure.

"And so I made my way, step by step, from tree to chicken coop, to bush, to shed and back again. That was a simple lesson he taught me, but it is a lesson that can take you a mighty long way."

That lesson that Lincoln spoke of reminds me of a famous hymn, "Lead Kindly Light," which was written by Cardinal Newman in 1833. He was a man who was often troubled, suffering much anxiety and fear. The thought of the future looming before him often filled him with dread. He spoke of a fear of the gloom coming to encircle and overwhelm him. His solution to all of this fearful worry was to come before the Lord in prayer. He discovered when he prayed that there was a way out of his fear. Here are the first words of this hymn:

Lead, Kindly Light, amidst th' encircling gloom,
Lead Thou me on!
The night is dark, and I am far from home,
Lead Thou me on!
Keep Thou my feet; I do not ask to see
The distant scene; one step enough for me.

Newman discovered what Lincoln's father had taught him – the way through fear is to take one step at a time. Like Lincoln holding up his lantern on that very dark night, all we have to do is to find enough light to take the next step. And an important truth that Cardinal Newman came to discover is that the light we hold up is not the light of a simple lantern. It is a person who called himself "the Light of the world." Although we may feel that we are in darkness and far from home, we are never far from Jesus who said, "I am with you always." By finding a bit of light so that we can see just the next step, we will eventually be led out of our fearful dark nights.

If you find yourself feeling overwhelmed, confused or lost; if you find yourself overcome by fear, perhaps you need simply to ask Jesus, the Kindly Light, to show you just the next step. If you do that, you will be taking your first step out of your fearful, dark night.

November 5th
Letters Full Of Love

I was visiting someone in the hospital a few weeks ago. As I watched the woman respond to her grandkids, I noticed how her eyes lit up when they came over to her and showed her the drawings they had made for her. "These are the most beautiful artworks I have ever seen in my life!" she said with tears in her eyes. Her grandkids beamed with pride. They were so glad to see their grandmother's big smile and you could see them "drinking in" her words of appreciation and her words of praise for the work they had done. It was an inspiring scene to witness and it set me thinking.

Earlier last week I had come across an essay on the lost art of letter writing. The author was explaining that in the age of e-mail, texting and instant-messaging, we seem to have lost an important art, the art of crafting words of encouragement and support for those we love. We are in such a rush these days, that we don't seem to have the time to sit down and with pen and paper express heart-felt words that touch the hearts of those we love.

A few years ago I copied down quotations from some very old letters that a woman had found in her grandmother's attic. The letters, which appear to have been written by a mother to one of her sons, are dated in the early years of the 1840s. The woman who wrote them was writing on behalf of herself and her husband to a son and his wife who were living somewhere near what is now Dayton, Ohio. I like three different remarks which I have taken from three different letters:

From a letter dated August 15, 1844: "You don't know how much your letter meant to us! When you left, I felt as if the sun itself had stopped shining."

From another letter, this one dated December 1, 1845: "The courage with which you are facing your current difficulties is certainly an inspiration to all of us. We are sure that you will be better for all that you have endured. Your strength has made your father and me very proud indeed."

And finally, from a letter that was not dated: "We all long to behold you in person! We are always so much the better when we can see you and hear your gentle laugh and your kindness never fails to make me blush with pride."

Aren't those wonderfully written expressions of affection? Those folks knew how to put words together so that even great distances could not get between them and those they loved. Can you imagine how the recipients of those letters felt after they read them? Such expressions of love and support must have helped them through some very difficult times. Those folks knew how to bless each other with finely crafted words.

Perhaps there is someone in your life who would be truly blessed to receive sentiments like those above in a note from you. Why not take a few moments this week to bless a loved-one's day with a thoughtful letter or note?

November 6th
Behold His Face!

St. Paul said some pretty remarkable things. In one letter he says that "both in life and in death we are the Lord's." It's a reminder to us that we need not fear death. In the past several weeks, there have been many people who have stopped in or have called to talk about death. Many people are quite frightened by it, others are merely puzzled, and still others have been overwhelmed by the death of a loved one.

Just how should we Christians look at death, and what will it be like? None of us will know what death itself is like until we experience it, but we can, as believers, know something of how to look at "the other side." Just last week someone gave me a copy of a funeral program for a Baptist minister, Reverend Jones, who died recently. The following verses on the inside cover explain rather nicely what our attitude ought to be.

St. Paul said, "For me, to die is gain." It means the gain of being with the Lord, which is far better. It means the gain of freedom from the troubles and heartaches of life. It means the gain of release from sickness and pain, and it means victory over death. It means the gain of seeing our Precious Redeemer face to face.

Not just to kneel with angels or see loved ones who have gone; not just to drink at the fountain under the great white throne; not for the crown that he giveth am I trying to run the race; All I want in heaven is just to behold His face!

Just to behold His face, yes, just to behold His face. All I want in heaven is just to behold His face.

Not just to join the chorus and sing with those who are blest and bathe my soul that is weary in the sea of heavenly rest; but I'll look for the One who saved me from a death of sin and disgrace. Twill be joy when I get up in Heaven, just to behold His face! That summed up Reverend Jones' faith. How would you express your own?

November 7th
God Has Given Us an Unfinished World

Have you been noticing how much negative talk there is in all the political campaigns? When you listen to candidates for any office, they are all saying what a terrible shape the country is in, that horrible things are looming on the horizon, and that the world is falling apart. None of the advertisements are uplifting, and none of them make us feel that anything can really be done to make the world a better place. The underlying message of all the ads is hopelessness. It's as if this world is in such a mess that nothing can help it, that somehow we've inherited a world gone mad, and that even God is out of ideas!

I've been thinking about these ads a lot lately, and I think that they have sold us a worthless bill of goods! What these ads fail to take into account is a fundamental truth that Christianity and the other major religions take for granted. That fundamental truth is that God has given us an UNFINISHED world. This world was never meant to be a perfect, finished place. We often talk about our dependence upon God. We fail to remember that God depends on us too. There are many things that God can't do without our cooperation.

God cannot make a peaceful world unless we, you and me, help him by rooting out the hatred and prejudices that linger in our own hearts. God cannot make our society a just one if we don't look into our own hearts and begin to question our basic attitudes.

God cannot give us a happy home if families don't cooperate by working on their attitudes about sharing, forgiving, compromising, and fostering mutual respect. God cannot forgive sin unless we cooperate and are truly sorry and truly willing to work to change what we need to change.

God wants to heal us, but He often chooses to use the skills of nurses, doctors, and other caregivers. God wants to heal, but are we willing to be partners with God in healing others and in allowing others to heal us? God can't make the world a nurturing place unless we cooperate by being nurturing people!

God helps the poor with the charity that we are willing to give; God cheers up the discouraged with the words that we speak and the deeds that we do to encourage others; God guides our children with the example we set; God comforts the hurting with the solace that we choose to give.

As I said, politicians would have us believe that the world is in terrible shape. If this world is in the horrible shape that they would have us believe, I don't think that God is to blame, or that the politicians alone are to blame. I think that we are all to blame if we as individuals are not cooperating with God's plan for us.

The reason that you and I have been placed in this moment in time, in this particular family, in this particular part of our world may simply be that God needs our talents to finish off His unfinished world! The next time you see one of those political ads decrying the terrible shape of the world, take a look at your own part of the world, the unfinished part, and make a resolution to do your part to cooperate with God in the work of creation!

November 8th

What's In Your Heart?

I once attended a conference given by an Indian Jesuit named Anthony De Mello. The talk I remember most was one he gave on the importance of finding God wherever you find yourself. To illustrate what he taught, he told a story from an ancient monastic tradition.

According to the story, a monk whose reputation for holiness was known far and wide was called in by the abbot who was quite angry with him. When the holy monk appeared before the abbot, the abbot accused the monk of giving scandal to the people of God. "How did I give such scandal?" the monk asked. "I have been told," the abbot replied "that you have been seen having many conversations with a most beautiful woman who herself has a very bad reputation. You must explain yourself at once!"

The holy monk paused before he spoke. Then in a quiet voice he spoke to the abbot: "Holy Father Abbot, we, the woman and I, spoke only of Jesus. Perhaps I should explain to you something I have learned over the years. I have always held that it is far better to speak to a pretty woman with one's thoughts set on God than to pray to God with one's thoughts fixed on a pretty woman. Furthermore, all of the Desert Fathers and Mothers have taught us that what fills one's heart is what one will find in the world around them. Thus, if a monk enters a tavern, the tavern becomes his cell, where he most easily finds God. When a drunk goes into a cell, the cell becomes his tavern. What is in your heart conditions what and how you see."

Father De Mello concluded his talk by saying that we can find God wherever we are, as long as our hearts are filled with God.

November 9th

Turned Away at the Door

In his autobiography, Mahatma Gandhi tells how in his youth he was a student in South Africa. It was during this time that he became very interested in Christianity and he spent many hours reading the Bible. He was especially taken by Jesus' words in the Sermon on the Mount.

Having read about Jesus and knowing some of the things that Jesus preached, Gandhi began to see that maybe the teachings of Jesus could help his people in India overcome the evils of the caste system that had been so destructive and humiliating to millions of his country's poor. He seriously considered becoming a Christian.

One day he went to a local church to attend Mass and to ask to get instructions so that he could get baptized. This was his intention when he was stopped at the front door of the church and told that this was no place for a "colored" person like him. He was told to go to a church that was reserved for blacks. He left that day, and never returned.

Later on in life he was asked about that experience. He was asked this question, "Why do you suppose you were treated the way you were?"

Gandhi replied by saying that he could not really know why that person had turned him away that day. He suspected that the one who turned him away was probably someone who knew quite a lot about Jesus and his teaching, and that the man probably thought that he was doing the right thing. But, on the other hand, Gandhi suspected that while the man had known a lot about Jesus, he probably had never really met Jesus or never really got to know the real Jesus. "Had the man really known Jesus, I am sure he would never have turned me away!" Gandhi said.

Every day we must be ready to welcome Jesus under many disguises. Everyday He comes to us in many ways and many of us miss the opportunity to welcome him.

Why not make this a time that you will devote to getting to know Jesus? Remember, when he first showed up, He, like Gandhi, was turned away at the door. This can be your chance to welcome Him into your life in a new way.

November 10th

Honesty and Integrity

I was in the public library the other day reading through some old magazines when I happened on an article/editorial about a teacher in Piper, Kansas. According to the article the teacher was at the center of a major scandal involving her students' grades.

The controversy began when the teacher discovered that at least a fourth of her sophomore students had cheated on their botany project. She gave each of the cheating students a zero on their project. This meant, of course, that each of them failed the semester. Parents were outraged and they complained mightily both to the teacher and to the school board. At the direction of the school board, the principal ordered the teacher to give the students passing grades.

Rather than do that, the teacher resigned her teaching position. At least a dozen of her fellow faculty members planned to resign as well in protest. The school board responded by accepting their resignations and hiring new teachers. One of the failing students told a reporter, "We've won!"

When asked why she went through with her resignation, the teacher responded by saying, "It's not just biology we teach; you're supposed to be teaching them a lot more than that. We are supposed to be teaching them to be honest people, to have integrity, and to be good people."

At the conclusion of the article, the journalist made a simple statement, "I wonder if the parents who complained so loudly held any stock in Enron? Perhaps those men who caused the collapse of that company because of their dishonesty had teachers or parents who didn't insist that they be people of integrity. I think it was Socrates who said that the greatest gift we can give the world and ourselves is a life lived in honesty and in integrity."

November 11th
"Grand"-Fathers

About a year ago, I was invited to give a talk to a group of men who meet early (6:00 AM!) on Friday mornings to pray, listen to speakers, and to consider what kind of husbands and fathers they have been and are becoming. The group is made up of about thirty men ranging in age from 23 to 77. They begin their sessions with a short prayer, then a guest speaker gives an inspirational talk, and then the men form small groups in which they talk about the speaker's words and exchange ideas about their own lives. It was wonderful to be a part of the group and to realize how seriously these men take their roles as husbands and fathers.

In the group of which I was a part, one of the men talked about how much he admired his grandfather. He told of how his grandfather always encouraged him to be a "giver" not just a "taker." He said that his grandfather had given him a plaque inscribed with these words: "We make a living by what we get, but we make a life by what we give." The man concluded his reflection by saying that he wanted to honor the memory of his grandfather by making sure that he was making a life for his family and not just making a living.

November 12th
Astonishing!

Someone sent me a note recently that had a "Hi and Lois" cartoon attached to it. I have always liked reading that cartoon, and this one was particularly good. In the first frame of the cartoon, Hi, the dad of the family is on his way to his office where he works as an accountant. Driving along the road he is saying to himself: "Here I go, another dumb day, going to the same dumb office, to look at the same dumb numbers that

I have worked on thousands of times before!"

In the cartoon's second frame, Lois, the family's mom, is shown mopping the floor and she is talking to herself: "Another dumb day, cleaning the same dumb floor, in the same dumb house that I have cleaned a thousand times before!"

In the next frame, the older kids of the family are shown riding the school bus. One kid is saying to the kid next to them, "Here we go again on another dumb day to the same dumb school, with the same dumb teachers, working on the same dumb math problems we've been working on a thousand times before!"

In the very last frame of the cartoon we see Trixie, the baby of the family, standing in her crib, wide awake, with her arms up in the air reaching for a sunbeam that is coming through the window; she is smiling and saying, "Yeah! Another new day!"

For that little girl, Trixie, every day is a new day with new adventures. She has not yet lost her enthusiasm for what each day may bring. She is still wide-eye with the wonder of creation. As some theologians would put it, she has not lost her instinct for astonishment. Even though she may not have the words to express it, Trixie finds each day chocked full with blessings and she enjoys them all.

Soon we will all be gathering with family and friends to celebrate Thanksgiving. This is a great time for those of us who may have fallen into the stupor of daily routines to stop to reconsider our lives. This is a great time for us to step back from the busyness of each day, from our "in a rut" mentality, to regain our basic human instinct for astonishment that we all had as young children.

Every day is chocked full of wonders that truly are blessings. Just take a long slow walk through nature, stop and look around you and you can't help but notice all of the wonders of God's creation. If you stop to look, to listen, to breathe deeply, you'll find yourself feeling astonished, and even blessed. Take a few moments to look at your family members – not with a critical eye that looks for faults, but with the eye that looks for the good that's in them. You'll find that you are blessed by them too.

As Thanksgiving Day approaches I think we would all enjoy that special day even more if we paused long enough to regain our childhood instinct for wonder and awe for God has surely blessed each of us with an astonishing world!

November 13th
Mining for Gold

I read an article the other day about Andrew Carnegie. According to the article, Carnegie attributed his vast wealth to the way he helped his employees to develop. He said that whenever he thought of the people who worked for him, he thought of gold mining. "In gold mining," he said "You literally move tons of dirt to find a single ounce of gold. However, you don't look for dirt – you look for the gold."

It sounds to me that Andrew Carnegie was on to something when it came to people skills. He knew that developing people was developing true wealth. I think he provides us with some food for thought. If you stop to think about the way you see each member of your family, or the way you look at your friends or co-workers, do you look for dirt or for gold? And, when you find the "gold" in them, how do you help to bring that gold out of them?

November 14th
A Missed Flight

How often in the last six months do you think you have been caught in a traffic jam? If you stop to think about it, it is probably a lot more often than you would ever want.

What typically happens to you when you are stuck in traffic? Most of us end up getting a little anxious or nervous, some get a bit annoyed or even angry, and a few people might even begin to head toward road rage. One thing is certain, none of us likes sitting in a traffic jam. But have you ever thought about your reactions to traffic delays?

I was talking to a friend the other day about the all too frequent traffic delays here in West Chester. She told me that she used to get so angry at the traffic that she often found herself in tears by the time she got to work. I asked her if she still got that upset over traffic. She said, "I used to be a mess when I got to work. One morning after a very long traffic snafu, I vowed that I would change my attitude even though I had no idea how I would ever do so."

"Have you been able to change your attitude?" I asked her.

"Yes, I had an experience one day when I had to catch an early flight out of the Cincinnati airport. I made a point of leaving early, but even so I ended up sitting on I-75. I was fuming. I turned on the radio and the 'traffic guy' was talking about the delay leading to the airport when he said something that has made all the difference."

"What did he say?" I asked.

"This is what he said, 'To all you folks heading to the airport, it's one thing to miss a plane, but it's quite another to miss the moment. Take a deep breath, listen to some music, and enjoy the moment. There's nothing you can do about the delay. Why be miserable? Enjoy some nice music. Spare yourself from worry, anxiety and a headache."

My friend went on to tell me how those words have changed her attitude about traffic. She said that she now packs some of her favorite CDs and a good book. Now she sees her trips to work as a chance for a bit of quiet time, good music, and maybe even a few lines from a good book.

There is some real wisdom in what that traffic reporter said. It is one thing to miss a plane, but quite another to miss the moment.

November 15th

Checking Our Baggage

Mother Teresa once said, "If it takes you longer than 15 minutes to pack, you have too much stuff." Probably most of us would think that she was crazy to say such a thing, yet there is some very important wisdom in her words. When was the last time you looked around at the things that you have accumulated over the years? Isn't it amazing how easily we can fill up any empty space in our homes or offices with lots of "stuff?" We somehow begin to collect lots of things almost without knowing it and in a relatively short period of time we are living in a very crowded space. I'll bet that the last time you moved you probably kept saying to yourself, "Where in the world did we get all of this stuff!" Stuff happens – and before you know it, you are living with clutter.

What is true on a physical level is also true on a spiritual level. Our hearts and souls can accumulate a lot of "stuff." We can store up bad memories, hurt feelings, and old wounds, to say nothing of prejudices, judgments, and jealousies so that our hearts are heavy with burdens. We can carry around feelings of inadequacy, anger, or disappointment; and all of these things can begin to weigh us down and choke off the life that is in us. Taking inventory of the things we have stored in our houses can be a very useful tool for simplifying our daily life by giving us a clutter-free place in which to grow. On a spiritual level, taking inventory of our hearts and taking the time to get rid of our unnecessary baggage can free us in ways we never thought possible.

Mother Teresa was a wise woman who knew how to "travel light" through life both on a physical level and on a spiritual one as well– we can all learn a lot from her.

November 16th

Alexander the Not So Great!

Recently I read a short biography of Alexander the Great. One thing I found to be fascinating about him is that although Alexander had finally conquered the whole known world of his times, there was one thing that he could not conquer. He could not conquer his temper. In his boyhood days he thought his temper was his greatest asset because it could, as he put it, "summon up a powerful rage that would destroy all who got in its way." Because of this powerful rage, Alexander would win just about any competition he entered.

On one occasion, however, Alexander the Great discovered and experienced something he had not known – being conquered. It happened one day that Cletus, one of Alexander's generals and a friend from his childhood, became drunk and started saying insulting things to Alexander in front of the troops. Alexander's carefully cultivated "powerful rage" began to grow within him. Finally, completely losing his temper, he grabbed a spear from one of the soldiers standing nearby and threw it with all of his might at Cletus, intending to scare him and to remind him that he had overstepped his place. That's what Alexander had intended, but that is not what happened. Blind rage caused him not to throw the spear near Cletus; it caused him to put it straight through his heart! Alexander could not be consoled—he had killed one of his closest friends, a loss he never got over.

He had been conquered not by some vast army, but by his own temper. He began to warn his friends, "learn to control your anger or it will control you, and cost you dearly!" Those are wise words from one who knows. Perhaps all of us can learn something from Alexander the Great.

November 17th

Simplify Your Life—Eat Some Ice Cream!

Back in the early 90's while I was on retreat at a monastery, a monk gave me a few passages from a book to take to my meditation. A Buddhist nun wrote the book from which the passages were taken, entitled The Wisdom of No Escape. After having taken them to my meditation, I must admit that the first two passages were beyond me, but the third passage gave me a great deal to think about. Here is that third passage: "Life is very brief. Even if we live to be a hundred, it's very brief. Also, its length is unpredictable. Our lives are impermanent. I myself have, at the most, thirty more years to live, maybe thirty-five, but that would be tops. Maybe I have only twenty more years to live. Maybe I don't even have one more day to live. It's sobering to me to think that I don't have all that long left. It makes me feel that I want to use it well. If you realize that you don't have that many more years to live, and you live your life as if you actually only had a day left, then the sense of impermanence heightens that feeling of preciousness and gratitude."

"I've used one of your passages in my meditation," I said to the monk when I saw him the next morning.

"Did you find it helpful?" the monk asked.

"I assume that you wanted me to learn some spiritual principle from that nun's writings, is that true? I guess you wanted me to become acquainted with the Buddhist principle of constant awareness. Is that right?" I asked. The monk smiled at me and said, "You're getting too far ahead of yourself. I am interested in teaching you to simplify your life, to not waste your life."

"In other words, you want me to do something useful with my life, to make a difference?" I asked.

"No. Not at all. You have missed the point of your meditation time if you think that's what that Buddhist nun was talking about," he said in a soft voice.

"So, you're telling me I'm a spiritual dolt!" I said.

"To put it bluntly – yes!" he answered much too quickly.

"Well then, tell me how I am to simplify my life," I said.

"This is how I want you to simplify your life. Go into town and buy yourself an ice cream sundae. Sit down at a table and take at least a half hour to eat your ice cream. Enjoy each spoonful, savoring every element of its flavor. If you do this, you will have begun the process of simplification."

That monk didn't have to ask me twice to drive into town for ice cream. I did as he said and really enjoyed the ice cream sundae. When I returned to the monastery and was walking through the gardens, the monk found me and asked how my trip to town had worked out. I told him I loved the ice cream, but I didn't get what this had to do with simplification.

The monk looked at me and seemed a bit frustrated, and then he went on, "Life is short, much too short, yet its shortness makes it rich. It is chocked full of wonderful gifts that most of us miss because we are trying to cram way too much activity into an already overly busy day. To simplify your life is to take your time with life. Don't rush through it. It means that you take time to enjoy each event of your day. For example, when a breeze blows across your face, take time to feel it move across your skin. When a thunderstorm crashes around you, take some time to enjoy all its aspects, the flashes of lightening, the rich smell of a fresh rainfall, and how cozy it feels to be in a warm dry house watching the rainfall. Or again, how about savoring those times sitting with a friend drinking coffee and talking about important things. Don't these things make life rich?

"To simplify your life means to realize that time is limited and the life we have must not be wasted on worry, or fretting, or running a rat-race to get ahead in life. If you want to be truly happy, and you want to be rich in blessings, learn to simplify. Take your time with life. Savor it, enjoy it, and don't take any of it for granted. Simplify!"

I think of that retreat whenever I eat ice cream. I invite you to have some ice cream, only take your time with it—life's too short to waste.

November 18th
Peace

November is the month the Church sets aside for us to remember the dead. In recent months there have been many deaths within our parish, and these deaths have left behind a great sea of grief. In addition, many people are dealing with serious illness, others are dealing with personal problems, family problems or unemployment, and still others are coping with a crisis of one kind or another that brings on depression. Many are heavily burdened and need comfort.

There is much pain and suffering around us, and sometimes we can be confused by it. A friend gave me a prayer this past week, which I think can help put all into perspective:

Lord, give all of us the grace to understand that this life is very short, that we all have a mission and a purpose, that we are all called to great holiness, that we are called to live with You for all eternity in Your kingdom, that the sufferings of this life are not worthy even to be considered in comparison to the glory that is to come. Let not the darkness and discouragement of the present moment prevent us from reaching for the heights. Let not our minds and views be darkened to the point where we forget that You DO exist; that there IS an eternity; that you HAVE called us to be with You forever.

Lord, give us the grace that keeps our eyes on Heaven, that allows us to live in the present world with the joy that no one can take away, and the peace that is ever present, even in the midst of turmoil. Amen.

Jesus promised to give us a gift that no one else can, the gift of peace.

His peace comes when no other sentiment, feeling or emotion will satisfy. Only His peace has the power to keep our eyes focused on heaven.

November 19th
Out of Death Comes New Life

Perhaps one of the most recognizable pieces of classical music is Beethoven's Ninth Symphony. Its "Ode to Joy" is sung throughout the world and it is often used to celebrate great feasts like Easter. What is amazing about this piece of music is that Beethoven wrote it when he was totally deaf, totally cut off from the world of external sound.

What is amazing to the world, however, is not really amazing to those of us who follow Jesus. We have come to know and are well-acquainted with the fact that God can do some of his greatest work only in the midst of what appears to be a hopeless situation. This month, which is a time we traditionally remember the dead with heartfelt prayers, is a reminder to us that Jesus has taught us that, with Him, out of death comes new life.

A great composer's loss of hearing appears to those without faith to be a complete disaster, but not to Christians. We have come to look at the events in our lives through the eyes of faith. Perhaps God used the "death" of Beethoven's hearing to give him new life, the ability to hear the music that was beyond his reach when he was distracted by the sounds of the external world. His deafness forced him to hear an internal music that he may have never been able to tap into had it not been for his hearing loss.

November 20th
Tomorrow's Fruit

A very old man in India noticed that the monsoon rains had begun, so he set about digging holes in the ground in the fields that he owned. A neighbor's son asked him, "What is it that you are doing there?"

"I am getting ready to plant some mango trees," the old man replied.

"Do you expect to be alive long enough to be able to eat mangoes from these young trees?" the boy asked him.

The old man quickly answered, "Oh no, no, I don't expect to live long enough to enjoy fruit from these trees, no, not at all. But it has occurred to me as I watched the coming of the monsoon rains, that for all the many seasons of the coming of the monsoons that have made up the length of my life, I have often enjoyed the fruit of the mango trees that other people planted long ago. I have been blessed by the hard work of people long dead. Planting these new trees, whose fruit I will never enjoy myself, is my way of showing gratitude to those who lovingly labored all those years ago so that I might have mangoes today." We all enjoy many blessings which are the result or "fruit" of the hard work of people we may have never even met or have not even known about. Yet, we benefit from all of their labors. Perhaps we, like that old Indian man, can show our gratitude by planting "new trees" that will bear fruit that will bless others in the future.

In your life right now, what kind of "trees" can you plant to provide a bountiful harvest for future generations?

November 21st

A Thanksgiving Pause

As Thanksgiving approaches I am reminded of something I heard Billy Graham say at a conference I attended. He said that when he was a boy, he and his family were eating in a little restaurant when they noticed a local farmer ordering his meal. When the farmer was served his food, he bowed his head and began to give thanks. Some uncouth guys who were not from the area sitting at a nearby table noticed the farmer's prayer and began to make fun of him and shouted, "Hey, Pops, does everybody here pray before they eat this slop?"

Their laughter stopped when the farmer, unmoved by their rudeness, answered, "Everybody but the pigs."

Billy Graham concluded by saying that he always thought it was the height of rudeness to fail to pause to thank God for everything that nourishes us. Perhaps a good preparation we can all make before Thanksgiving is to consider how we are all hungry in so many different ways, yet how often

God meets our needs. The least any of us can do in the face of such generosity is to take a "thanksgiving pause."

How does one take a "thanksgiving pause"? Well, you just take a few minutes right now to consider how many needs God has already met for you just since you got out of bed this morning, and then you pause to give thanks! So, go ahead … take a pause!

November 22nd
A Day of Thanksgiving, a Day of Trust

Soon we will gather with friends and families to celebrate Thanksgiving. For many people, this is a great day to have a good meal with loved ones, but for us, it needs to be much more than that. We must not let this day pass without considering some important facts. We ought to take a few moments to consider the first Thanksgiving and how our pilgrim Mothers and Fathers took time to consider their journey to that point and to give thanks for all of their blessings. At first glance we might think that those first pilgrims were giving thanks because they had been so successful and had produced such a bountiful harvest. But first glances can be deceptive.

Those first pilgrims had suffered terribly on their long journey for freedom. Their sojourn had begun in the English countryside and ended on the rocky shores of New England. One of the two ships which had set out for America literally began to fall apart within the first miles from shore, so that they had to turn that boat around and half of those who had started had to be crammed onto the Mayflower. The other half of the passengers and crew were too sick to continue. The now over-crowded Mayflower then set sail and made for freedom in the New World. Once fully under way, they encountered one horrible storm after another, and for most of the trip, the travelers had to remain below deck where nearly everyone was sick. Ventilation was poor, sanitation even worse, and the smell unbearable. Morale was certainly at a low ebb.

Once they had arrived and after their first harvest season was completed, they gathered for the first Thanksgiving. As they looked around on that day, fully half of their number had already died. Life in the wilderness was surely difficult; daily, they endured one hardship after another. Yet in the midst of it all there was this tiny whispering voice that moved them to consider how many blessings had come their way even in the sea of suffering they had been through. They made a point of praising God and thanking God for the abundance of blessings that they knew they had received and that they trusted were still to come. They knew in their hearts that God had been with them through every danger, hardship, illness and difficulty. They knew too that God would never abandon them. Thanksgiving Day for them was not just a nice holiday – it was a public statement of trust in God.

This month as we pause to celebrate Thanksgiving, perhaps we too might use that day as an opportunity to make a statement of trust in God that whatever we may be enduring, we will always be aware that we are truly blessed by a God who never abandons us.

November 23rd
God's Children

The readings for these last weeks of the liturgical year are about the end of the world and the final coming of Jesus in glory, concluding with the Feast of Christ the King. All of these readings are meant to "put us in our place." Let me explain what I mean.

A man who was recently elected to the U.S. Congress was taking his seven-year-old daughter through the Capitol Building to the chambers of the House of Representatives. As the new congressman watched his little girl looking around the huge House chamber, he asked her what she was thinking. "Daddy, you know what?" she asked. "I think you look a lot bigger in our kitchen at home than you do here!" The congressman looked around and began to see where he was through his daughter's eyes and he was suddenly overwhelmed with a sense of the awesome responsibility that had recently been placed on his shoulders. He immediately realized that he must get God's help if he were ever to measure up to the trust that had been placed on him by the voters.

Like that little girl's comment, the readings that the Church places before us about the end of the world serve to remind us just who we are. They bring us down to size and remind us that we aren't as big and powerful as we like to think. As time draws to a close and Jesus returns, we will realize just who we are. We are God's own children, creatures in our loving God's hands.

November 24th
If Not, Why Not?

I've read most of the books that President Jimmy Carter has written, but there is one passage from his writings that I think about. In it, he tells about the time, after he had graduated from the U.S. Naval Academy, when he had applied for duty with the nuclear submarine program.

In order to enter that program, he had to be interviewed by Admiral Hyman Rickover, the founder and commander of the nuclear submarine fleet. The admiral looked over Jimmy Carter's file as he began the interview, and then asked, "What was your standing in your class at the Naval Academy?"

Carter proudly answered, "Sir, I was 52nd out of a class of 820." He expected that the admiral would be impressed by his class rank and waited for some comment.

Admiral Rickover stared at him and appeared to be looking right through him, when he asked, "Well, Mr. Carter, did you do your best?"

Jimmy Carter said that he was about to say "yes," but thought he had better tell the truth. "There were times, sir, when I did not always do my best," he said.

With that, Admiral Rickover sat in silence for a few minutes and said in a whisper, "Why not?"

Jimmy Carter said that he often thought back to that interview and to that question and he wondered if God were to ask him a similar question – "Have you done your best as a son, husband, father, friend or Christian?" – if he would have to admit the same thing to God as he had to admit to Admiral Rickover. "From that day on," Jimmy Carter said, "I have always tried my very best because God deserves at least that much."The question we all have to answer is "Are you giving God your best?" If not, why not?

November 25th
Trying to Read the Book

There is a story told of St. Anthony the Great, the desert hermit. It happened that one day he was sitting by the side of the road, under an old tree reading a book. A stranger happened by and said, "Oh, you are that holy man everyone talks about. What are you reading?" St. Anthony replied, "I am reading an old Sacred Book."

"So, what is the book about?" asked the stranger.

"It's about God Himself," answered St. Anthony.

"Who is God?" the stranger asked.

"God," said the St. Anthony, "Is the Lord of the Universe."

To this the stranger replied, "I only believe in those things I can see with my own eyes. Where is this God you are reading about? Where does this 'Lord of the Universe' live? Like many things in my life, this makes no sense to me."

With that St. Anthony stood up, walked ten paces away from the man, turned around and held the book open for the stranger to see. "Read this book to me," St. Anthony commanded. "How can I read that book to you when you hold it at such a far distance from me?" asked the stranger.

St. Anthony then held the open book so close to the stranger's face that it literally was touching his nose. "Read the book to me now," St. Anthony said."

"But how could I ever be able to read this book when it is so close to my face? I cannot see anything clearly," the stranger replied.

"Indeed you cannot see," St. Anthony said. "You cannot see and you cannot focus your eyes on the print because you are blinded by faulty perspective."

If you are going through a period of time in which you find yourself questioning things or not fully understanding what is happening in your life, perhaps you, like the stranger above, are finding it difficult to 'read the book.' Maybe this is a good time to check your perspective. Maybe it is time to read some Scripture and pray with it. Maybe this would be a good time to consult with someone whose perspective you trust. Talking things over with a good friend may give you a fresh perspective and a new lease on life. Why not give it a try and see what happens?

November 26th

Old and Frayed Ropes

One of my favorite stories from my time as a hermit in the desert in Israel is one that a monk told me about his visit to a monastery in Portugal.

The monastery he had visited is a unique one in that it is located on top of a 3,000 foot cliff. The only way to get to the monastery is by climbing into a basket that sways in the breeze as several very strong monks pull it up to the top! The monk told me that he is terrified of heights and that his getting into that basket took all of the faith and strength he had as well as a good stiff drink. As he was being pulled to the top of the cliff, the young monk noticed that the rope was old and frayed. He asked the attending monk who was with him in the basket about the rope. "How often do you replace that rope?" he asked. The attending monk rather matter-of-factly said, "Oh, well, we replace it only when it breaks." The visiting monk did not find much comfort in the answer.

I was thinking of that story of that monk in the basket this week during a marriage counseling situation in which a distraught husband said tearfully, "Why did we have to wait till everything fell apart, before we came for help? Why did it take such a catastrophic mess for us to realize how important we are to each other?"

Why is it that we so often wait too long to do the important things? There are probably as many answers to that question as there are people, but it is quite true – too often we simply wait too long. If you did an inventory of your life right now, are there relationships in your life in which the rope is old and frayed? Wouldn't it be better to tend to those "frayed" situations now rather than waiting until they break? Some other questions we might ask ourselves: "Is the 'rope frayed' with regard to my health? Are there things I should be doing right now concerning preventive health care rather than waiting for a health crisis to occur? And then there are similar questions we might ask ourselves about our faith life, too.

As the year is winding down, and Advent is near, wouldn't it be a good idea to take some time to consider if there are any "old and frayed ropes" in your life that need tending?

November 27th

Meeting Him in the Garden

The famous Danish theologian and philosopher, Soren Kierkegaard, wrote about a wealthy woman who felt a very strong call from God to the religious life. She knew what God wanted and she knew that following God's call would require that she would have to give up her vast wealth. She felt that she would be able to give up everything she owned, with one exception. She had a garden that was very special to her. It was her place to be alone. It was in that garden that she found strength to face life's difficulties. It was in that garden that she knew she would find refreshment and true peace. Her garden was her place of refuge. As she thought about giving up all her possessions, she knew that all of them meant very little to her, but the key to her garden meant everything.

What that young woman had not realized as she struggled with her decision was that her true garden, her true source of strength and her true place of refuge was not the physical garden that she owned. It was that place in her heart where God lives. This was her true garden. She may have thought that it was the physical garden that produced the strength she needed to face life. She may have thought it was the garden that provided the solitude she experienced; she may have thought it was the garden that produced refreshment and peace; but it was not.

The true source of these gifts was not the garden, but the One person who joined her in that Garden, the Lord. Yet, the garden was important because it did provide the place for her to meet the Lord. Do you have a garden? Is there a place in your home or yard where you go to find peace, solace, and refreshment? If not, is it possible for you to create such a place? I have found over the years that having such a place has made it much easier for me to find the garden in my heart. When you find that garden in your heart, you can be anywhere and you'll be in touch with the One who gives true peace.

Having a physical place, like a garden, can truly help us find a refuge from the hectic pace our world often imposes upon us. Why not treat yourself this Summer to a little garden oasis where you can find the Living God. I promise you that once you have done this and once you are committed to spending time there, you will discover how much easier it is to find God when you are not in that garden.

November 28th
A Man Who Refused to Be Caught by a Fish

I came upon a curious story. It is a story of a rather prosperous CEO who went out for a walk along the beach. As he walked along, the sight of a fisherman sitting lazily beside his boat disturbed him. Even though what the fisherman was doing was none of his business, the CEO decided he needed to give the man some sage advice.

"Why aren't you out there fishing?" he asked angrily.

The fisherman, a bit startled by the stranger's question, looked up at him from under his hat and said, "Because I've caught enough fish for today."

"Well why don't you get out there and catch more fish than you need and be even more productive?" the CEO asked.

"What in the world would I do with them?" the fisherman replied.

"Isn't it rather obvious," came the impatient reply. "With more fish you could buy a better boat so you could fish in deeper waters and catch even more fish. You could then purchase some stronger nylon nets, catch even more fish and make even more money! Soon you would have a whole fleet of boats and you would be rich like me."

The fisherman scratched his head and asked, "Then what would I do?"

"If you became as rich as I am you could sit down, relax and really enjoy life!" said the exasperated CEO.

"What do you think I'm doing right now?" the fisherman replied.

From time to time it is good for us to take a moment to focus on our life's goals. The fisherman above knew that his goal in life was to catch fish not to be caught by the fish. He knew that there is more to life than amassing vast wealth. He knew that to be truly wealthy is to be aware enough to drink in the beauty and the many gifts that God places all around us. With our noses too close to the grindstone, we can often miss out on the true riches that life has to offer. As the temperatures begin to fall, as the trees begin to drop their leaves, why not slow down a bit yourself, sit down, relax and really enjoy all the gifts.

November 29th
Need Directions?

I read a story the other day about a man who went on a business trip. Being a bit unfamiliar with the route, it wasn't too long before he was completely lost. He was so confused that every time he came to an intersection, he would just turn left. Finally, when he realized that the situation was getting worse he decided that as much as he didn't want to, he had to stop and ask for directions. He pulled into a gas station and spoke to the cashier, "Pardon me," he said, "I'm lost, can you help me?" "

Just where are you headed?" asked the cashier. "I'm headed to St. Louis for a business meeting," replied the traveler.

To which the cashier replied, "Then you are not lost, you just need directions."

Reading that story reminded me that we are all in the same boat as that traveling businessman when it comes to our life of faith. We all know where we want to go, but every now and then we lose our way and need directions. Sometimes as we make our way through life we can feel like we are going in circles – or that we are completely off course. Other times we begin to realize that we have stopped traveling altogether. It's then that we have to decide to ask for help.

November 30th

Feel the Quiet

A police officer tells the story of an experience he had with a mentally disturbed man. The man had gone on a rampage and had torn up the living room of his family to such an extent that his family was completely terrorized. The police were called and it took five officers to subdue the deranged man. When they arrived at a local hospital, it took all five officers to control the man as he violently lashed out at everyone who came near him. Dragging him down a corridor and into one of the examining rooms, they forced him to sit in a chair and ordered him to be quiet. The more they tried to calm him down however, the more enraged he became.

A cleaning woman who happened to be mopping the hallway looked in at all the commotion. The woman calmly walked toward the man and gently put her hand on his shoulder. He turned violently to look at her, but when he saw the look of compassion on her face, he became completely still. He relaxed. She kissed him on the top of his head and said, "Why, you could be my son. Let's you and me just sit here a while and talk with one another quiet-like. Let's just feel the peace and quiet that we both need so much." As she spoke, not one sound could be heard except for her quiet, calming voice. "Do you hear the quiet?" She asked him. He nodded very slowly. "Yes, I hear it too," she said as she touched the side of his face. "And ain't it so beautiful to sit here and listen to that quiet? It makes us feel peaceful inside, don't it?" Everyone was amazed at how she had brought peace to such a troubled man.

The time of year called Advent is the season when we await the arrival of the Prince of Peace. This Advent, why not spend some time thinking about peace. Who has brought you the gift of peace? Are you being called to bring peace to someone or to some situation? Could you walk into a storm-like commotion and be an instrument of calm and peace? Are you at peace with yourself, with your spouse, your children, family or friends? Are there steps you can take during this time of preparation to deepen your experience of peace? Are there steps you can take that will bring peace to your family and friends? Jesus, the Prince of Peace, is calling each of us to be instruments of peace. Are you ready to take the first step to bring peace to another?

December 1st

Patience and Encouragement

The American painter, Benjamin West, told the story of how, as a very young boy, he decided that he was going to paint a picture of his sister. Since his mother was not at home, and he knew where the bottles of ink were stored, he got them and set to work. As he worked with the bottles of ink, he began to mix the colors together. As it is with all children, he was not very neat with his "mixing," and a great deal of it ended up on everything. He had created an awful mess.

When Benjamin's mother returned and saw the terrible scene, she didn't raise her voice or scold him. She chose to pick up young Benjamin's painting and said, "Benjamin, what a wonderful picture of your sister!" Then she kissed him, and the two of them went on to have the painting framed.

Later in his life, Benjamin West said of that day, "With that kiss, I became a painter."

Have you ever stopped to consider how much good the various members of your family have drawn out of you by their love, encouragement, and their acceptance. This is a good time, too, to decide to do the same for each member of your family. Who knows how many future painters or other gifted people will be "born" by words of encouragement and acceptance.

December 2nd

Clean Hearts

A mechanic looked the old car over very carefully and turned to the man who had brought the car in for an oil change and said, "Joe, I think it would be better if you'd keep the oil and change the car!"

Did you ever have the experience of cleaning out the garage or the attic when all at once you became overwhelmed by the amount of "stuff" that you had accumulated? It was difficult to know what to keep and what to throw away, so you were tempted to put it all back where you found it and simply walk away.

Just as it is difficult sometimes to know which possessions to keep and which to throw away, so it is sometimes with feelings. Sometimes we hold onto feelings or grudges too long and they can cause a great deal of damage. Often we can hold on to a very judgmental opinion about someone or something long after that opinion has been disproved simply because we cannot admit that we are wrong.

During this Season of Advent, when we prepare our hearts for Christmas, perhaps we need to "clean out our hearts" and throw away those feelings, grudges or resentments that hold us hostage. If we do that, perhaps this Christmas there will be "room at the inn" for Jesus in our hearts.

December 3rd
Profitless Waste

Recently I was reading an article about the Grand Canyon. I was amazed at an account of one observer who was part of a scientific study investigating that area of the country. A young U.S. Army officer by the name of Lieutenant Ives made an entry in his report to his superiors about his findings. Here is part of his report:

"This region we last explored (the Grand Canyon) is, of course, altogether valueless. It can be approached only from the south, and after entering it, there is nothing to do but leave. Ours has been the first and doubtless the last party of whites to visit this profitless waste of locality. It seems intended that the Colorado River and along the greater portion of its lonely and majestic way, shall be forever unvisited and undisturbed."

Lieutenant Ives' report is a great illustration of how easy it is to be so short-sighted that you could actually fail to see the gift of great beauty and wonder of the Grand Canyon! Advent is a good time for us to check our "sightedness." We may not be walking through the Grand Canyon, but every day we are exposed to the wonderful gift of the people that God brings into our lives. Each of our family members, our friends, our neighbors and even those we've just met are as great a gift of beauty and wonder as the Grand Canyon. Lieutenant Ives could only see as "a profitless waste." Take some time this week really to "see" your spouse, your children, grandchildren, friends and neighbors in a new way.

December 4th

What He Has Done For You

There is a novel entitled *"Rough Justice"* by C.E. Montague in which a little boy is listening in church to the preacher tell the story of the crucifixion of Jesus. As the preacher continues describing the crucifixion, the little boy quietly begins to cry. In fact, the little boy is so taken by the story that his quiet tears turn into very audible sobs. His sobs grow so loud that people turn around to look at him. The little one's mother begins to feel a bit uncomfortable with everyone looking at her son, so she leans down and says to him "Don't take what the preacher is saying so seriously. What will people think?"

Isn't that just what we are often told by the world around us? "Don't take your faith so seriously or you'll become a fanatic!" So often we are made to feel "odd" if we begin to show that our faith is real or strong. Yet, following Jesus and living the Gospel He preached is strong stuff. It requires us to take it seriously and to choose to be deeply affected by it.

Are you deeply affected by Jesus? Does it show? Are you overly concerned about what others may think if your practice of your faith gets people to "turn around and notice you"? Some of the best preaching ever done is by ordinary people letting other people see how deeply the life of Jesus has touched them. Be proud of the faith you have. Be proud of Jesus and what He has done for you.

December 5th
Safely Home

I recently finished reading a biography of Thomas Jefferson. The book was based on personal diaries of people who knew him well. In one such diary, there was an account of an event that took place when Jefferson was president.

It happened that the President and some companions were traveling across the country on horseback. They came to a river which had recently left its banks due to heavy rains. The swollen river had washed the bridge away, so that each rider was forced to ford the river on horseback, fighting against the rapids. The very real possibility of death threatened each man as he crossed the river. A traveler who was not part of the group watched as each one tried to cross. He was very nervous because he could not swim. After several riders had plunged into the river and after much struggling had made it to the other side, the stranger asked President Jefferson if he would help him cross to the other side. Jefferson invited the stranger to get on his horse with him. The man climbed on, and shortly thereafter, the two of them made it safely to the other side.

As the stranger slid off the back of the saddle onto dry ground, one in the group asked him, "Tell me, why did you ask the President to ferry you over the river?" The stranger was shocked to learn that the man who had helped him over the river was the President of the United States.

"All I knew," the man said, "was that on most of your faces was written the answer 'no,' but on his face was the answer 'yes.' I knew he would get me to the other side safely. I knew I could trust him."

Jesus is the One sent from the Father with "Yes" on His face. He is the one we can all trust to get us across the dangerous rivers in our life. He invites each of us to "climb aboard" and allow Him to lead us safely home. If you are facing difficulties at this time in your life, now is the time to recall what Advent and Christmas is all about. God chose to make a home with us. Jesus is born for each of us. Jesus is here for you!

December 6th
The Feast of St. Nicholas

Today, December 6, is the Feast of St. Nicholas. St. Nick was a fourth century bishop who was well known for his charity to the poor, and he is the inspiration for gift giving at Christmas. Nicholas was not just generous in giving money to the poor; he also is said to have spent a lot of time considering just what gift would make each person more aware of the goodness of God. In other words, he didn't just throw money at the poor, he went out of his way to learn what a person most needed or what would bring the most happiness. Nicholas tried his best to give gifts that would allow others to be free from fear, worry, or anxiety.

If you were St. Nicholas for your family, what gift would you give to each member of your family that might free them from fear or worry? Is there anything you can do for others that would make them truly happy?

As you prepare for Christmas, prepare some special gifts this year – a word of encouragement, a note of consolation to a grieving person, a short visit with a relative you haven't seen for awhile, or maybe an apology you owe someone, or perhaps you could forgive someone who's wronged you. Wouldn't those be great gifts to give and receive?

If those are the kinds of gifts that St. Nicholas gave, it's no wonder they call him "Jolly Old St. Nick"!

December 7th
In Your Hands

The Season of Advent is a season of hope. It teaches us to look expectantly to God and the future to all that God has in store for us. It is also, in a way, the season when God looks in hope towards us. It is the season in which we remember that God has entrusted people and the world to us for our safekeeping. I was thinking about this the other day when a friend of mine gave me a thank-you card with the following words printed on the front:

"When a child puts his or her hand into yours, it may be smeared with ice cream or jelly, and there may be a wart on the right thumb, or a Band-aid on a little finger. But the most important thing about this little hand is that it is the hand of the future.

"This hand may some day hold a Bible or a gun; play the church organ or spin a gambling wheel; gently dress a wound or shake terribly as it grasps a needle full of drugs.

"Right now, that hand is in yours. It represents a full-fledged personality in miniature, to be respected as a separate individual whose day-to-day growth into adulthood is your responsibility."

Whose hand are you holding right now in your life? Who is holding yours?

December 8th

God Entrusted His Son to Mary

Consider this. If someone you love, perhaps a spouse or a child or a brother or sister, was ill or needed some kind of special care or attention, to whom would you entrust them? If you had to put one of your children in someone else's care for either an extended period of time or even permanently, in whose care would you put them? How would you go about choosing that person? What qualities would you look for and what skills would you want them to have? I bring this up because a friend of mine was telling me that he and his wife were making new wills and in the process had to indicate in whose care they would want their children to be placed in the event that some horrible accident should leave them orphaned. He said it was a scary thing to decide, because, as he put it, "Who could ever love our kids the way my wife and I do?"

Entrusting those we love to others takes a great deal of courage. We can only hope that these trusted ones would love and cherish the precious gifts we are committing to their care. The people we choose to care for our loved ones reflect something about ourselves. If you are a parent, you know how deeply you love your children and how carefully you select those who baby-sit them, who teach them, or care for them in any way. Your choice of a particular caregiver says that you trust that person with what is most precious to you. Your choice reflects your love.

Where am I going with all this? I'm headed toward today's major Feast Day, the Feast of the Immaculate Conception, which honors the Blessed Virgin Mary. Take some time to please consider this: When God the Father was looking for someone to whom He could entrust His son, whom did God choose? He chose the simple young woman, Mary of Nazareth. God is a parent too, and he deeply loves His Son. When God chose that young girl from Nazareth to care for His Son, God was saying something about her. Some thirty years later when the Son knew He was returning to His Father, and He was making out his "last will and testament," he looked around from His cross and entrusted to the same woman from Nazareth those He loved and cherished – US!

As we prepare to celebrate the birth of God's Son, let us take time this week to praise and thank God for the great gift He has given us in Mary, to whom he entrusted His Son and us too.

December 9th

Life Through One Another

I love to read biographies. Reading about another person's life can give you great insights into your own life. This past week, I read a biography of Louis Pasteur, the famous scientist and immunologist. Pasteur was horrified that many thousands of people, especially children, died from rabies. He worked for many years on a vaccine, but did not have a subject on which to test his work. He was about to experiment on himself when a neighbor's young son, named Joseph Meister, was bitten by a rabid dog. The boy's mother begged Pasteur to try his vaccine on her son. Reluctantly, and only because there was no apparent hope for the boy otherwise, Louis Pasteur administered the vaccine. The boy lived.

Years later, as Louis Pasteur was very ill and preparations were being made for his tombstone, he was asked if there were any words that he wanted etched on his headstone. Pasteur answered, "Just three words would sum up what was the most important work of my life – 'Joseph Meister lived!' "

If you were to look over your whole life, whose life has been significantly altered for the better because of your influence? Are there people in your past who are "alive" in a new way because of you? Then again, is there a "Louis Pasteur" in your life who made such an impression that you are "alive" in a new way?

The season of Advent provides us with opportunities to reflect on how Jesus came so that we might "have life and have it to the fullest." As we prepare for the season of gift-giving, let us be aware of the gifts of life and new life that God has given us through one another.

December 10th
Waiting For You and Me

There is an old Hasidic story that the rabbis in Israel used to tell their students about a grandfather who came upon his grandson who was sitting under a bridge crying uncontrollably. The old grandfather asked his young grandson, "Why are you crying so bitterly?"

The boy just went on crying, and then after a long silent pause to catch his breath, he looked up at his grandpa and said, "Grandpapa, my friends and I have been playing hide and seek. I have been hiding here under this bridge for a very long time. They have not come to look for me, and I am here all alone!"

The old man thought for a while, then said, "Yes, this is a terrible feeling – to feel that you are all alone, and no one is looking for you. Perhaps you can learn something of value from this disappointment. Remember this, our God is much like you. God is waiting to be noticed, to be found, and the human race has gone off in search of other things. God sends us prophets to remind us that God is here, waiting for us. Maybe you are having this disappointing experience because God wants you to be his prophet to tell everyone to look for God."

We are in the midst of the Advent Season, and our thoughts turn to John the Baptist, the greatest prophet who ever lived. His message for us is the same as that old grandpapa's little talk with his grandson: God is waiting for you and me. Have we gone off in search of other things?

December 11th
Time Each Day

Can you believe how quickly Thanksgiving came and went this year, and how rapidly Christmas is rushing towards us? I can't count the number of conversations I've had this past week with various people about the holidays. A quiet panic seems to be settling in around us. People are getting nervous trying to figure out how to get everything done. They're worried about buying gifts, putting up decorations, making cookies, looking for the right Christmas cards, writing letters to out-of-town relatives and friends, planning meals, etc. Not only is it beginning to look a lot like Christmas, it's also beginning to feel a lot like a big rush!

Wouldn't it be great if we could slow this down a bit? It would be wonderful if we all took a breather, but unfortunately many people feel that they are just too busy to justify taking a moment, to be quiet, to think, or to pray. They claim that too many important things would go undone. Because they think there is so much to do, they rush around and miss the best part of life. Many people are so busy getting ready for Christmas that they miss the quiet contemplative season of Advent, and that's a real shame.

I made a resolution that this year would be different. I came to the conclusion that no matter what I am doing, no matter how busy I get, I will not give up my quiet prayer time. I've learned the importance of that time from one of the greatest men of American history, Abraham Lincoln.

Lincoln knew himself quite well. He knew that if he didn't tend to his mind and to his heart and soul, he wouldn't be worth much as President. Every day, even in the midst of the Civil War, Lincoln would spend an hour each afternoon, sitting in his rocking chair on the porch of the White House thinking. It was during this time of thinking, praying and meditating that Lincoln came up with his greatest ideas.

Because of the quiet time, Abraham Lincoln was able to bring some great ideas and eventually some peace to the most chaotic time of our nation's history. In the rush of his day, Mr. Lincoln knew there had to be a place of peace.

In the rush of this season, in the rush of our everyday lives, there has to be a place of peace. Why not take advantage of the season of Advent? Give yourself a half hour of prayer time each day. That would be the greatest Christmas present you could ever give yourself.

December 12th

A River of Love and Generosity

A woman lost her husband to cancer and was devastated by the loss. She fell into a very deep and long period of grief. She took flowers to the cemetery every Sunday and would spend hours just sitting by the grave weeping. She began to seclude herself, dropped out of the organizations and activities which had been a big part of her life before her husband died. She even stopped visiting with her friends and family. When she was at home she would draw the drapes, and she even began not to answer the telephone when it rang. The world seemed a cold, dark, unhealthy place to her. In a short time her own health began to fail. It seemed she was always sick. Eventually her illnesses drove her to see her doctor for some relief.

After the doctor examined her, he began to ask her about her life as he suspected that there was an underlying cause to illnesses. He asked her if she ever left her home. She replied that she only left her home to go to the cemetery. He listened to her and then began to tell her about two of his patients who were in a nearby long-term care hospital. They did not have families to visit them. They were completely alone in the world. The doctor then wrote out a prescription and handed it to her. The woman took the script from the doctor and was surprised to see what he had written on it: "Every Sunday for the next two months, instead of taking flowers to the cemetery, take them to those two lonely patients of mine. Say hello to them and see if they need anything. See what you can do for them."

"How is this supposed to cure my illness?" she asked the doctor.

"Your unresolved grief has caused your heart to grow cold. This will warm it up a bit. As your heart grows warmer with each act of generosity and kindness, you'll see a marked improvement in your over-all health, I assure you," the doctor replied.

Sure enough, after the month, the woman's outlook on life was completely changed and her physical ailments disappeared as well. Astonished by the results, the woman asked her doctor, "How did you know this would work?"

"I knew it would work," he said, "because it's basic – if the river of love and generosity in your heart stops flowing, it stagnates and before you know it, you're sick. From now on, keep the river of love and generosity in your heart flowing freely and you will discover that the world is not that cold, dark, unhealthy place you thought it was."

That woman had a true healer for a doctor. His wisdom is a wisdom we all need to hear from time to time. Now is a good time for us to check our heart condition. Is there a river of love and generosity flowing freely in your heart? Are we aware of the great amount of need there is in the world right around us? Are we responding to that need as generously as we can? Are there people in your own family or neighborhood or parish who need your talent or gifts to help them get through a tough time? Are there talents that you have that might serve a wider community in some way? Are you willing to share that talent? Or again, has God gifted you with spiritual and material gifts that could benefit many people? Is the river flowing in your heart?

December 13th

The Season of Orange Barrels

This is the time of getting ready for the Lord's coming. It's the time of the prophets who call out that "He is near!" and that we have to "Make straight the highways for our God!" Don't you just love that kind of talk, all that John the Baptist stuff about going out to the desert to get ready for God's coming by reforming and letting go of sin and so on?

The season of Advent can be a bit deceiving, because of how much we emphasize Christmas. You can really feel the excitement build as we make all of our preparations for the big day. The problem with that is that we often miss Advent, because we spend the four weeks thinking about Christmas and not about our relationship with God.

I had an insight into this last week as I was away on retreat. I drove to

Georgia to a Trappist Monastery in order to spend time in deeper prayer. The retreat was wonderful, and I really did feel closer to the Lord. The only problem with the retreat was the drive down there. The Holy Spirit Monastery is 520 miles from here, and in order to get there, I had to endure about a billion orange barrels!

Don't you just hate those barrels? I do. I hate the sight of those stupid things because they mean delays, slow-downs, and time spent just sitting. It was during one of those "just sitting spells" that I began to think of how close Christmas is and how much there is to do between now and then. I thought of all the gifts I have to buy, Christmas cards, parties, schedules, liturgical duties, and on and on. I thought of all that there was to do, and then I got annoyed that I was just sitting there, doing nothing because of those stupid barrels! Then it hit me. The Season of Advent is the Season of the Orange Barrels. It's God's way of getting us to "just sit for a spell" to consider if there is room for Him in our schedule, if there is enough time for Him.

Let today be the first day of "orange barrel time!" Before you run off to all the things you have to get done between now and Christmas, why not make up your mind to put some extra time in your schedule each day to "just sit in traffic with God"? If you don't spend time with Him this way, you may not recognize Him when He comes.

December 14th
Beautiful

As Christmas draws near, it's good for us to think about the meaning of Jesus becoming one with us. I read the other day about a black woman, 87-year-old Oseola McCarthy, who knew, as she put it, "only how to do one thing in life." The one thing she learned to do as a little girl was laundry. She earned her living by doing wealthy families' laundry at 50 cents per load. Most of her work was done in Hattiesburg, Mississippi, where she preferred a washboard over an electric washing machine. She said that every week she would put some of her earnings into a savings account so that some day she could be of some help to somebody who really needed it. "Jesus," she said, "taught us that we should be like Him, and help people wherever we find 'em. Maybe my little bit of money could turn somebody's miserable life into a happy life. I truly hope so. If I can do that, I will have made good use of my life."

When Oseola finally retired in 1996, she went to the bank to find out how much money she had saved over all the years. To her astonishment, the banker told her that she had saved over $250,000! She was in shock. "That's more that I can use, and I can't carry any of it into the promised land of the next life. So I will give it to some young folks who would like to go to school. When I lay down in death, I can finally rest, 'cause someone will be smarter because of all those loads of laundry! The work was worth it if that happens. I am so happy. What a beautiful life God gave me! I want to share some of its beauty with the world."

Few of us would ever say that a life of hard work doing countless loads of laundry would be a "beautiful life," yet Oseola found it to be so. After years of hard work, Oseola discovered in her bank account the possibility of helping some turn their life around. It was working hard so that others might have a better life that led Oseola to discover the beauty that can be found in life. Jesus came "that we may have life." Oseola and those like her certainly have life. They have life because they know how to find the beauty of sharing what they have with others. As Christmas draws near, open your heart to others, and you, too, will discover how beautiful life can be.

December 15th

Truly Important

As Christmas draws closer, most of us begin to rush around a lot. It seems that the closer Christmas gets, the more hectic our lives get and the more urgent our tasks become. When this happens, we may miss the most important part of Christmas.

Arthur Gordon tells the story of how, when he was thirteen and his brother was ten, his father promised to take them to the circus. As they were about to leave, the telephone rang. It was Mr. Gordon's secretary informing him that some urgent business had come up that required him to come to work at once. Arthur and his brother started taking off their coats – they thought that the trip to the circus wouldn't happen after all. Their mother told them, "Now you boys know that the circus always comes back."

Before they could reply to their mother, Dad said, "Yes, the circus comes back, but childhood doesn't ... we're going to the circus; work can wait!"

Arthur Gordon concludes the story by saying that his father taught him a valuable lesson that day: "Give your attention to the truly important things, not to the merely urgent."

As Christmas draws near, remember to pay close attention to what is truly important, and not to what is merely urgent.

December 16th
Following Jesus

A first grade teacher was sitting at her desk grading papers when her class came back from lunch. One of her students named Alice came to her and said, "Mrs. Johnson, Chad isn't coming back with us because he had to go to the principal's office."

"I wonder why?" the teacher asked.

"Because he is a following person," little Alice replied.

"A what?" the teacher asked her.

It came over the loudspeaker, "The following persons are to go to the principal's office."

As we continue to prepare ourselves to celebrate the birth of our Savior, it is probably a good idea to take some time to ask ourselves if we are "following persons." Can others readily recognize that we are true followers of Jesus? Is there evidence in the way we live and in the way that we treat people that we take Jesus' invitation to "come follow me" seriously?

As the season of giving and receiving gifts approaches, don't forget to take time to thank God for the one great gift He gave us when He sent His Son who invited us to be His followers. You and I are indeed "following persons" and that makes all the difference. We are indeed blessed.

December 17th

That One Gift

How are you doing with your Christmas shopping? Have you made a list of gifts you would like to give each important person in your life? When I was a child, making a "gift list" meant writing out what I wanted Santa to bring me. I'd write out a long list, making sure my mom and dad knew what was on it. But now my "gift list" refers to the gifts that I want to give to others. From time to time though, it may not be a bad idea for us to make out a list of the gifts we would like to receive. Let me explain what I mean.

About ten years ago, I led an Advent retreat for high school students. One of the retreat talks was about gifts. In preparation for the talk, I asked each participant to write out a "wish list," listing the gifts they would like to ask God (not Santa Claus) to give them at Christmas. As you can imagine, those lists were quite interesting. There was one young man in particular who gave an answer that became the basis for my talk on gifts. He wrote: "The one gift I want more than anything else from God is to love myself, to accept myself as I am, to be able to change what I know I need to change and not to care what other people think ... and if I can't have this, then I want a big-screen TV. That way, I can watch sports and not have to think too much."

How's that for profound insight? Isn't self-acceptance a gift we all could use? Self-acceptance is one of the building blocks of peace – peace of heart, peace of mind, and peace in the soul. How differently would we treat others if we loved ourselves? If we truly loved ourselves, the peace of heart that flows out of that would certainly flow into loving others more profoundly. This would lead to peace in families and peace throughout the world. What a gift! What a blessing!

December 18th
Big Empty House

There's a wonderful story about a woman who was called away to take care of her mother, who lived out of town. Her mother's illness meant that the woman would be gone for at least six months. She hated to be away from her family for so long, but her mother needed her. She wondered how her husband and children would do during her absence.

Every day or so, her husband and children would call to let her know how well they were doing. She felt content … at first. As time went on, however, she began to wonder whether or not they missed her at all since everyone seemed to be managing so well without her.

Then one day a letter arrived from her 11-year-old son, in which he said: "Dear Mom, this is the biggest, emptiest house I ever saw since you went away." With that letter, she knew she was missed.

As Christmas draws near, it is important for us to realize just how big and empty our "house" would be if Jesus didn't have a place in it.

December 19th
What He Wants From Us

"What are you going to get your parents for Christmas this year?" I asked one of our servers this past weekend. "Well, I had bought them a video that they said they wanted, but then they gave me their 'wish list' and it wasn't on there." "I guess you're going to have to take the movie back to the store, aren't you?" "No way!" he grumbled. "I can't possibly get them anything on their stupid list, so they'll just have to like the video I bought them."

"What was on their list that would be impossible to get them?"

"They had stupid stuff on their list, like they want me to get two A's next report card, to come in on time, to do things the first time I'm told, and not to hang on the phone all the time. That's not fair to ask a guy to do that kind of stuff for a Christmas present. It won't cost me any money, but it would make me miserable. They are going to have to just like the movie.

My parents are weird!"

Mass was about to begin, so we never finished our conversation, but it made me think again about whether the gifts we give are meant to please those to whom we give them, or are they meant to please us? What gift would your family truly appreciate from you?

What gift could you give God that would truly honor Him? Going to special services during Advent and Christmas time, being with family and singing Christmas carols might be good gifts to give God, but wouldn't a renewed dedication to prayer all through the year truly give Him honor and praise? Donating a turkey to a poor family at Christmas might be a great gift to God, but wouldn't contributing to the poor all year long be an even better gift to God?

We all know what we would like to give God, but have you consulted God's "wish list" to see what He wants from you?

December 20th

Most Valuable

The other day I was looking through some old magazines when I found an interview with Erma Bombeck. When she was asked about what she considered to be her most valuable possession, she replied, "I would have to say my wedding ring. For years it has done its job. It has reminded me every day of the last thirty years that I have someone who loves me."

In a few days, most of us will be giving and receiving many gifts. Perhaps it might be good for us to take a little time to consider that gift which is most precious to us – Jesus. This week as we all gather to celebrate His birth on Christmas, let us remember to give thanks for our most valuable possession, our faith, which serves to remind us that we have "Someone" who loves us (literally) to death.

As you prepare to give gifts to all of your loved ones, consider the gift you might give to the One whose birth is the reason for all of our gift giving.

December 21st
Your Own Words and Witness

I came across an article the other day in which Billy Graham was interviewed. The interviewer asked Dr. Graham many questions about how the famous minister is feeling in these closing years of his life. Billy Graham said that he had become more reflective about his past ministry of preaching and hoped that the Gospel he preached had taken root in some of the people he had invited to "come to Jesus."

Mr. Graham went on to tell of some of the research that his ministry has done. He said that their research shows that 2 percent of the people they surveyed said that had come to be believers through non-personal advertising (TV, radio, print ads etc.), 6 percent because of the personal influence of their pastor, 6 percent came to know the Lord from the outreach of some local church. But 86 percent of those who had come to know true faith came to it as a result of a friend or relative inviting them to come to church or simply talking with them about Jesus and His influence on their life. Billy Graham concluded by saying that a Gallup Poll showed that 63 percent of all un-churched Americans have never been invited to church by their friends. "Just think," he said, "what would happen if each one of us would invite just one of our friends to come to church? It would be a new awakening for the church today. It would be like the early days of the church right after Pentecost – when thousands were added!"

Sometimes we assume that the missionary activity of the church takes place overseas, yet I think that the greatest missionary work that needs to be done today is right around us, among our own friends. Have your friends ever shared their faith with you? Have you ever shared your faith with any of your friends? As we get ready to celebrate the birth of Jesus, why not allow someone to experience him through your own words and witness?

December 22nd

Make Room

In a few days we shall all be gathering to celebrate Christmas. I just want to give you a little thought to ponder this week as the big day approaches. As you consider what gifts you are going to give to others, take some time to consider for a moment just what gifts you want from God. When you have finally considered what you most want God to give you, stop again and consider not what gift you want, but rather what gift you think God might want to give you. I say this because we can sometimes be so full of what we need or want that there is no room in us for anything that God might want to give us or do for us.

God wants to give you some great gifts. Is there room in your life for what God intends to give you? Why not use these last days before Christmas to clear out space in your heart to "make room" for what God wants to give you?

December 23rd

What Does the Word Ignore Mean?

There is a story about a four-year-old boy who had the habit of asking a lot of "why?" questions. One day, as the boy was helping his dad with the Christmas decorations, he began to ask about everything they unpacked. "Daddy, why do we have so many lights?" he asked.

"Because we need them to put on the Christmas tree" His father replied. "Why are you testing all of these lights?" came the boy's next question.

"Because," his dad explained, "we don't want to put them all onto the tree if some of them don't work."

"Did you help your daddy put up Christmas decorations when you were little?"

"Yes, I did, and I had a great time too," his dad said excitedly.

The boy and his dad worked for over an hour together, listening to Christmas music as they did so, when the little one asked his dad, "What does the word ignore mean?"

The father explained, "Ignore means to not pay attention to people when they call you."

Immediately the little boy looked up at his daddy and said, "I don't think we should ignore Jesus."

Puzzled, the father sat down on the floor next to his son and said, "I don't think we should ignore Jesus either. Why do you think we are ignoring Jesus?"

"Because that's what that Christmas song just said – 'Oh come, let us ignore him!'"

Although that little story brings a smile to anyone who reads it, that little boy sure had some powerful wisdom in his statement, "I don't think we should ignore Jesus." How easy it is for us to lose sight of our faith, to get caught up in the exterior aspects of Christmas and forget the "heart" of it all – Jesus. As we prepare to celebrate the birth of our Savior, let us make sure we don't ignore Jesus. Why not make plans to pay closer attention to Him? It will make a big difference in your Christmas if you do. By spending a little bit of time each day in quiet prayer, realizing that Jesus has called us and wants us to be his own, we can assure that we will never ignore Him and that when Christmas finally comes, then our song can truly be "Oh come let us adore him!"

December 24th
When You Care Enough

There is a story that is said to have been told by Mother Teresa whenever she was instructing her nuns about generosity to the poor. She said that when she was a little girl she remembered her mother always wearing the same cloth coat year after year. She never seemed to get a new one. So a group of relatives bought her a brand new fur coat that was quite warm.

At the next family gathering, the relatives noticed that Mother Teresa's mother was wearing her old cloth coat, not her new one. So they quietly asked her about the coat they had bought for her.

"Oh, well, I met this poor young girl in the street the other day, and she had no coat. I thought for sure she would catch cold. So I took her home with me, fed her lunch and then as she was leaving, I gave her my fur coat."

"Why didn't you give her your cloth coat?" they asked her.

She ended the conversation with a smile and then remarked, "I've always been taught that we should give our best to the poor, not our worst things. Wouldn't you want a nice warm, fur coat if you were poor and very cold?"

Mother Teresa is said to have told this story when her novices were ready to make their first steps in learning to serve the poor. "They deserve your best," she would tell them.

As we celebrate Christmas, those words could serve as a great meditation for all of us.

Do we give the people around us whom God has entrusted to our care our best? I've written the words, "They deserve our best" on a post-it-note and put it on my computer to serve as a good reminder. Perhaps a post-it-note strategically placed somewhere in your home or office might serve as a good reminder for you as well.

December 25th
Christmas

I recently read a commentary on Christmas by a noted British preacher, Reverend. W.E. Sangster. He told of having been invited to a party celebrating a wedding. He arrived late and really didn't know anyone except the friend who had invited him. Everyone was in high spirits. There was dancing, laughter and singing.

As the evening progressed, the clergyman noticed a young woman sitting by herself. No one was paying her any attention. When the preacher asked his friend who she was, the friend replied, "Don't you know? I must introduce her to you. She's the bride."

Rev. Sangster concluded his Christmas commentary by remarking, "Can you imagine being left alone and unnoticed at your own wedding party? That is how Jesus must feel at Christmas. Most of the celebration of His birth has little to do with Him."

When I first read Rev. Sangster's words, I first agreed with him. After a few days, however, I am certain that he is wrong. In recent days, many people have written me notes or stopped to tell me how Christmas affords them an opportunity to "be public" about their faith in Jesus. In the past week, four people have anonymously left small donations here at church. One had a note attached with the message, "Jesus isn't in a manger any more; He's in the poor. Please see that the poor get fed through your pantry." People at several local businesses have taken up collections for our "Giving Tree" program. When the people dropped off their donations they said things like, "God has done so much for us, it's the least we can do." In addition, I have received quite a few Christmas cards in which people have said that they have experienced God in a new way recently, and that they have begun to set time aside each day to pray more.

I'm not sure just what experiences led Rev. Sangster to see Christmas the way he does, but I do know that because of my experiences with many of you, I disagree with him. Even though it may be true that much of contemporary society doesn't fully understand the true meaning of Christmas, there are quite a few people among us who really do understand. May our continuing celebration of His birth lead many others to come to know Him.

Merry Christmas!

December 26th
Comfort

At a nursing conference, each nurse was asked what experience in their career had helped them the most to be good nurses. One retired nurse told of one day early in her career in which she was in the room when a priest was attending to the spiritual needs of a dying patient. After the priest had anointed the dying man, the nurse spoke to the priest. "Father, if he dies, I don't know what I can say to his wife. I don't think I'll ever have the right words. Maybe I shouldn't be a nurse."

The priest smiled at her and said, "You don't have to say much at all. If this man dies, go to the man's wife and bring her a cup of coffee, and just sit with her. That's all you have to do. Let your actions be your words."

There will be times in life when we will be called to 'speak' words of comfort to family, friends, or perhaps even strangers. The most profound words that can be offered to someone in need, however, may not be words at all. A simple act of kindness can be a true healing ointment for the most serious of wounds.

Sometimes we can be tempted to run away from situations in which suffering and sorrow, pain and affliction seem to overwhelm. Running away, however, would simply multiply the sadness. A simple act of kindness offered to one in pain or sorrow can quickly cut the misery in two and begin the healing process. God has given each of us great power to heal one another through simple kindnesses offered in love. When you find yourself confronting sorrow, be sure to take some time to 'speak' a word of comfort.

December the 27th
Your Bonus

This week we will celebrate the end of one year and the beginning of another. A few years ago I came across an article in a Senior Citizens' Newsletter which asked the readers to send in ideas based on this question: "If God gave you one extra day this year, what would you do with it?" Here is one person's response to that question:

"Suppose everyone in the world would receive that extra day and would celebrate it as 'God's Day'! Suppose everyone would give the wages they earned that day or the services they rendered to a helpless or homeless person or to some definite cause that they feel is God's work! Or what if for twenty-four hours we would not think any negative thoughts, or have any hatred or resentments, fear, anger, jealousy or envy? Instead, what if we only had thoughts of good will, courage, peace, faith, so that love and trust would be vibrating through the air? What wonderful TV and radio programs would be broadcast that day! What wonderful news stories could be told that day! What wonderful human encounters would take place; what wonderful exchanges between world leaders would occur! What wonderful family gatherings would result! How much love would be poured into every task undertaken that day! I am certain that I would make my bonus day, God's Day. And what a day that would be!"

That response was submitted by a woman named Molly Pickens, age 94. The vision that Molly has for "God's Bonus Day" is certainly the vision that Jesus has for us and our world. As you gather with friends and family to celebrate the New Year this week, why not take a few moments to consider this entire coming new year as a "Bonus Year" from God. What will you do with your bonus?

December 28th
Resolutions

At a faculty meeting, an elementary school principal made this suggestion to his teachers: "Since the end of the year is fast approaching and we will begin to think about a new year, let's all write some resolutions about how we can be better teachers. I'll post them on our staff bulletin board and in that way, we can help each other to keep our resolutions and we will end up being better people."

The teachers agreed, and when the resolutions were posted, they all crowded around the bulletin board to read them. One of the younger teachers suddenly became very angry and in a loud voice said, "He didn't even put up my resolution. I know it was one of the first ones in, but he didn't even bother to post it. He doesn't care about me. It just goes to show you what it's like around here!" On and on she ranted and raved. The principal, who couldn't help but hear her outburst, was mortified. He really didn't mean to exclude the young teacher's resolution. Looking quickly through the papers on his desk, the principal found the young teacher's resolution and immediately went to the bulletin board and tacked it up. The resolution read: "I resolve not to let little things upset me anymore and not to turn little things into big things."

As a new year approaches, we get a "fresh start" in our spiritual life. Perhaps it's time for us to make a few spiritual New Year's resolutions. If you were to take a spiritual inventory, would you find some areas in your spiritual life that need some attention? Has your relationship with God deepened in this past year? How do you need to go even deeper in your life with God in the coming year? Maybe this is the year to take your spiritual life more seriously. Maybe this is the time to make sure that your resolutions become reality.

December 29th

The Beginning Is Near

Do you ever worry about the end of the world? It's no wonder that you do. With all of the stuff that's been going on in the Middle East and with all of the other stories that fill the newscasts these days, it's amazing that we ever think about anything else. Not only that, each week there is always some new movie about Armageddon, the next great world war, or some other calamity that will destroy the world and all that we know. And then there are those "prophets" who keep warning us that the end is near. So, it's no surprise that the end of the world might be on our minds.

Yet, we are all still here. I think that from the very beginning of time itself there have been people scaring each other with worries about the end of the world. I don't think that Jesus wants us to be worried about the end of things; I think he wants us to be enthused about the beginning of things. Every morning offers us a new opportunity, a new beginning. Each day offers us an opportunity to try something new, to undo the harm we may have done yesterday, or to create something new today.

We are people who were created for new beginnings. Think of yourself as a little child exploring the wonders of the new world all around you, or think of your first day of school, your first day on a new job, the day you got engaged, the day you married, the day your first child was born – weren't each of those new beginnings a gift?

God is the great Creator, and we who are made in God's image are at our best when we are creative. Creativity by its very nature leads to the joy of a fresh start, a fresh approach to life. This is what God wants for each of us – to be filled with enthusiasm for life and for all of its new beginnings, not filled with feelings of dread, worry and woe about the end of the world.

Does this mean that we should ignore the horrible tragedies that are going on all around us? No. What it means is that we must not allow the calamities of life to rob of us who we are. If we remember to be creative, to be full of hope, to look for new beginnings, who knows what goodness might triumph to bring solutions to so many challenging world events? We are not meant to live in fear; we are called to live in hope. We are not called to worry about the end, but rather we are called to bring about a new beginning. Instead of walking around carrying signs that say "the end is near!" we ought to carry signs that say "the beginning is near!"

December 30th
Just Over the Horizon

In some of my reading this past week I came across a piece about the wife of the Scottish novelist Robert Louis Stevenson. The article related how much she admired her husband, not only for his great talent as an author, but also because of the way she had seen him live his daily life. She marveled at the way he could face the most difficult things that life handed him with such courage and optimism.

For much of his life, Robert Louis Stevenson spent his time confined to bed. Even though he was quite ill, it did not change his attitude about life. In fact, one day, Mrs. Stevenson heard him coughing so violently that she thought he would collapse and die on the spot. This lasted for about 15 minutes and at the end of the coughing fit, she said rather sarcastically, "I suppose you still believe it's a wonderful day!" He looked up and saw rays of sunshine pouring through the windows.

He paused for a moment to catch his breath and said, "I do think it's a wonderful day." As he looked around at his bedside table he added, "I'll never let a row of medicine bottles block my horizon. Something good is always just over the horizon."

As you go through difficult times, do those difficulties block your horizons? Are you able to look beyond what threatens to overwhelm you to see that something good is just over the horizon? I can see why Mrs. Stevenson admired her husband so much.

December 31st
Re-created

I was in Dayton this past week preaching a Parish Mission. After one of the evening sessions, I was talking with a group of school children who were discussing a class assignment they were working on together. They had to find quotes from famous people giving reasons why going to college was so important. Some of them had quotations from Thomas Jefferson and others cited Ben Franklin. I think the best quotation of all those they showed me, however, was from Muhammed Ali:

> *"Go to college, get the knowledge. Stay there till you're through.*
> *If they can make penicillin out of moldy bread,*
> *Think what they can make out of you!"*

I think it's certainly true, that college can make us into new people. Imagine, if a mere human institution like a college can "re-create" us, just think how much the Holy Spirit can mold and shape us into new creations. As we begin a new year, why not use this coming week as a week of prayer to ask the Holy Spirit to "re-create" you? If we are open to the workings of the Holy Spirit, there's no telling just what great things might happen in us this New Year.